BEARS

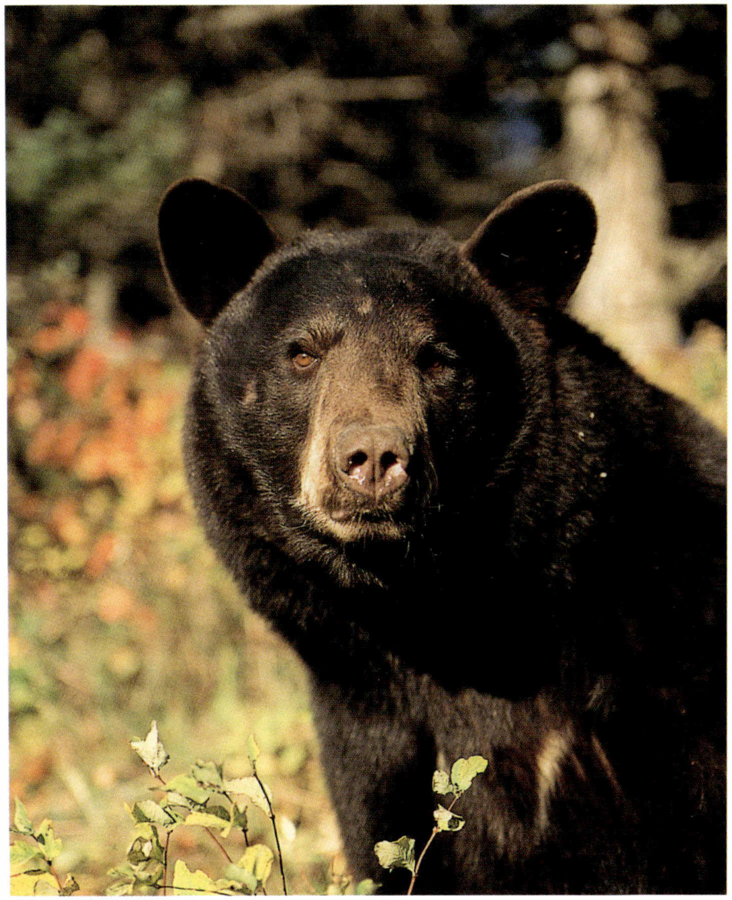

First published in Great Britain in 2000 by
Colin Baxter Photography Ltd
Grantown-on Spey
PH26 3NA
Scotland
www.worldlifelibrary.co.uk

A CIP Catalogue record for this book is available from the British Library

ISBN 1-84107-062-9
Front Cover Photograph: Grizzly bear
Page 1 Photograph: Black bear
Page 4 Photograph: Polar bear walking in sea surrounded by lumps of ice.
Back Cover Photograph: Polar bears, Manitoba, Canada

Printed in China

BEARS

Lance Craighead

Colin Baxter Photography Ltd, Grantown-on-Spey, Scotland

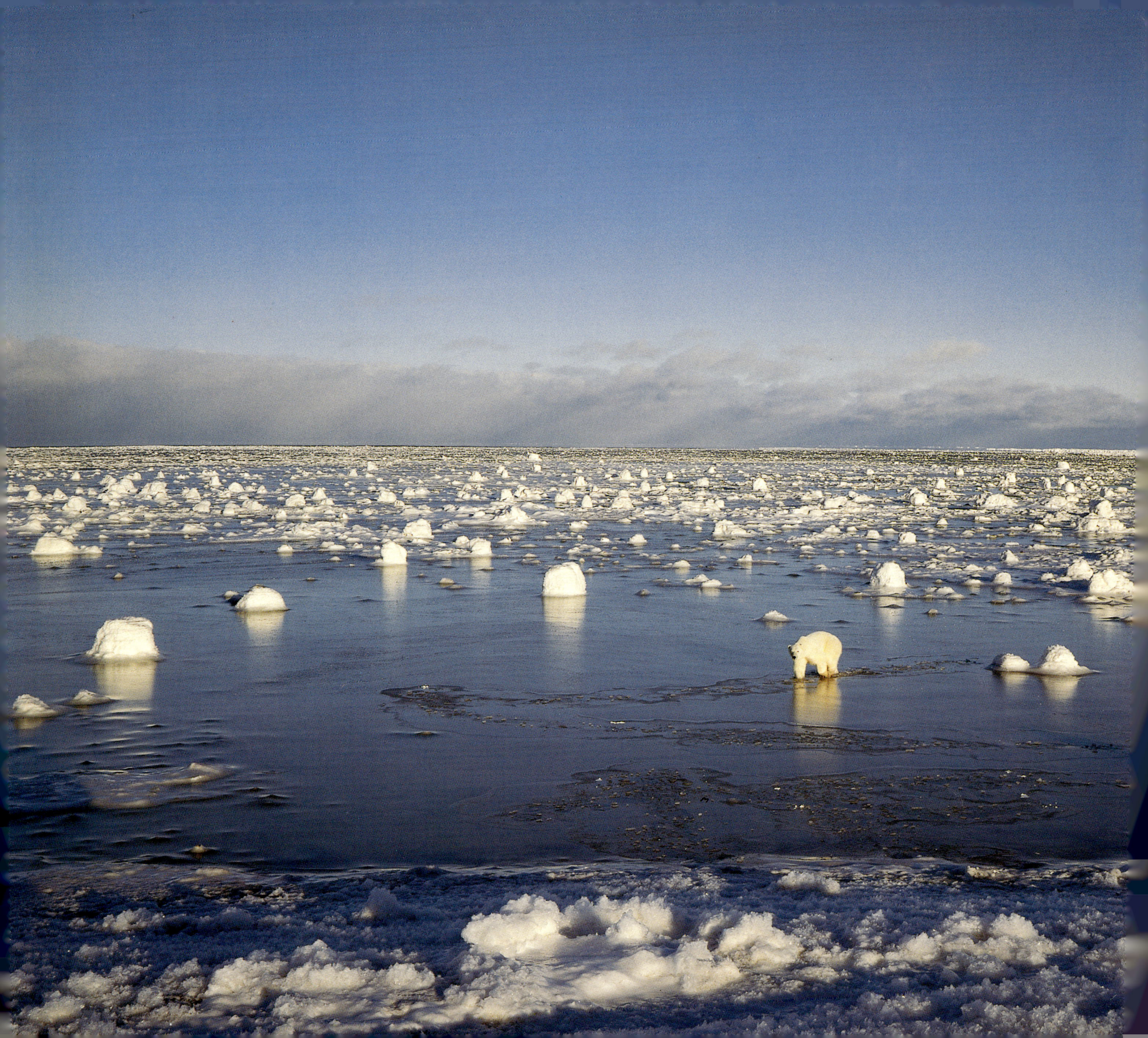

Contents

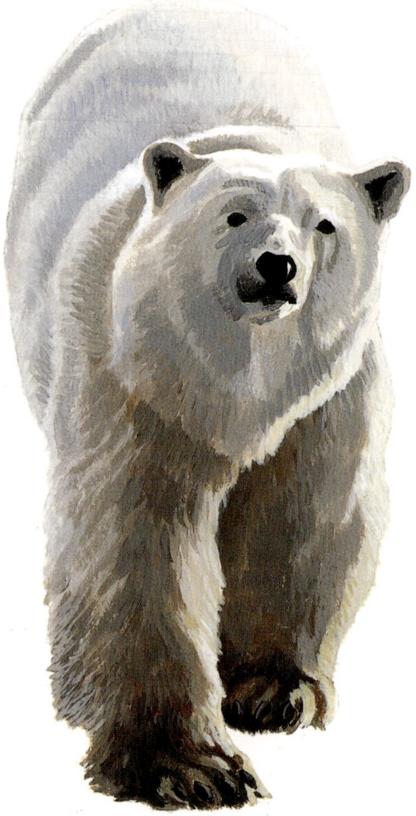

Polar Bear

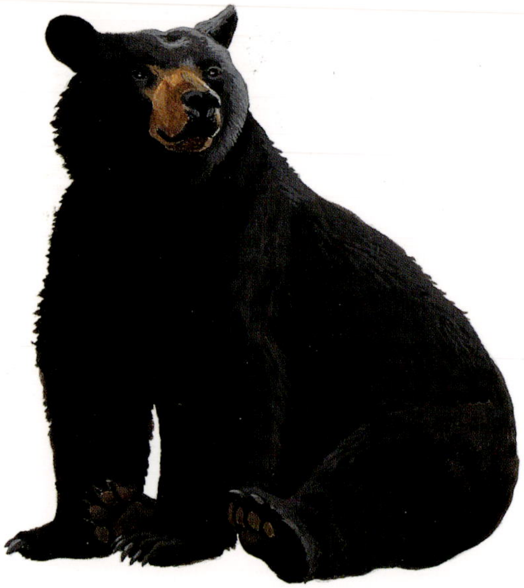

American Black Bear

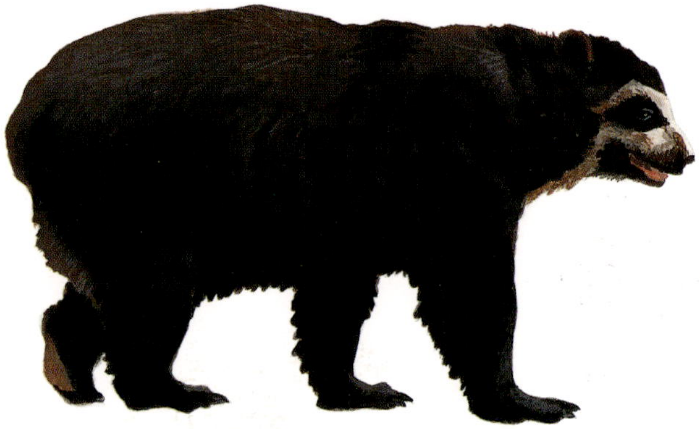

Spectacled Bear

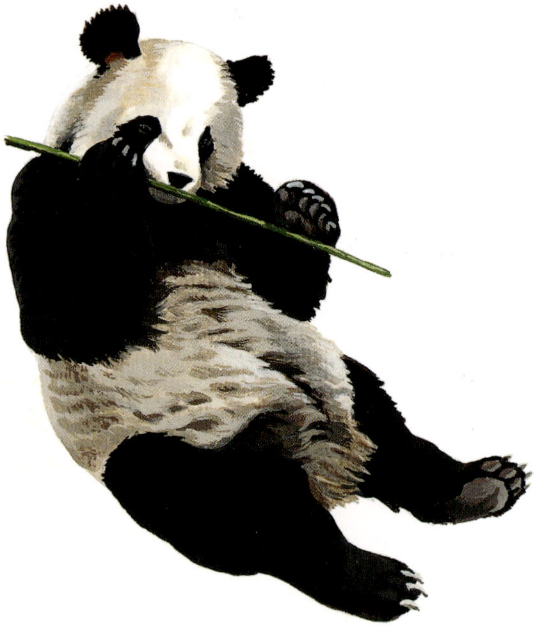

Giant Panda

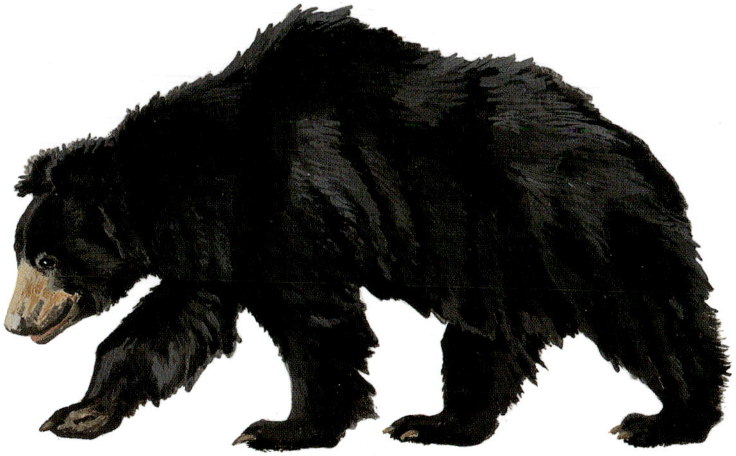

Sloth Bear

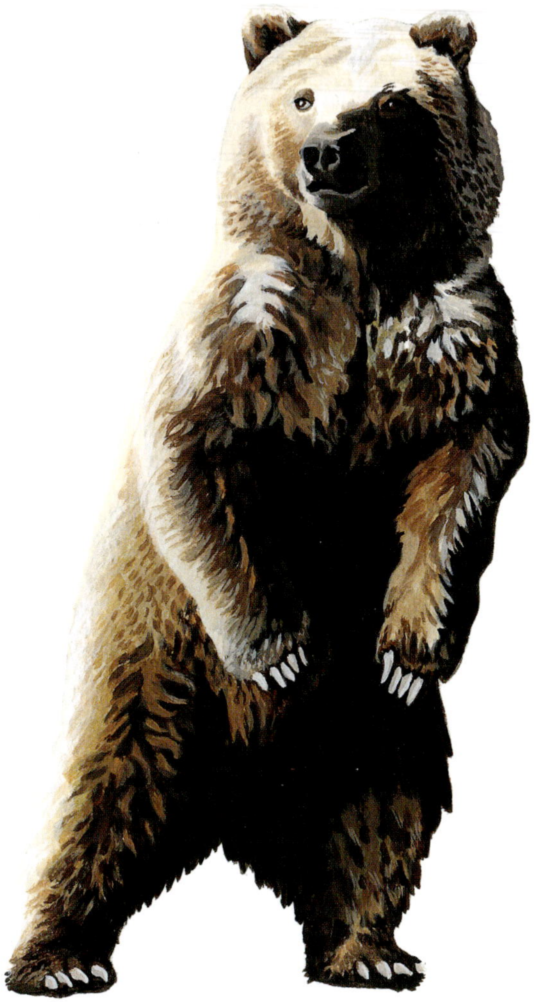

Grizzly or Brown Bear

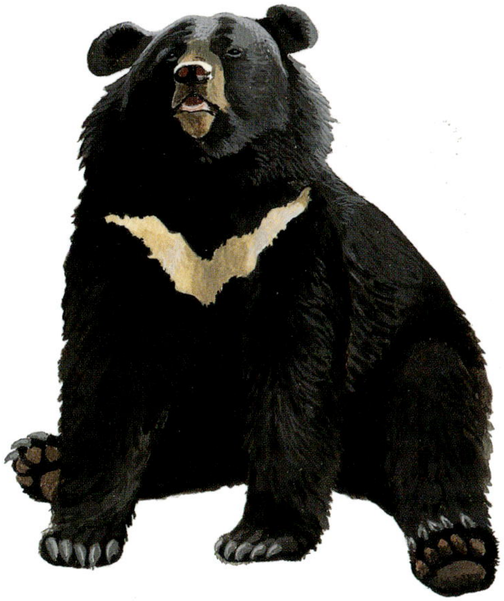

Asiatic Black Bear

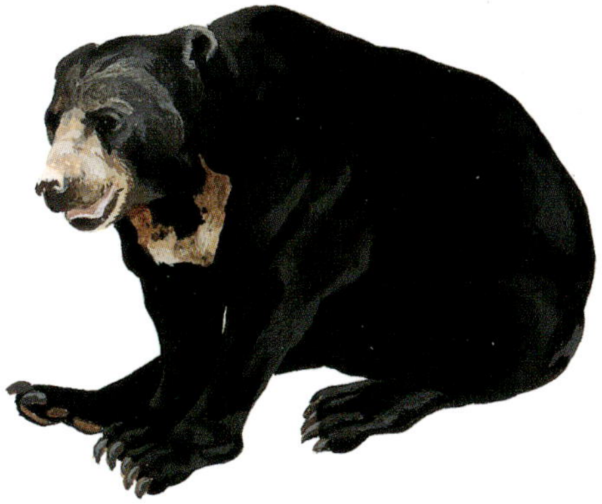

Sun Bear

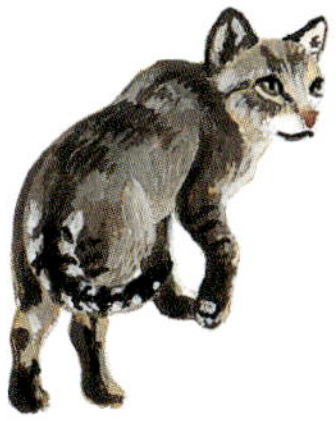

Scale:
c½ in = 1 ft
c13 mm = 0.3 m

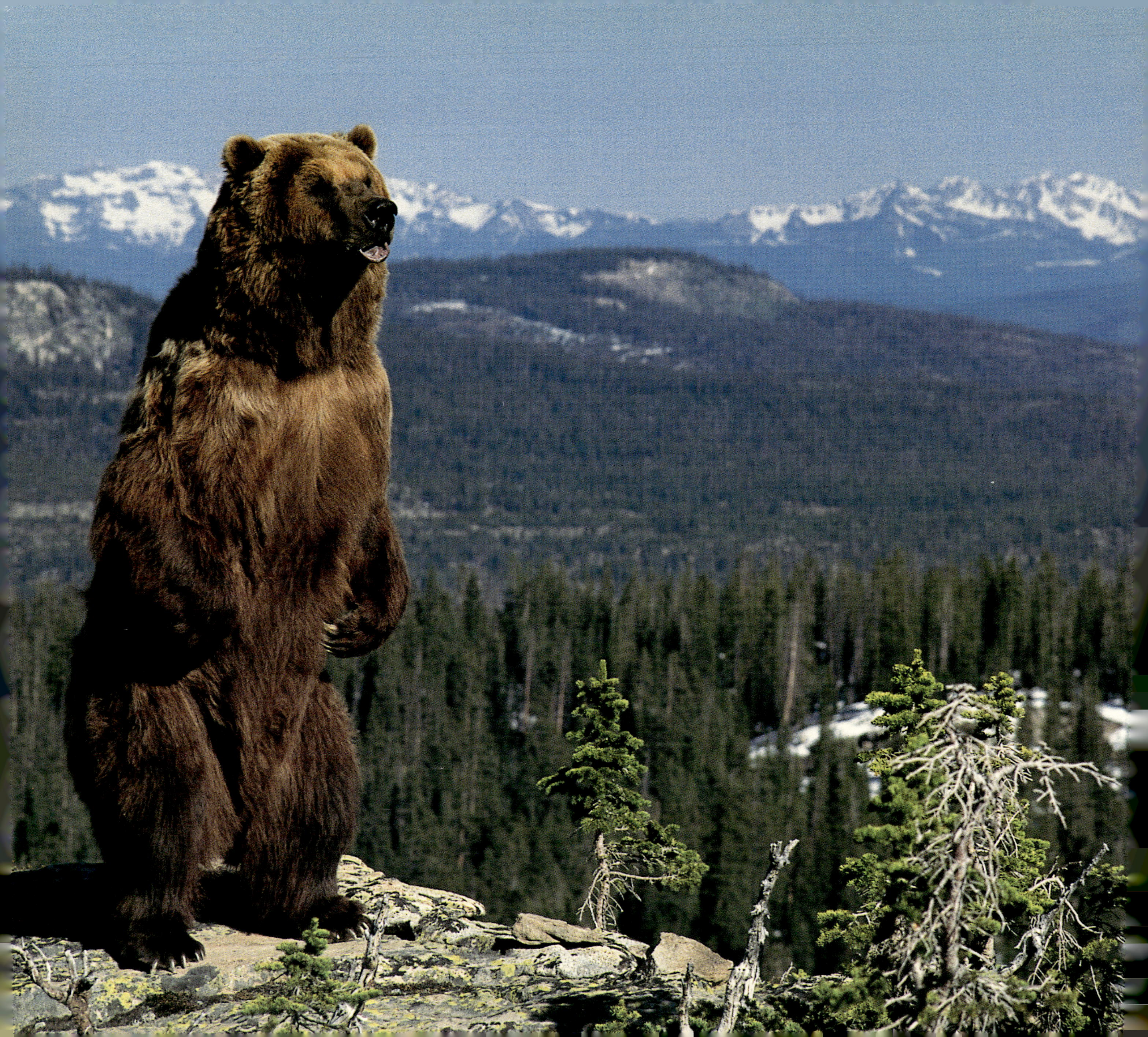

Introduction

Bears have fascinated and frightened people since our ancestors long ago walked north out of equatorial Africa and began to encounter them. Humans and bears have shared a long history of coexistence in Europe and Asia, and both species colonized the New World in the same fashion; migrating there on foot. The bears occupied the northern hemisphere before humans, and were also first to reach North America. Our history together has primarily been one of wary and respectful tolerance; two top predators sharing the same food sources, each able to harm the other but also likely to get hurt in the process. Because of our similarities we feel a kinship with bears. We eat the same foods, both plant and animal. We both can stand upright. We nurture and protect our children. Because of our differences we fear and revere the bear. Bears are incredibly powerful. They have big teeth and claws. They can outrun us. Bears in turn have learned to fear and respect us. We have always been able to kill them, but it was much more difficult and dangerous before the advent of modern firearms. It has become too easy to kill bears; we stopped trying to live with them, as we had for tens of thousands of years, and merely removed them whenever we encountered them. Now many of them are almost gone; only two of the eight species of bears are not widely considered to be endangered. We need to revere bears again, and stop fearing them irrationally (a healthy fear in appropriate situations is a good thing). We're smarter and more adaptable than they are and it is time to let our intelligence overcome our instincts. We can tolerate bears and understand their behavior well enough to coexist with them. The first step is to leave them enough space to survive.

Although I have studied bears, hiked among bears, and camped in bear country for almost 40 years, I have never been injured or even seriously threatened. I have always tried to keep my eyes open and to let the bears know that I was there. Given the choice, bears have almost always chosen to leave me alone. That's not to say that I have not been frightened. I think the most frightening encounter I ever had was also one of the most distant. I was camping on a ridge in Alaska; on the North Slope of the Brooks Range, in the foothills. A friend and I were watching bears as the caribou migrated through. Two other volunteers were camped a couple of miles away on another ridge. We were hoping to record instances of predation by grizzlies on caribou calves, many of whom were still too young to outrun a bear. So far we'd only seen one calf get run down and eaten by a bear; a safe half mile away.

One evening (it stayed light for 24 hours) we decided to walk over to the other camp for a visit, and so we started out along the ridge top. As we walked along on solid, smooth terrain I realized that we had not bothered to bring along the shotgun. Bear spray deterrent was not yet available. I didn't think much about it though; the bears we had encountered had run off as soon as they figured out what we were. I had seldom carried guns in bear country further south; climbing trees there was an option to give the bear more space and time to leave gracefully. Here there were no trees, however. The tallest plants were 3 inches (8 cm) high.

Suddenly, out there in the middle of nowhere, we saw a grizzly bear. Like us he had come up onto the ridge where the traveling was easier. Like us he had a goal in mind and was moving along with a purpose. Unlike us, he moved very fast. Luckily, it was a very wide ridge and so he was about 250 yards (230 m) away. He was upwind of us though, and wouldn't catch our scent. If he saw us, he'd probably trot on over to find out what we were. If he got too close before he identified us he might attack rather than run. All in all it was an unnerving experience. I don't recall breathing.

All that we could do was to crouch down and stay still; quietly hoping

A standing grizzly bear is not necessarily threatening; he's probably trying to see or smell something he's unsure of.

that he would continue on his way without even noticing us. That is what he did. For those endless, brief, moments I was transported back in time and viewed that bear through the eyes of my Stone-Age ancestors. I was hopelessly outmatched in strength and speed; the bear's agility and fluidity of motion across the landscape were awesome. Even with a spear or arrows I would scarcely have had a chance against him. He weighed three times as much as I did, and was at least ten times as strong. I felt naked and fragile; my Swiss army knife was no consolation. He was up on the ridge with us, he danced across it in about 60 seconds, and then he was gone. However, I can see him still.

If he had seen us, and if he had approached, he most likely would have run away. He had no way of knowing we were unarmed, and he had probably learned to fear humans. We're probably not that good to eat either, unless the bear is very hungry. On the other hand, if he got too close, within his 'fight' rather than 'flight' distance, fear would have given way to aggression and he would have charged. This is the way many of the casualties caused by bears occur. These are the kinds of encounters that we can avoid in most cases.

This innate, visceral fear of bears lives somewhere inside all of us. Stone-Age man still hunkers in the cave of our emotions and his survival is still threatened by predators. If we don't acknowledge this innate fear, try to understand it, and overcome it, we will end up continuing to destroy all of the bears we encounter. In many cases we end up searching out and eliminating bears to preclude any possibility of encountering them. And we find that many people today oppose reintroducing bears into areas where they once lived because of the fear of encountering them. This Stone-Age fear will always exist, but we can control it with understanding. I hope to help in some small way to increase the understanding, and tolerance, of people for bears. I'd like to share my wonder at the variety and beauty and grandeur of bears and the intricacies of the bear's world. I hope to make it easier to coexist with bears, because without them our lives will be greatly diminished.

Like the other books in this series, *Bears* is not a field guide or an encyclopedia or a scientific dissertation. It is a look at what we know about bears; a view through the eyes of biologists; a view that I feel is interesting and can offer the best explanation for the scientific facts through the process of evolution. I hope it will be interesting and thought-provoking. In doing this I will take the liberty to speculate upon many things that have not been rigorously examined from a scientific point of view, but which seem to make scientific sense. Such things – for example, the basis for cub-killing behavior – will be difficult to ever prove conclusively. The purpose of this book is to raise more questions than it answers.

To a large extent this book is a history of bears. Like most histories it is based upon some facts. I have colored my interpretations of the facts with my own personal biases, which may be fairly apparent; I like bears and want to keep them around for future generations of humans to be acquainted with.

As I grew up in the Rocky Mountains of Wyoming and Montana I had a wonderful opportunity to learn about bears and other wildlife. With my siblings and cousins I followed my father, Frank, and my uncle John Craighead around Yellowstone Park while they conducted the first long-term study of grizzly bears. Later I was able to follow some of their graduate students around in Alaska and other wild parts of the world. It wasn't until I started to write about some of my experiences that I began to realize that not everyone had a childhood like mine. Not everybody grows up with a chance to experience the natural order of things in the wild, or has the time and opportunity to even think about it. Most people today live and grow up in urban environments and have few chances to visit the little wilderness that is left. I hope to impart, in some fashion, some of the things I've had a chance to think about and experience, and to help fill some of the gaps of understanding that come from spending too much time surrounded by too many people. Life hasn't always been that way.

Coastal grizzlies are generally called brown bears: this one is looking for salmon inland from the coast along the Brooks River in Alaska.

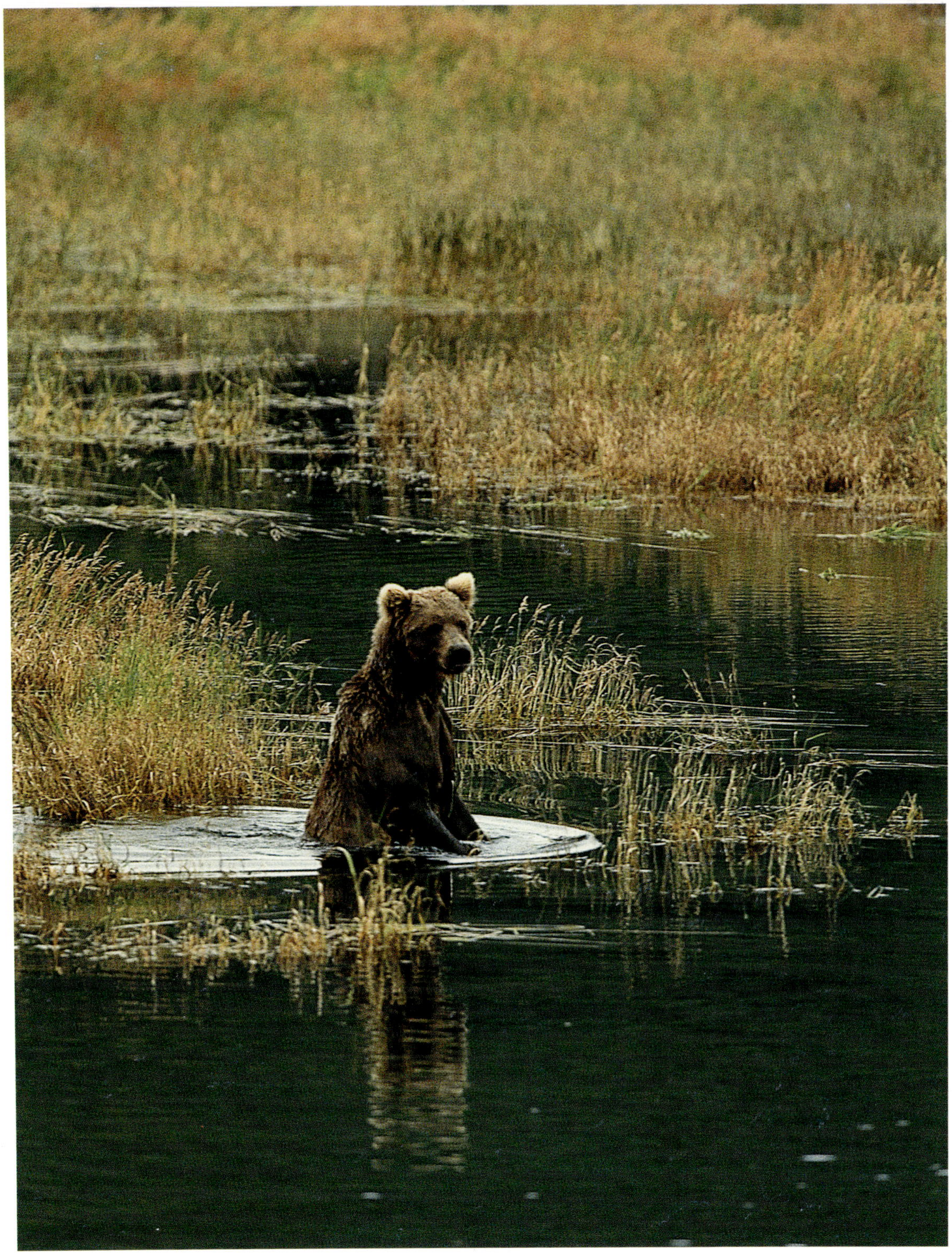

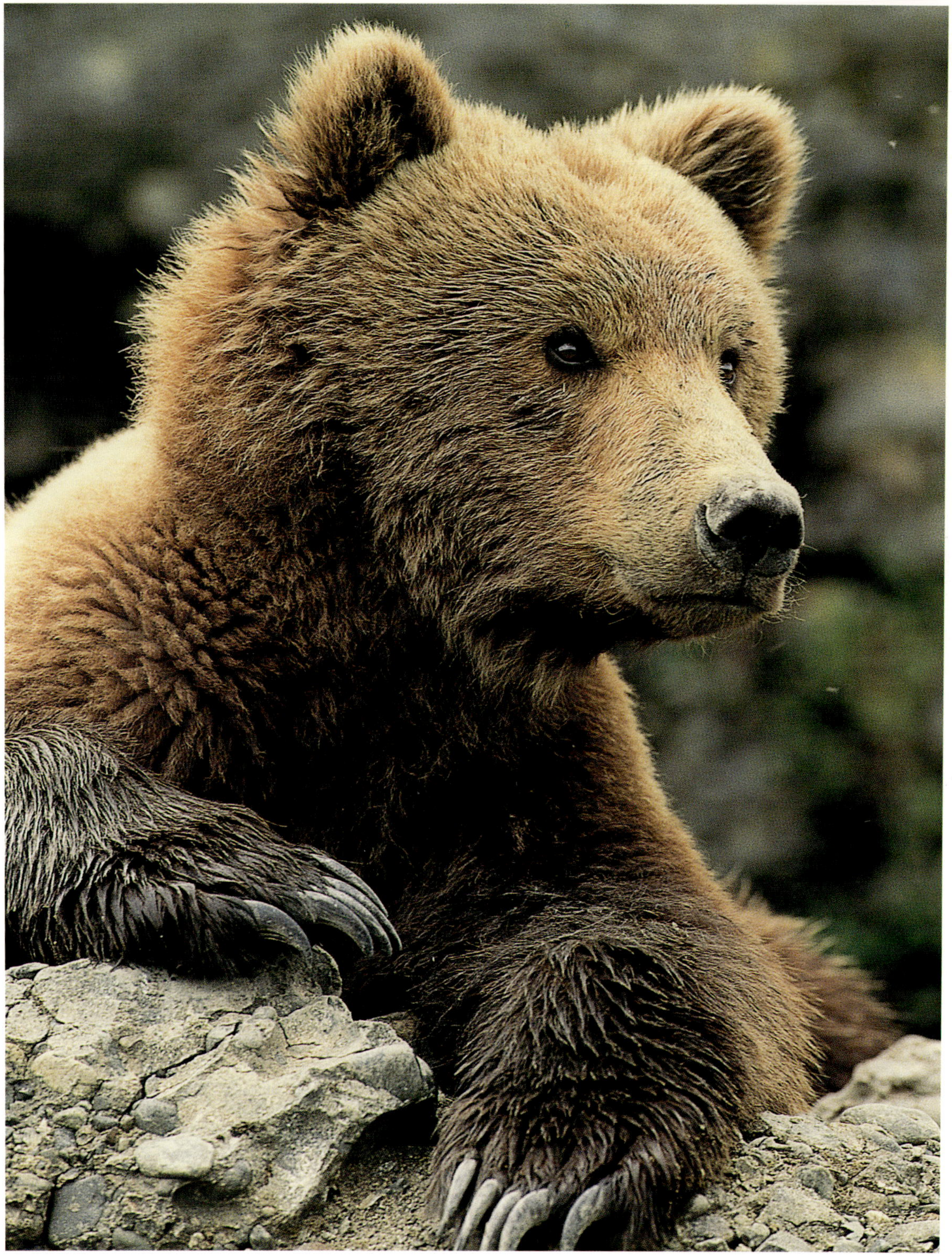

Origins and Evolution

All eight of the species of bears living today had a common ancestor, *Ursavus*, that lived during the Miocene period over 20 million years ago. The evolutionary routes (phylogeny) that bears took to reach their present positions make an interesting story, which will undoubtedly change as new evidence becomes available. Two lines of evidence for bear phylogeny are presently available: paleontological (fossil) and molecular. Both sets of data are in general agreement as to the timing of speciation (the formation of new species) events. The fossil data suggest that *Ursavus* and his relatives were forest-dwelling carnivores that probably lived much as foxes or raccoons do today. They had warm fur coats that enabled them to live in cool climates with cold winters. They ate meat, but probably also fed on a variety of plant foods, especially when prey was not available. Their teeth were primarily the teeth of carnivores; sharp, cutting teeth adapted for tearing and ripping, but they were beginning to develop teeth for grinding plant foods. During winter periods, they were probably restricted to areas where their prey could also survive.

The evolutionary process has been at work shaping the animals we call bears for over 20 million years. The formation of new species is a continuous process that takes place over long periods of time. Generally a new species is formed from a population of animals after they become isolated from other populations of the species. At some point, after about half a million years or so, the isolated population becomes so different genetically that it is unable to reproduce with its parent population, which has also diverged over time. This is called reproductive isolation.

Many groups of animals that we all would consider to be distinct species are actually able to breed successfully with other species on a physiological and genetic basis. In some cases they are prevented from doing so because they have developed distinct breeding behaviors which keep them from 'recognizing' the other species and consummating the reproductive act. This is called behavioral isolation.

In other cases they are separated by geographic barriers that effectively prevent any individuals from the two groups from coming in contact with each other. If this geographic isolation lasts long enough, they may become behaviorally or reproductively isolated, or both. Grizzly bears and polar bears are a case in point. Their genetic lineages diverged less than one million years ago according to the evidence of mitochondrial DNA. They have produced viable offspring from matings in zoos; in one case a male polar bear accidentally got into an enclosure with a female Kodiak bear at the U.S. National Zoo in 1936. They mated and had three hybrid offspring. A breeding experiment was then conducted and the hybrid offspring proved able to breed successfully with each other, indicating that these two species of bears were much more closely related than previously expected. In fact all the species in the subfamily Ursinae (all bears except the giant panda and the spectacled bear) probably have the ability to cross-breed, and several combinations have actually occurred.

In the wild, grizzly and polar bears rarely come in contact with each other, and they may have difficulty recognizing each other as potential mates. Few biologists today would argue that they should be considered the same species: from morphological and behavioral points of view they are completely distinct. More discussion about species, subspecies, evolutionarily significant units, and management units can be found in the chapter on brown bears.

Fossil Evidence

The fossil record of most large, rare animals like bears consists of a few scattered records; a fragment of bone, a jaw, a disjointed portion of a skeleton. Rarely is an intact skull or complete skeleton discovered.

After weaning and before reaching maturity, bears such as this curious brown bear at McNeil River, Alaska, are called subadults.

From these tiny clues, and using techniques to determine the age of the fossil or the layer of soil in which it was found, paleontologists construct the history of an animal's past. Naturally enough, different scientists may come to somewhat different conclusions regarding who evolved from whom and when it happened. I've tried to synthesize the various theories and lineages (which do not differ greatly) into a reasonable outline in this section and to paint pictures of how bears might have evolved.

Although fossils of bears are quite rare, microscopic fossils are extremely numerous. The most common insect fossils are parts of beetles. The most common fossils on land are plant pollen fossils. Most of our understanding of the vegetation of the past comes from pollen fossils, with which other microfossils give clues to the climate, the environmental conditions, and the ecology that existed when they were deposited in sediment.

Fossils are dated primarily by using a technique called carbon-dating. However, not all materials can be carbon-dated; in that case, other specimens such as plant material are generally taken from the same soil strata as the specimen of interest and those are dated instead. Recently, there are newer and more accurate methods of dating material using accelerator mass spectrometry. Older techniques are accurate only to about 40,000 years ago. Given this variation in techniques and interpretation, the dates that are used in this book are approximate; they are not intended to be taken literally, but should serve as a relative measure (within two thousand years) of what happened when.

Today there are only eight living species of bears worldwide. *Ursavus* was the first truly bear-like ancestor. *Ursavus* seems to have exploited a generalized diet which included both plants and meat. During the early Miocene the *Ursavus* lineage split into two subfamilies. One of these ancestral bear-dogs, Indarctos, gave rise to the Ailuropodinae (which ultimately developed into the plant-eating giant panda, *Ailuropoda melanoleuca*).

Another ancestral bear-dog, Agriotherium, evolved to fill a more predatory niche. Agriotherium's lineage evolved into the omnivorous Ursidae during the early Miocene. About 15 million years ago the ancestral Ursidae diverged to form two other lineages; the Tremarctinae, and the group we now call the 'true bears', the Ursinae.

The ancestral short-faced bears, the Tremarctinae, crossed the Bering Land Bridge into the New World about 15 million years ago. The short-faced bears that remained in the Old World went extinct during the Pliocene. The New World group became isolated as sea levels rose and they evolved into two genera, *Tremarctos* and *Arctodus*. One of these lineages produced the giant short-faced bear *Arctodus simus*. The short-faced bears eventually became extinct in North America at the end of the Pleistocene, but the lineage survives in South America as the spectacled bear, *Tremarctos ornatus*.

The ancestral Ursinae gave rise to the six modern species of the true bears: the subfamily Ursinae. Modern true bears (the genus *Ursus*) first appeared during the Pliocene. They arose in the Old World, probably in Eurasia. One of the oldest forms was discovered in Spain. The early Ursine bears migrated east and south across Asia. During the Pliocene, about 3.5 million years ago, the first ancestral Ursine bear migrated into the New World. The fossil record indicates that it evolved into the American black bear, *Ursus americanus*, and was a separate species by at least 1.5 to 2.5 million years ago. This early black bear had established itself south of the ice sheets by the time of the Pleistocene glaciations (which began about 2 million years ago and lasted until just 10,000 years ago). The black bear shared this area with three species of short-faced bears. However, *Ursus americanus*, the American black bear, is the most commonly found Pleistocene bear species among the fossils from this period. The early black bears were larger than they are today.

The lineage which led to the black bear also remained in the Old World and diverged there. These bears radiated into southern Asia,

Black bears and brown bears are sometimes misidentified; this large black bear does not have a prominent hump.

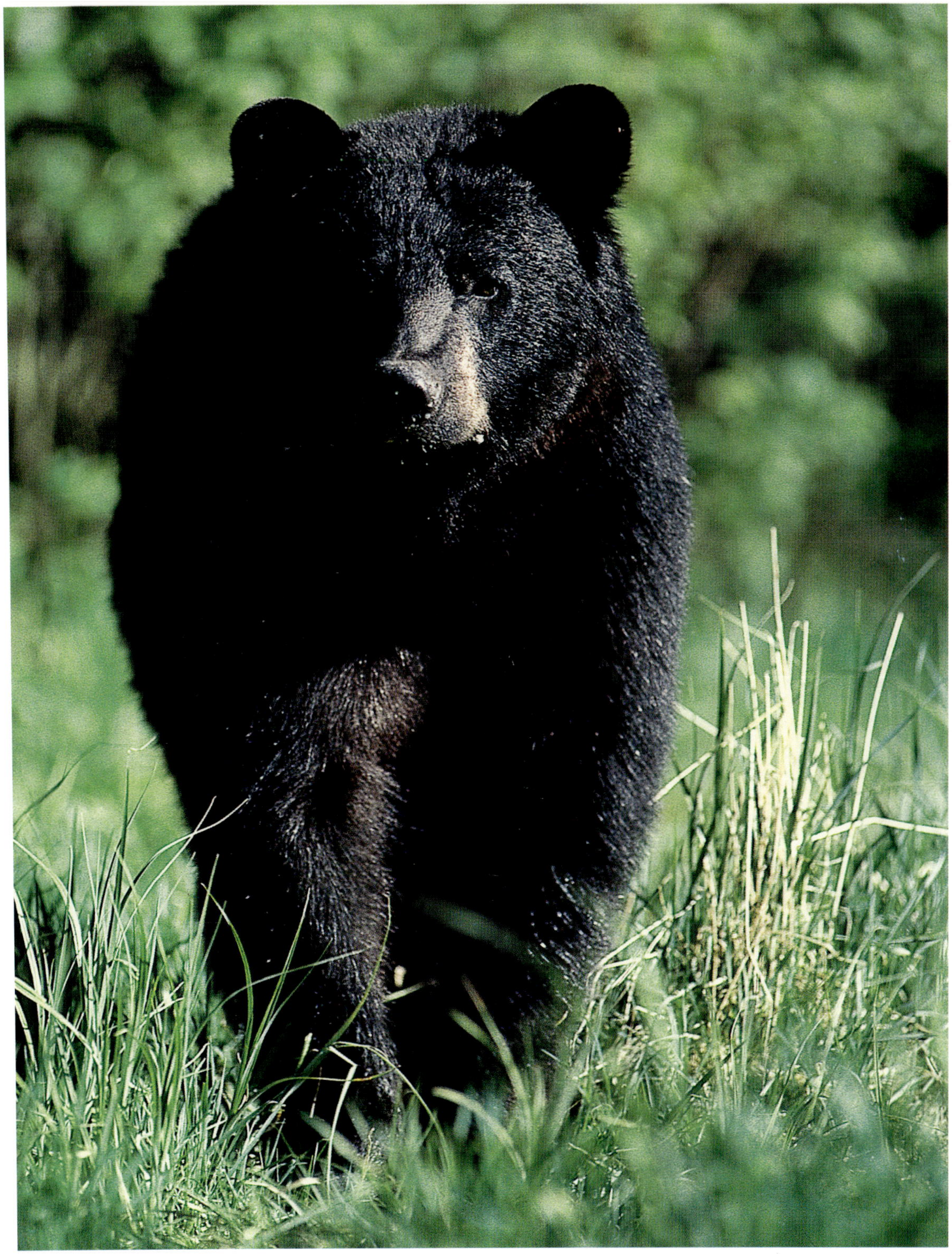

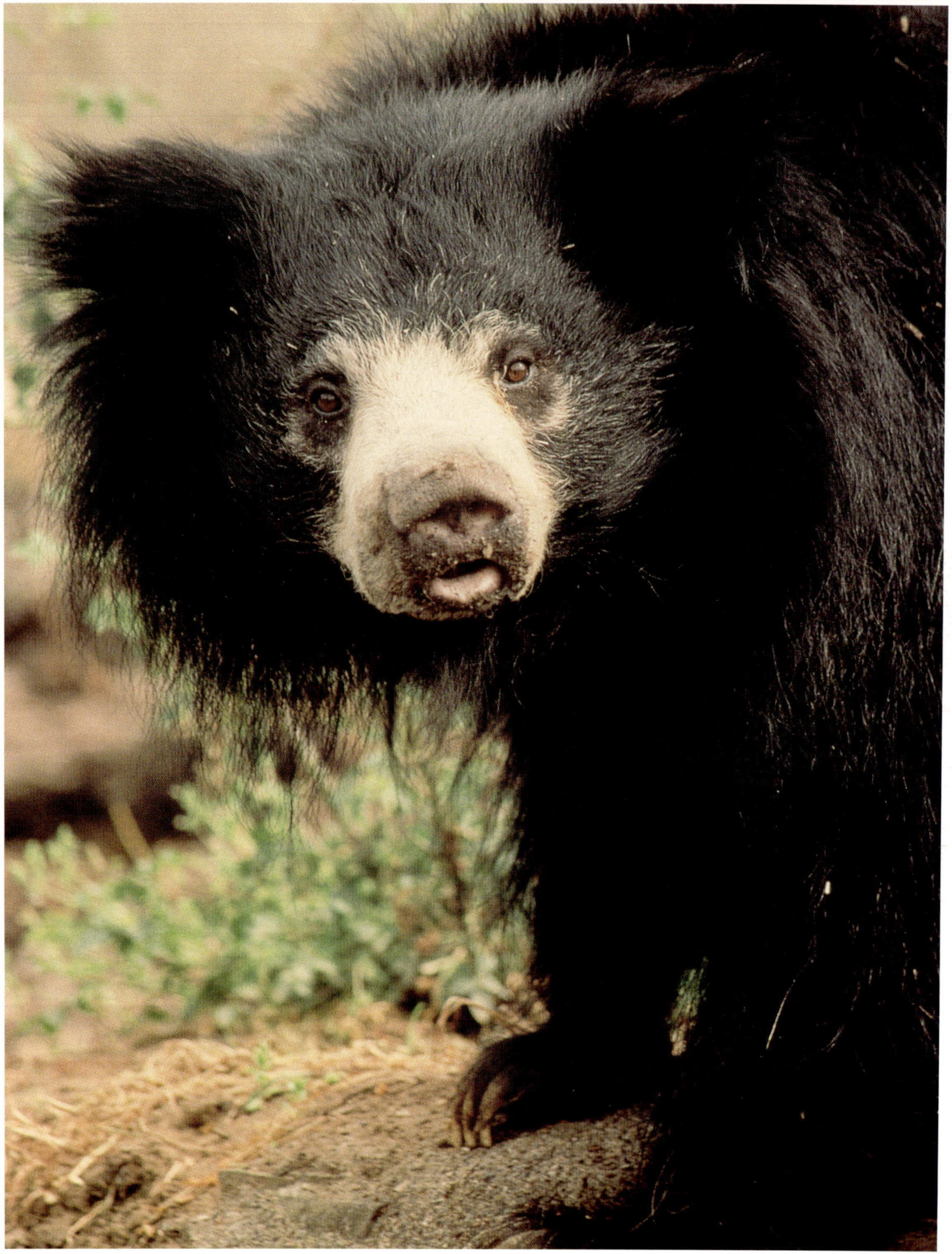

also during the Pliocene, and evolved into two or more lineages that are represented by three extant species: the Malaysian sun bear, *Helarctos malayanus*, which probably became isolated on the Malay Peninsula; the Asiatic or Indian sloth bear, *Melursus ursinus*, which probably became isolated on the Indian subcontinent; and the Asiatic black bear, *Ursus thibetanus*, which may have become isolated on the Tibetan plateau or elsewhere in the Himalayas.

Although the American black bear was more numerous, the giant short-faced bear, *Arctodus simus*, was the most wide-ranging bear species during the Pleistocene in North America, and was present in Alaska and the Yukon during the late Pleistocene. The giant short-faced bear was the reigning monarch of North America at the time when the grizzly or brown bear migrated across the Bering Land Bridge into the New World.

The grizzly or brown bear, *Ursus arctos*, began to evolve in the Old World from the ancestral *Ursus etruscus* during the middle Pleistocene about 1.6 million years ago. The oldest known fossils of today's brown bears were found in France and are about 900,000 years old. A more recent fossil was found in China, and is about 500,000 years old. This and other fossil data suggest that brown bears were well established in Europe by the mid Pleistocene about 800,000 years ago. They may have also been in central Asia at that time. They subsequently dispersed into eastern Asia and eventually into North America following the route taken by the black bears.

This was a time of giant mammals. The Northern Hemisphere was populated with incredible creatures like the saber-toothed tiger, the North American lion, the giant short-faced bear, the giant sloth, ancestral horses and camels, and of course the wooly mammoth and the mastodon. Periodic changes in climate gave rise to land bridges between continents, and mammals moved across; then after a hundred thousand years or so the land bridges were covered with water again. This migration, mixing, and isolation set the stage for a wide diversity of bear species to evolve; and then to fade away. At the end of this period, after the last ice age, as the modern or Holocene epoch began, only eight bear species were left on the earth.

Fossil evidence suggests that the ancestral brown bear lineage split over 300,000 years ago to form the polar bear, *Ursus maritimus*, probably in northern Asia. It is likely that coastal brown bears in north-eastern Siberia share a common ancestor with polar bears. A group of early brown bears became isolated on or near the ice and then one group of these brown bears branched off to become polar bears while other populations of brown bears continued on with the original lineage. Polar bears adapted to living on the pack ice, while the brown or grizzly bears remained on land. Populations of grizzlies then crossed the Bering Land Bridge during the late Pleistocene glaciations. Numerous black bear fossils indicate that both species coexisted along the coast. Brown bears survived on mainland Alaska and on the coastal islands during the height of the glacial periods when the ice sheets were at their largest and sea levels were lowest. Black bears apparently did not reach Alaska until after the last glacial period. The maximum extent of the Wisconsinan period occurred 18,000 years ago.

During the Pleistocene, the grizzly was only found north of the continental ice sheets in North America. At this time a continuous brown bear population probably existed all across Eurasia and into Alaska connected by the Bering Land Bridge. In essence, Alaska was a part of Siberia. North-eastern Siberia, the Bering Land Bridge, and Alaska formed a region we call Beringia. It was at one end of a single, vast continent that was cut in two by a huge ice sheet over North America, Northern Europe, and north-western Eurasia. The climate of Beringia 18,000 years ago was arctic: cold and dry. The southern coast of Beringia, as well as the interior, had no trees, it was a rocky landscape with a thin layer of tundra or tundra steppe (grassland) lying over permafrost. There were low beaches from Siberia to what is now

Sloth bears use their large mobile lips for sucking ants and termites out of the ground.

the Aleutian Peninsula where the Cordilleran Ice Sheet reached the sea. Along the edge of the ice sheet there were islands of dry land that served as refugia for species which could survive there. The ABC Islands (Admiralty, Baranoff, and Chichagoff), the Queen Charlotte Islands (Haida Gwai), and Vancouver Island were among them.

There were two Ice Sheets over North America at the height of

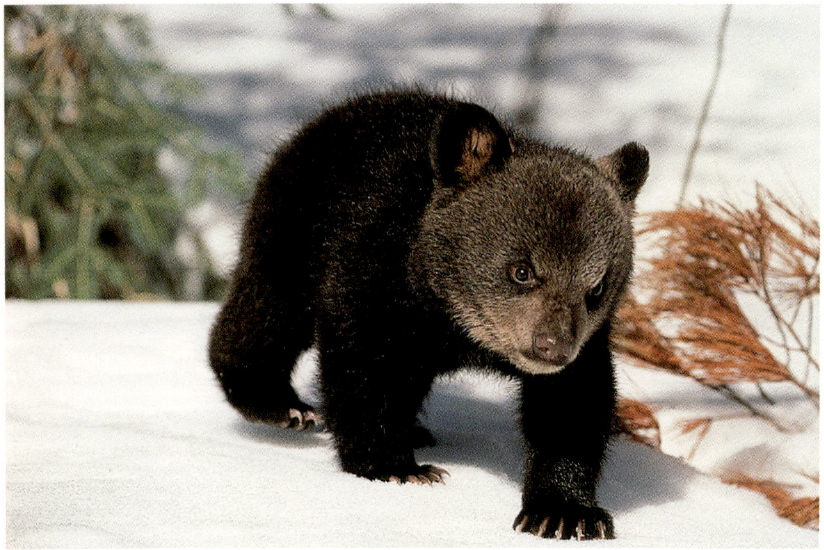

Black bear cubs remain in the den for several months.

the last Ice Age (the Last Glacial Maximum). The larger, Laurentide ice sheet began to recede about 18,000 years ago. However, the Cordilleran ice sheet along the coast continued to expand until 15,000 years ago. There was no interior route south until about 11,000 years ago although the coastal islands may have served as stepping stones for some species long before then. An interesting question is whether there were salmon along the ice-free portions of the coast. Almost certainly there were. Beringia was primarily low and flat and may have had few streams, but as the ice receded, salmon eventually colonized the rivers that were formed. Both brown bears and early humans would have relied heavily on salmon whenever and wherever they became available.

The brown bear also coexisted with the giant short-faced bear, *Arctodus simus*, during the last part of this epoch in the Alaska-Yukon region, and finally migrated below the ice sheets only during the last phase of glaciation as the ice sheets receded and the Mackenzie Corridor (a pathway between the two large masses of the continental ice sheet) opened up. The only known association of these two species south of Alaska is from Little Box Elder Cave near Douglas, Wyoming. The grizzly was probably in competition with the giant short-faced bear throughout its range and eventually replaced it. The earliest records of brown bears below the ice sheet are around 13,000 years ago. The latest fossil record for the giant short-faced bear is about 13,000 years ago from Lubbock Lake in Texas.

Bear populations expand slowly; one female home range at a time. As grizzlies expanded their range south of the ice sheets they competed with the black bear and in some cases restricted the black bears' range. By the time of the earliest historical records, the grizzlies had expanded as far south as central Mexico.

Genetic Evidence

The genetic data that relates one species to another (phylogeny) is largely based upon proteins and mitochondrial DNA which is found in most cells. Mitochondrial DNA (or mtDNA) contains only the blueprint for the mitochondria: single-celled organelles that function primarily in providing energy to the cell. Mitochondrial DNA is passed on, from generation to generation, only by the female. Mitochondrial DNA has helped us learn about the differences that have been found between bear species, which bears came first, which bears evolved from other bears, and approximately how long ago two bears species diverged from a common ancestor. Nuclear DNA contains the blueprint for the individual animal. Studying nucleur DNA can tell us about differences between individuals and between populations.

Using mtDNA and proteins to compare species, geneticists have determined, or confirmed, many important relationships, ie: giant pandas are true bears, while red pandas are more like raccoons. The giant panda lineage is the oldest of all the bears and is the only species with 42 chromosomes; the original bear group split from the Procyonids (raccoons) about 32 million years ago. Then the ancestral pandas (family Ailuripodinae) split off about 20 million years ago.

The next oldest group of bears are the Tremarctinae or short-faced bears, of which the spectacled bear in South America is the only living species. The spectacled bear has 52 chromosomes. The short-faced bears split off from the Ursids about 15 million years ago. One group subsequently invaded South America and then all the North America species became extinct.

All other bears have 74 chromosomes and are classified as the family Ursidae. This group began to branch off from a common ancestor within the last four to eight million years. Most mtDNA evidence suggests that the sloth bears diverged first around 8 million years ago. Sun bears evolved later, about 5 million years ago.

One study suggests that a group of bears split off from the same lineage as sloth bears about 6 million years ago and that American black bears and sun bears resulted as sister taxa from that new lineage; later the Asiatic black bears split off from the main lineage. Another study suggests that a black bear lineage split about a million years after the sun bear and eventually formed two species of black bear; the sister taxa of American black bears and Asiatic black bears. A third study could not find any statistical differences among the sun bear, American black bear and Asiatic black bear lineages. Regardless of whether they were part of a sun bear lineage, or an Asiatic black bear lineage, one group of ancestral bears migrated across the Bering Land Bridge to North America about 3.5 million years ago. As the connection with Asia was severed during the Pliocene by rising sea levels, the American black bear became a separate species while its relatives in northern Asia went their own way.

At about the same time, somewhere around 4 to 5 million years ago, another group of bears diverged to form the lineage leading to brown (or grizzly) and polar bears. Grizzly bears and polar bears

APPROXIMATE DATES OF ORIGIN OF THE SPECIES OF BEARS

Species	Date of Origin From Fossil Evidence	Date of Origin From Genetic Evidence	Area of Origin
True Bear Family Ursidae	> 5 MYA* *Ursus minimus*	4-8 MYA	Northern Asia
Polar Bear *Ursus maritimus*	c 300,000 years ago	1 MYA	Northern Siberia
Brown Bear *Ursus arctos*	> 500,000 years ago-China > 900,000 years ago-France	1 MYA	Northern Asia
American Black Bear *Ursus americanus*	> 3.5 MYA	5 MYA	North America
Asiatic Black Bear *Ursus thibetanus*		5 MYA	Central Asia (Himalayas?)
Sloth Bear *Ursus ursinus*		7 MYA	South-central Asia (India?)
Sun Bear *Ursus malayanus*		5 MYA	South-east Asia (Islands?)
Cave Bear *Ursus spelaus*	> 300,000 years ago-Europe		Europe
Short-faced Bear SuperFamily Tremarctinae	> 6 MYA *Plionarctos*	12-15 MYA	North America
Giant Short-faced Bear *Arctodus simus*			North America
Spectacled Bear *Tremarctos ornatus*			South America
Panda Bear SuperFamily Ailuropodinae	> 15 MYA *Agriarctos*	18-22 MYA	Central Asia
Giant Panda *Ailuropoda melanoleuca*	> 600,000 years ago		Central Asia (China?)

* million years ago

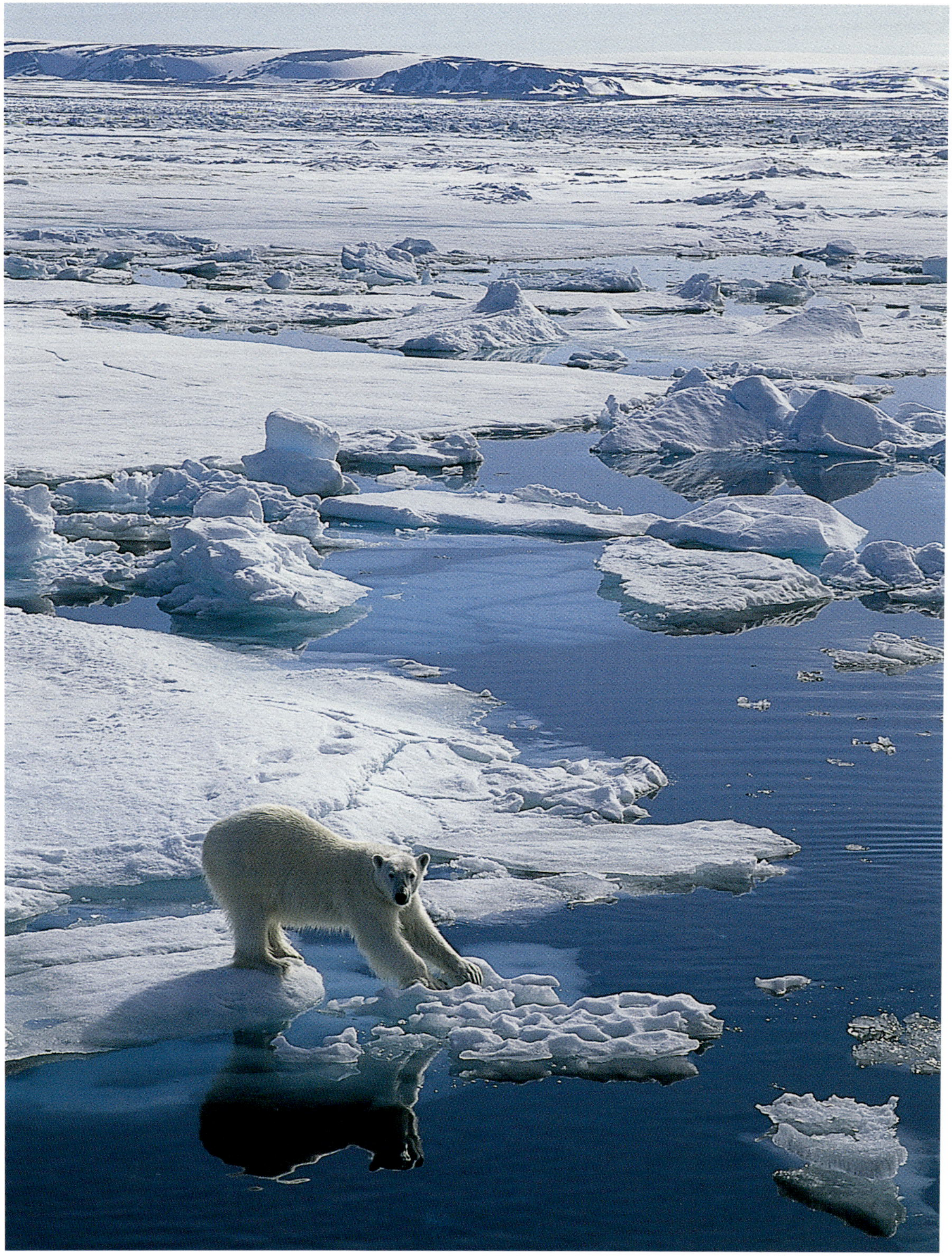

appear to have diverged from each other about one million years ago according to the DNA evidence. This is an earlier date than the fossil record suggests, but may be due to the scarcity of fossils from that period. The picture that emerges from the combination of DNA and fossil evidence shows that during warm periods new habitats open up which bears can colonize. During cold periods the habitat shrinks and bears were often isolated in islands of habitat (or refugia) for long enough periods to become genetically distinct. Important migrations took place during the transition from cold to warm periods; bears had to cross the Bering Land Bridge and other land bridges during cold periods when sea levels were low (the water was frozen in glaciers and ice packs). But they could probably do this most easily near the ending of a cold period as new habitat became available when the glaciers retreated but sea levels had not fully risen. Polar bears too may have diverged during transition periods when there was pack ice near shore for hunting seals, but when the pack ice receded it may have isolated a group of bears stranded on the ice away from land, or at least away from brown bear populations, for many thousands of years.

Half a million years ago, ancestral brown/grizzly bears ranged all across northern Eurasia. At about this time, the European cave bear was also present. Cave bears probably evolved earlier and they went extinct as brown bears increased. According to the DNA evidence, different groups of ancestral brown bears in Europe diverged about 850,000 years ago during the first Ice Age. Apparently, two major groups became isolated in refugia as the ice covered the land; one refuge was in western Europe (the Iberian refugium), and the other was in eastern Europe (the Balkan refugium). There were other refugia on the Italian peninsula and in Turkey, but bears from those areas did not re-colonize Europe. The location of these refugia has been determined by the recovery of fossils from those regions, and the legacy of isolation can be found today in the DNA evidence. As the climate warmed and the ice retreated, the plants and animals began slowly recolonizing the land that the glaciers uncovered. Descendants of the two brown bear populations expanded until they reached territory occupied by other brown bears, and then they began slowly to interbreed. The evidence for this remains as two distinct lineages (or clades) of mitochondrial DNA in European brown bears. Sweden is one such contact zone where the two distinct mtDNA lineages have only recently met.

There are at least five distinct brown bear mtDNA clades worldwide; two in Eurasia and three in North America. As genetic data accumulated, at first it was thought that the three clades in North America were probably formed by three separate migration events. The first wave of migration from the Old World may have occurred as long as 300,000 years ago prior to the last, Wisconsinan, glaciation. For a period of time, both brown bears and giant short-faced bears competed in the vast plains of Beringia. However, as the glaciation proceeded, the mammoths, horses, ground sloths and short-faced bears eventually went extinct. During an early glaciation this group of brown bears survived as an isolated population on the ABC islands of south-east Alaska. When conditions became favorable again, it was thought that a second wave of brown bears migrated across the Bering Land Bridge. It appeared that the ABC bears, at least the females, remained on the islands which were probably surrounded by deep water during warmer periods, and did not interbreed with the second wave of colonizing brown bears. Somewhat later, a third wave of migrants was thought to have crossed from Asia. Humans also colonized the New World at this time. The last wave of brown bears was originally thought to have occupied the western part of Alaska, including Kodiak Island. The previous group of bears moved farther east and south into what is now Canada and the Lower-48 States as the ice sheets receded.

Currently however, a different picture has emerged. Recent mtDNA evidence has been analyzed from bear remains that were

A polar bear waits by a polynya, or patch of open water; whales use these openings for breathing.

frozen in the permafrost of eastern Beringia. These mtDNA data indicate that brown bears inhabited eastern Beringia 35,000-40,000 years ago during a time when the entire continent was ice free. All three lineages were present in the population at the same time. They had migrated over from Asia about 50,000-70,000 years ago. Apparently they had not migrated much further south before the glaciers blocked this route about 18,000 years ago.

At least one lineage of brown bears appears to have become established on coastal islands where the bears survived the height of the Ice Age. Since mtDNA is passed on only the egg, from a mother to her offspring, a fascinating picture emerges. Small groups of females probably colonized the island refugia; maybe even a single female. Thus a single female lineage eventually occupied the ABC Islands in Alaska. It appears likely that another female lineage survived the glacial maximum further south on another island refugium although no samples have yet been found.

After the ice began to recede, the southernmost lineage expanded all across what is now the western contiguous United States and Mexico. The lineage on the ABC Islands has remained there; males dispersed away from the islands to the mainland, but females, who remain close to their mothers when they reach adulthood, have never successfully left the islands. The brown bear lineage that survived the Ice Age in eastern Beringia never migrated into the Lower-48 but has expanded across Alaska.

American black bear genetics also tell an interesting story. Black bears were found all across North America below the ice sheets for over 3 million years. Then, about 11,000 years ago when the ice receded, brown bears expanded southward, and black bears expanded northward, along with the forests, into uncolonized lands that both bear species managed to share. Both species may have survived the last Ice Age on coastal island refugia; brown bears almost certainly occupied the ABC islands at that time.

Black bear genetics have received less scrutiny but mtDNA studies indicate that there are two ancient lineages, or clades, in North America. One group is currently centered on the west coast and extends into the Canadian Rockies. The other group is found everywhere else from Alaska to Florida. There is hybridization of the two groups in the Northern Rocky Mountains. It is likely that these two ancient lineages were formed about 2 million years ago when the North American forests became separated into an Eastern and interior forest and a Western coastal forest by a colder and drier climate than we have today. The Eastern lineage was distributed over a much larger area where the populations remained connected and gene flow continued.

More samples of black bears need to be analyzed from different regions to clarify this picture, but it appears that during the Pleistocene one group of black bears was isolated along the Pacific coast perhaps in Washington or British Columbia about 350,000 years ago, while another group occupied inland areas during interglacial periods. The fact that there are only two distinct mtDNA clades of black bears, but there are 16 recognized subspecies (based on morphological, behavioral, and other differences) illustrates the fact that genetic data alone does not tell the whole story as far as ecological differences are concerned. All the available information is often used by taxonomists to separate animals into subspecies. It is likely that the changes which have occurred in the various black bear subspecies have occurred relatively recently (perhaps only since the last glaciation about 11,000 years ago) as black bears adapted to local environments. There has not been a long enough time for mtDNA changes to occur, but studies of nuclear DNA should reveal important differences.

There have been several genetic studies of polar bears using allozymes (proteins), mitochondrial DNA, and nuclear DNA. Only the nuclear DNA studies revealed enough detail to detect differences.

Spectacled bears are the last living species of the short-faced bears (Tremarctinae); they are excellent tree climbers.

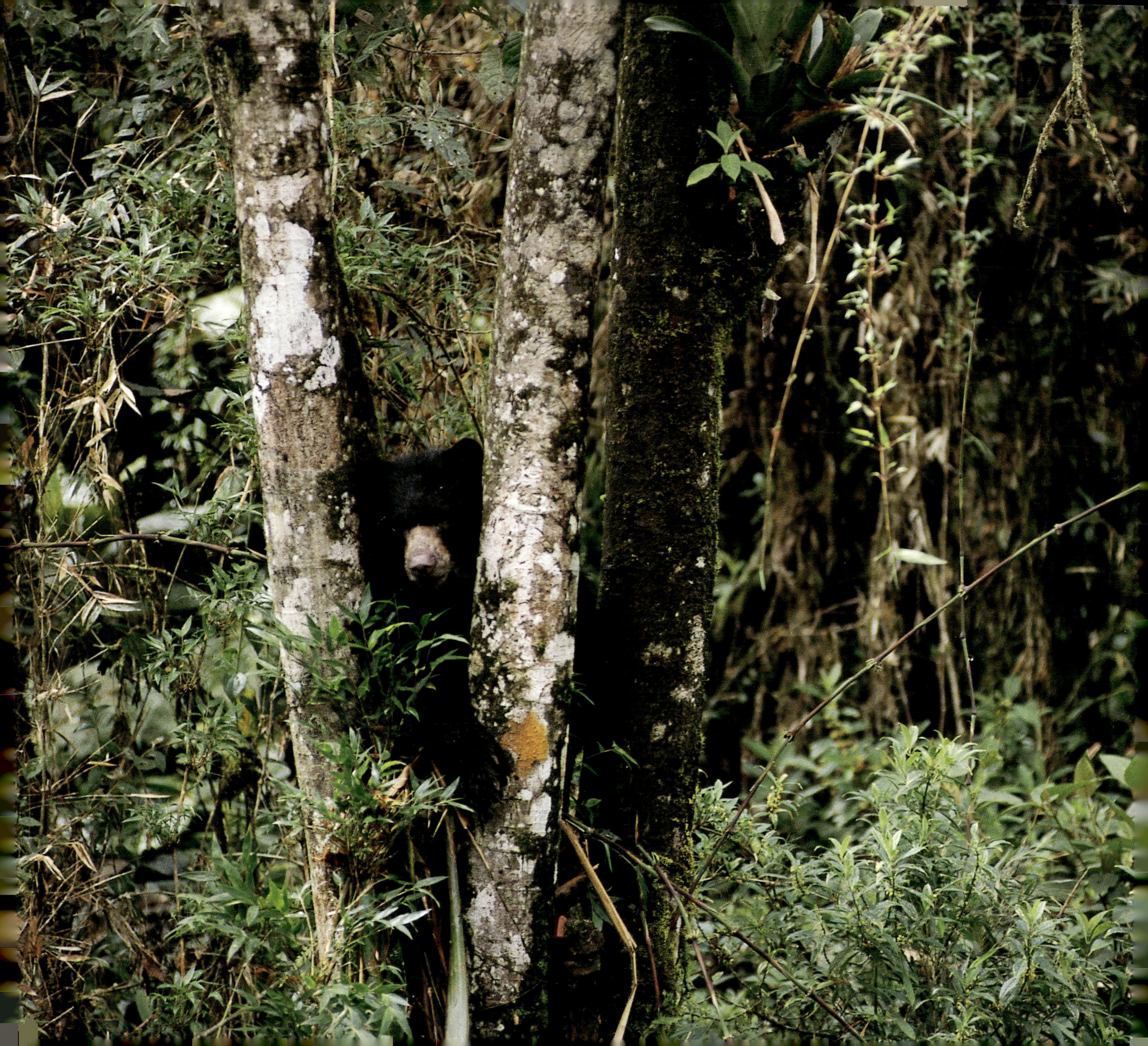

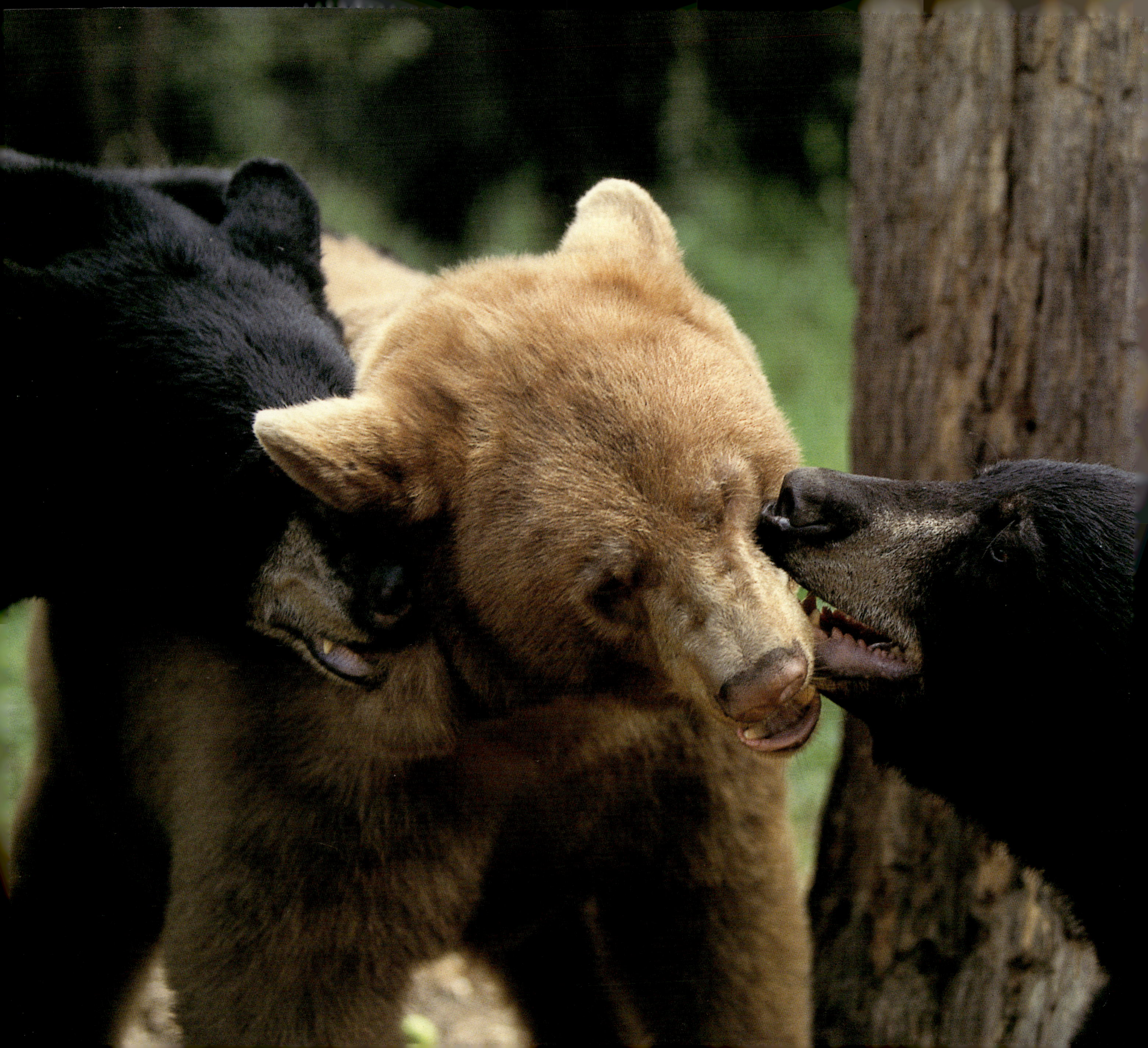

Behavior

Over time bears have evolved a diversity of adaptations; morphological, physiological, and behavioral; which allow them to survive and reproduce. Each species has developed different approaches to survival and reproduction and these techniques have been fine-tuned in the workshop of natural selection to operate at a nearly optimal level in the environment.

The bears, as a group, have remained mostly generalists, mostly omnivorous. The giant panda, whose lineage branched off long ago, is the only true herbivore: and the polar bear is the only true carnivore among bears. Sloth bears and sun bears feed primarily on fruit and insects. The brown or grizzly bear, which feeds on both plants and animals, still occupies the greatest natural geographical range of any large mammal except wolves and man. It ranges from the edge of the Arctic ice, to the Himalayas, to the edge of the Gobi desert and was once found even in northern Africa.

To understand why the different bear species are the way they are it is helpful to consider two important points; 1) they evolved from carnivores and developed herbivorous adaptations from a basically carnivorous form, and 2) they evolved relatively recently and needed to exploit ecological opportunities (or niches) that were not already taken by the other, older, carnivores. The big cats – lions and tigers – had already specialized enough to monopolize the strictly carnivorous niches for larger prey, and the dogs were more efficient at capturing small and medium-sized prey. As the bears evolved, they changed to take advantage of whatever underutilized food sources were available in the particular environment they found themselves in. In this way, the sloth bears evolved in the Indian subcontinent. Lions, tigers, and cheetahs were well established. Fruits were extremely seasonal and could not provide a year-round food source. However, insects such as termites and ants were high in calories, constantly available, and under utilized. Over time, the ancestors of the sloth bear developed adaptations such as highly mobile lips, hairless muzzles, and missing teeth so that they could utilize insects as a reliable, year-round food source.

The other bear species evolved in a similar fashion. Sun bears became very good at climbing trees and feeding on fruits and honey. Pandas exploited the wide availability of bamboo; although they are strictly herbivorous they still retain the canine and incisor teeth of their carnivorous ancestors. Both species evolved where tigers ruled. The brown bears evolved in the northern hemisphere where wolves were the top carnivores in more recent times. The fast-moving herbivores were already being taken by those equally fast, and cooperative hunters. The brown bears settled for strength, size, and quickness to take prey when available, and to rely on more stable plant foods and the seasonally available salmon. The polar bear then evolved from a brown-bear-like ancestor, a generalist, in order to exploit an unused carnivorous niche; the marine mammals of the polar ice pack.

The ability to climb trees probably appeared very early in the evolution of bears. The skeletal structure and musculature of all bears predisposes them for climbing trees; the species that don't often climb are those that do not have much need for climbing.

Avoidance Behavior

As predators developed their arsenals of weapons through evolution – their sharp teeth, claws, speed and other attributes which gave them the ability to catch and kill prey animals – they needed to simultaneously develop ways to prevent using them on their own species. Animals that kill their own kind reduce their chances of passing on their own genes; they may kill their own offspring, or reduce the population enough that the entire population goes locally

Black bear color phases vary greatly; these black and cinnamon bears are playing and all may be from the same litter.

extinct. Over hundreds of generations, genes which allowed predators to kill their own kind became very rare or were lost completely. At the same time, predators which did not kill their own species had higher survival rates and larger populations. Any genetic component of this restraint behavior was maintained and those individuals passed on more of their genes than kin-killers. These behavioral adaptations became genetically determined (at least in part), and ingrained in predatory behavior.

Nothing is absolute, particularly where behavior is concerned, and there are situations in which predators will kill their own kind. However, in general, predators have evolved ways to avoid killing their kin and even unrelated members of their own species. One important exception is cub-killing behavior.

Some of the most well-known avoidance behaviors are aggressive displays which allow competitors to size each other up, and perhaps to spar with each other and gauge each other's strength, without fighting to the death. Bears will often fight ferociously with rivals that match them closely, and they often carry impressive scars on their head and neck. However, when one bear involved in a fight accepts defeat and shows the proper submissive behavior, the dominant bear will usually allow him to back off and run away. In many cases the loser will turn his head to the side and look down, exposing his neck to the other. Submissive behaviors such as this are common among many predators and must have evolved long ago in the earliest carnivores. After being defeated, the loser will generally avoid encounters in the future, and will relinquish food or potential mates when more dominant bears arrive. Aggression is more common among male bears, which are larger and stronger than females, and they will fight to establish dominance hierarchies within social groups. These 'pecking orders' are most easily observed where bears congregate in high densities to feed on concentrated food sources such as salmon spawning streams.

It is clear that bears have developed behaviors to avoid unnecessary injury to themselves or to other bears. Less well known, and much more difficult to observe, is avoidance behavior determined primarily by scent-marking. Grizzly bears are known to establish traditional trails that follow topographical features and in some well-traveled areas these trails are worn a foot or more deep into the soil. Along these trails, and in other areas of common use, scent-marking trees where bears rub, bite, and/or claw the tree have also become established. As bears pass these sites they will sniff to see who has passed recently and perhaps leave their own scent for other bears to find. The strength of the scent enables an experienced bear to determine how recently another bear has passed, and thus how close that individual may be. This enables bears to avoid each other, and also to find each other during the breeding season. Bite marks and claw marks have been suggested as a means of estimating the size of other bears; the higher a bear has clawed a tree and the size of the claw marks may provide visual clues to go with the scent that was left. Traditional scent-marking sites are more effective in some types of habitat than others and will be discussed in more detail in the chapter on grizzly bears.

Much less is known about the scent-marking behavior of some of the other bear species, but it is likely that it is an important signaling mechanism among all species.

Cub-killing Behavior

Predatory species have developed mechanisms to reduce or avoid injury or death in inter-species competition. However, there is also a type of behavior which does just the opposite; this is the killing of young animals. At first glance, such behavior does not seem to make sense from the standpoint of survival. One of the most extreme cases is found in African lions. When dominant males grow older and weaker they become vulnerable to takeovers by younger males;

Grizzly bears in the Rocky Mountains mark trees with their scent and often leave claw or bite marks.

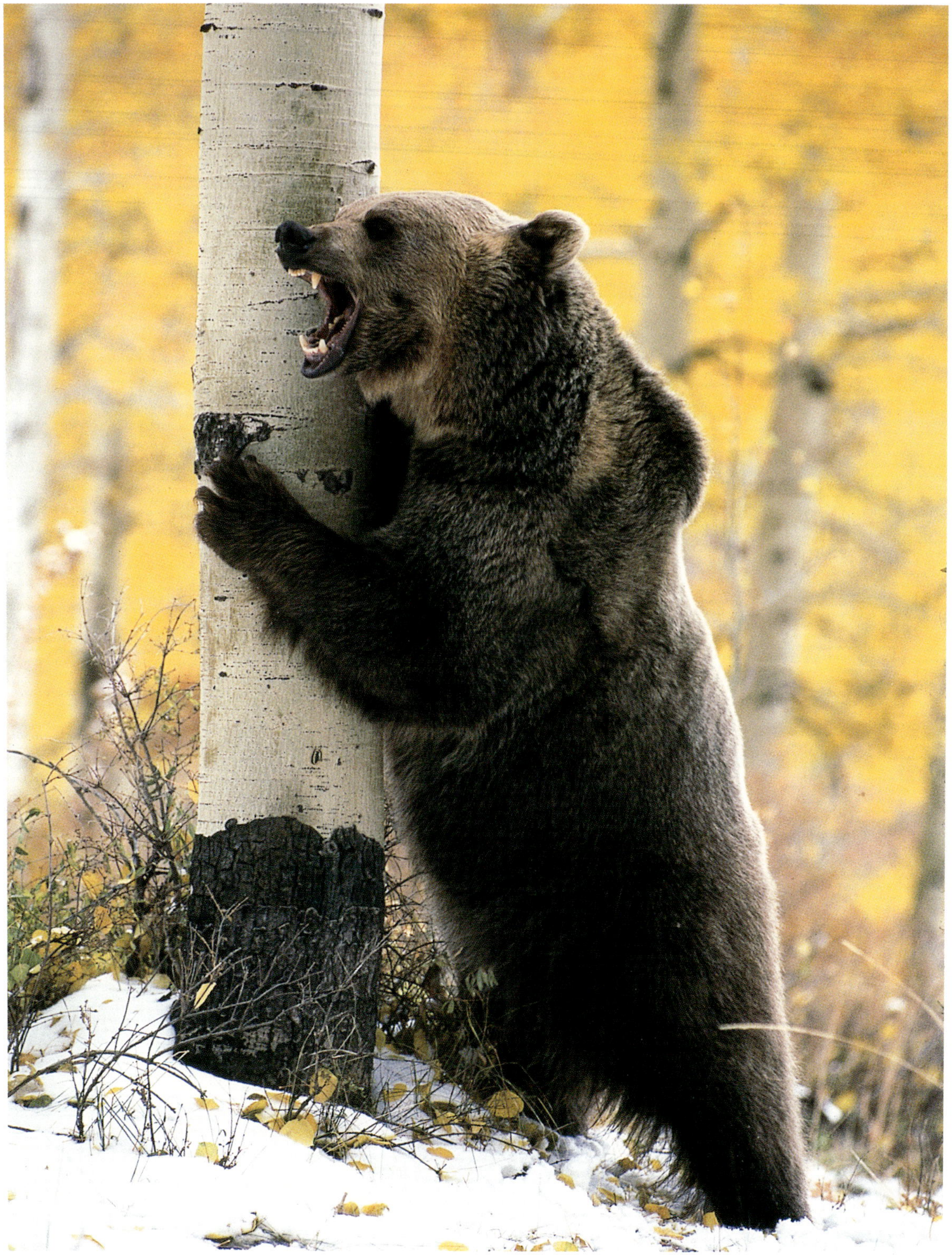

often a group of male siblings will disperse from a pride and challenge an old monarch; driving him away from his pride. Although they may not kill the previous ruler, they will invariably kill all the cubs in the pride. From a population standpoint this reduces the size of the population and may increase the risk of local extinction. However, from an evolutionary standpoint, this behavior makes sense

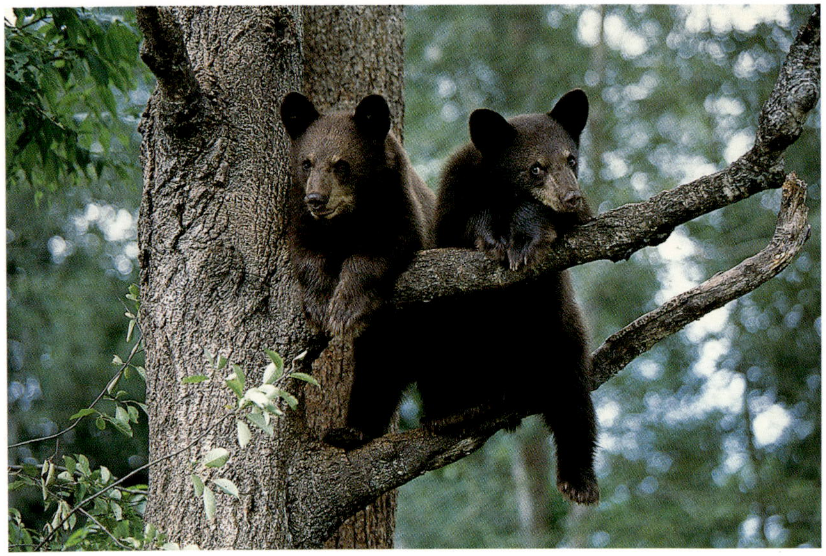

Black bear cubs climb trees when danger threatens.

in that the new arrivals are maximizing their own fitness. By killing the cubs that were sired by the previous monarch they are removing his genes from the next generation and reducing the amount of prey needed to maintain the pride during the transition period. As the females in the pride come into estrous, the new dominant male passes on his own genes. Any genes that govern this cub-killing behavior are passed on as well and the behavior is perpetuated.

A similar behavior is found in bear species; especially in the brown or grizzly bears. Cubs are constantly at risk of being killed by male bears and mothers are wary and vigilant. A female with cubs is very aggressive and can often drive off much larger males when her cubs are threatened. In some cases, however, males may even kill the mother. The reasons for this behavior are not well understood. Cub killing may be a mechanism for increasing a male's fitness. However, it makes more sense in the case of lions, since females will readily come into estrous again at any time of the year. Female bears only come into estrous during spring. Some biologists have suggested that the killing of cubs can hasten the onset of estrous in the mother; without a cub to care for the female will become sexually receptive sooner than if she raised the cub to the age of weaning. When this happens, the cub-killer can mate with her and promote his own genes.

There are several difficulties with this theory, but it may explain some of this behavior. To begin with, the male must be able to recognize his own cubs (or at least the females he has previously mated with) and refrain from killing them. This is very difficult to demonstrate. Then, he must be the one to successfully breed with the female when she comes into heat or else the killing has been in vain. This is also very difficult to obtain data about. In genetic studies of low-density Arctic populations, even the most successful males were found to have sired only about 11 per cent of the known cubs. In such cases, even random cub killing could remove more competing genes than his own from the population. However, the chances that he would be the one to successfully pass on his genes with those females when they next bred, are very low.

The theories of genetic advantage in cub killing are confounded by hunger. In most cases, when cubs are killed by male grizzly bears, they are also eaten. It appears that cubs are also a source of food. Male bears in the Arctic will also occasionally kill and eat female bears; with or without cubs. Cannibalistic behavior, especially in species with low density and low reproductive rate, is not an evolutionary option. If bears killed and ate other bears for food they would soon become extinct. However, it may have survival advantage in cases where food resources are very scarce. In such cases, at least some bears would survive, rather than all of them starving to death. In fact, most documented cases of cub and/or female killing by males seem to be from areas where food is scarce and population densities are low. Coastal brown bears, that are well fed on salmon, are not nearly as aggressive towards cubs and mothers as their Arctic counterparts.

The causes of cub-killing behavior are probably some combination of these two factors: genetic advantage and plain hunger, and are further determined by individual differences in aggressiveness in male bears. Some males kill cubs while others don't. There are also differences among species. Grizzlies, American black bears, and polar bears are the most well-studied species and all may sometimes kill cubs; less is known about the other species. It is possible that the more carnivorous a species is, the more likely that hunger plays a role. Some of these mysteries may eventually be explained by detailed genetic studies of bears with known kinship, but the whole story may never be completely understood.

Learning Behavior

In addition to claws, teeth, and strong back muscles, perhaps the greatest adaptation that bears have in common is the high capacity for learning and memory. They are relatively long-lived, with an extended development period. Perhaps more than any other predator, bears learn from their mothers how to survive. Their biggest challenge is to learn about plants. Because bears have inherited a carnivorous metabolism and intestinal tract from their distant ancestors, they cannot efficiently digest cellulose and other plant fibers like elk, deer, and cattle can. They need to find and consume growing plants during the short pre-flowering stage when the growing plant contains more protein and has its highest nutritional value. Later, when this energy has been stored by the plant in seeds or nuts, it is again a valuable food source for bears.

As cubs, bears learn where to find dozens of species of plants as they emerge in the spring and grow, and they remember those places for the rest of their lives. They learn to find corms, roots, or tubers of dozens of other species when they are also at their highest nutritional state. And bears learn to find and return to, year after year, habitats with mast crops (nuts and berries) in the fall when they need to put on fat for hibernation. Spilled wheat and other grains along railroad tracks will attract bears, and they will often return to search along the rails; many have been killed by trains. Once a bear finds dog food on a porch, or groceries in an empty cabin, or French fries in a garbage can, he will remember it for the rest of his life, and his life will be shorter because of it.

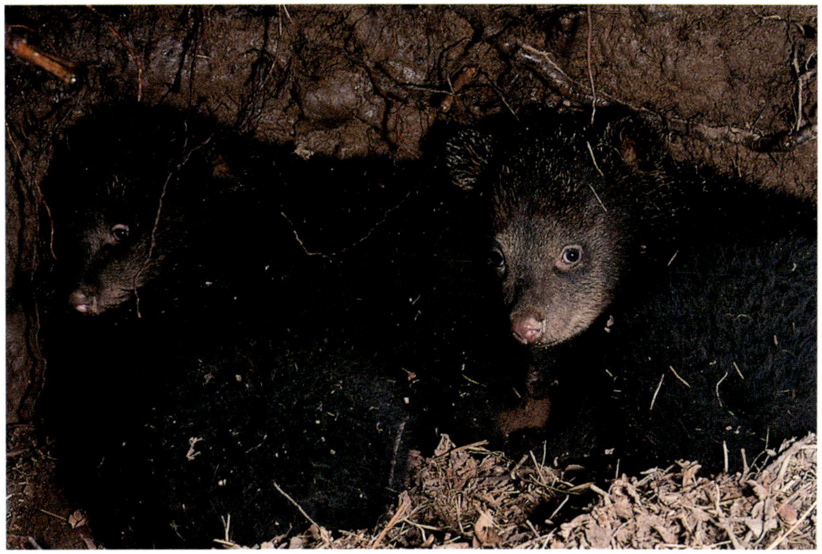

These black bear cubs grew this large entirely on their mother's milk.

Hibernation

The northern species of bears have adapted to the cold by entering a state of dormancy when food is unavailable. Bear researchers generally agree that the term 'hibernation' is appropriate for the dormant stage, although 'winter sleep' is often used. Brown bears remain continuously dormant for up to seven months. Other 'hibernating' species such as ground squirrels wake up every four to ten days in order to feed, defecate, and urinate. However, bears hibernate near body temperature (37–38°C) while other species may drop to just above freezing. Brown bear and black bear heart rates drop from 40–50 beats per minute to less than ten during hibernation. Polar bears that lack food in winter enter a similar dormant state but the heart rate only drops to about 27 beats per minute.

Brown and black bear metabolic rates are only 68 per cent of normal on average while dormant polar bears average 73 per cent of normal. The lowest metabolic rates recorded are 33 per cent in black bears and 40 per cent in polar bears. This low rate of metabolism provides enough water to supply the bears' needs; to keep plasma and red blood cells hydrated. Most of the blood is shunted to the heart, lungs, and brain as the heart beat and available oxygen drops. The concentration of protein, uric acid, and urea remains constant in the blood, but creatinine concentration doubles. Urea, a normally toxic substance derived from the digestion of proteins, is recycled.

During hibernation bears may lose up to a quarter of their predenning weight. Losses of more than 2 lb (1 kg) per day have been recorded. Fat, protein, and bone are metabolized. However, muscle mass and bone mass generally remain constant because the metabolized protein and bone are recycled. The ability to conserve protein seems to depend upon the amount of fat that the bear attained before hibernating; if there was insufficient fat, some loss of protein for energy can occur.

In addition to the energy demands of survival, pregnant female northern bears also must provide energy for the development of the fetus and the production of milk. Bears have developed a process of delayed implantation and a reduced gestation period. The eggs are fertilized during the spring mating period, but the fertilized egg does not become attached to the placenta until fall. The embryo quickly develops and the weak and helpless young are born in January. As an implanted embryo, the baby bear is fed on proteins from the mother's blood supply. The digestion of these proteins creates toxic compounds such as urea and creatinine which must be recycled in hibernating bears. The tropical bears continue to feed and spend only a short period of time in the birthing den; they continue to excrete the waste products of metabolism.

By giving birth early, and caring for the helpless infant in the den, the mother bear shifts from the burden of metabolizing protein, to feeding the cub with milk, outside her body, using the fatty acids she has stored which are not metabolized. In the first few days of life, the newborn cubs have short thin hair and their eyes are closed. They weigh about ten per cent less than the young of other mammals in proportion to the size of their mother. They cuddle close to their sleeping mothers and drink her milk as they grow. Their hair grows rapidly but their eyes remain closed until they are fully developed. The mother produces her rich, viscous milk while continuing to fast; converting her fat supplies to provide her own needs plus the needs of her cub.

Bear milk is similar to the milk of marine mammals, richer in fat and protein than other terrestrial carnivores. It has about three times the energy of that of humans or cattle. Polar bears have the richest milk, followed by brown bears and black bears. The milk of tropical bears, sun bears, pandas, and sloth bears is less rich, perhaps because less energy is required to combat cold temperatures. The tropical bears do not hibernate, but they may enter a somewhat dormant or lethargic state while giving birth and beginning to nurse. Their cubs are tiny, and they undergo delayed implantation and short gestation like the northern bears.

This suggests that the entire reproductive cycle, from delayed implantation, to short gestation, to nurture of the newborn, is an adaptation that arose early in evolution, in synch with the requirements of hibernation. As tropical bears adapted to warmer climates, they lost the ability to hibernate but the reproductive cycle has remained relatively unchanged.

In southeast Alaska black bears like these occupy almost all except the three largest islands, where grizzly bears reign supreme.

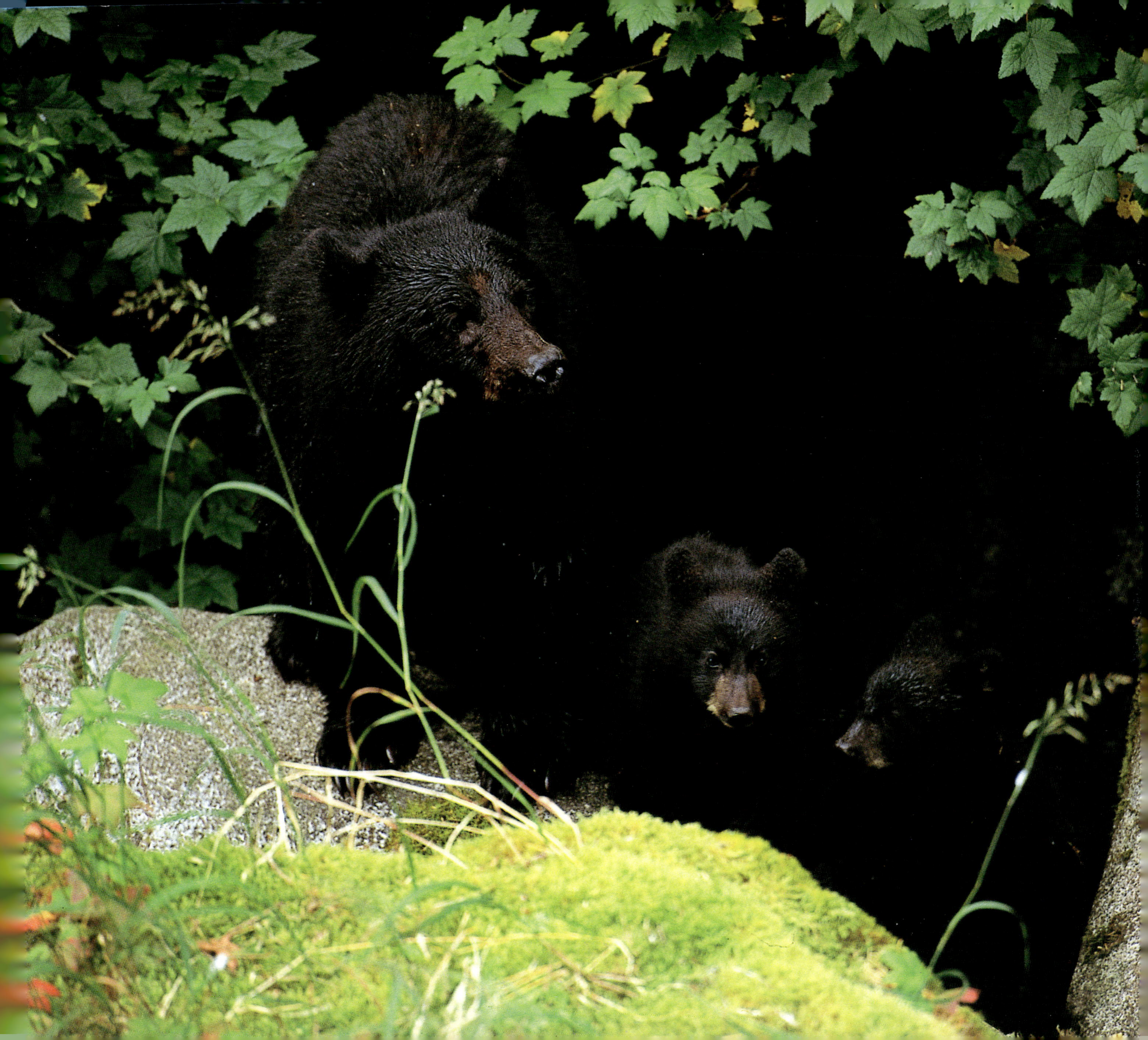

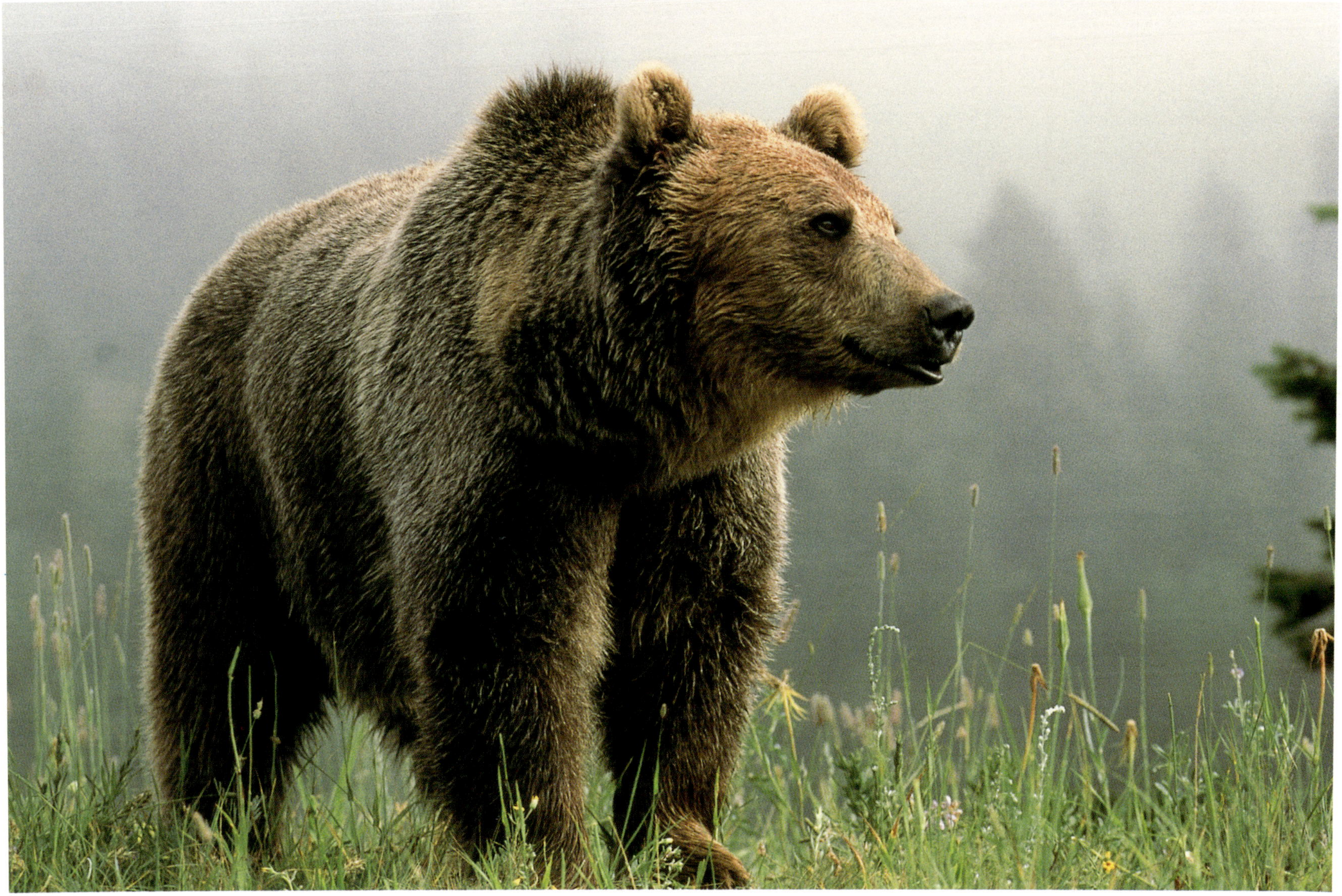

The Grizzly or Brown Bear

Scientifically, more is known about the brown bear than any of the other bear species except for the American black bear. The brown (or grizzly) bear and the other five species of the Ursid family of bears have evolved recently and share many similarities. In popular terms, the name brown bear generally refers to coastal and Eurasian populations, while grizzly bear refers to interior populations in North America; all of them have the scientific name *Ursus arctos*.

The grizzly or brown bear is the most widely distributed of the extant (living) bear species. Because much of what is known about them – behavior, life history, physiology – applies to some degree to the other bear species, brown bears will be discussed in much greater detail than the others. There are wide variations in color and size which appear to be due primarily to environmental differences. Size is probably correlated closely with the amount of nutrition available in the diet; thus coastal bears with access to salmon, a richer variety of plant foods, and milder weather conditions with a longer period for feeding, are about one-third again larger than bears in interior populations.

Brown bears can be thought of as direct descendants of the main lineage of the family Ursidae. Their ancestors have evolved from the ancient *Ursavus* 'bear dogs' primarily in Asia. Over time, this lineage gradually evolved to adapt to the colder climates in the north. Among the more important adaptations were the ability to hibernate during periods of food shortage and the ability to store large amounts of fat.

Brown bears are generally considered to undergo four annual stages of biochemical and physiological change. 1) The dormant stage is termed winter 'sleep' or 'hibernation' and is discussed in greater detail in the chapter 'Behavior'. 2) A modified dormancy, termed walking hibernation, is a transitional stage between hibernation and normal activity. 3) During normal activity brown bears cannot suddenly switch on the state of hibernation; if they are deprived of food they will begin to starve and utilize muscle tissue to survive. If deprived of water they will become dehydrated. During the normal state bears feed, sleep, defecate, urinate, and breed. 4) As the period of hibernation approaches, bears greatly increase their food intake in the stage called hyperphagia. The excess food is deposited as fat, or adipose tissue, and they gain weight. The layers of fat provide a source of energy during hibernation and insulate the bear from the cold. Fat is especially critical for the first few weeks after emergence from the den in spring, when food is generally scarce, but the bear's metabolic demands have increased. It is at this time that bears will starve to death if they were too lean during the previous fall.

Brown, or grizzly, bears have adapted to diverse habitats, from the Arctic tundra to the edges of the Gobi Desert. Wherever they live, they have the same requirements as other animals; adequate food, shelter, protection from predators, and the opportunity to find a mate and produce offspring. Although tigers, wolves, and mountain lions may have the ability to kill brown bears (especially cubs), their only real enemy is man. And men are such effective killers of bears that even though an area may have everything else that brown bears need, if it is easily accessible to people, brown bears will probably not use it. The exception to this is in areas where bears are totally protected such as National Parks. In these areas, where bears have not learned to immediately fear humans, they are able to coexist with man.

Bears are very intelligent animals; the experience of zookeepers and animal trainers indicates that they are smarter than dogs. This intelligence has enabled them to live in extreme environmental conditions and to exploit and learn an encyclopedic array of food species and local places. They spend several years with their mother learning from her what plants are good to eat and where to find them. They

A typical grizzly, or brown bear, has a prominent hump: muscles used primarily for digging.

also learn by themselves from experimentation. Orphaned cubs have learned how to catch and eat salmon on their own. By the time that subadult bears leave their mothers and take off on their own they know what plant foods are available at each time of the season, and they know what habitats are likely to have those foods over a very large area. As they leave their mothers and move into new areas they learn and remember where food is available. This knowledge is critical. Food sources change drastically from year to year depending upon weather and climate. A grizzly bear is often required to remember a type of food and where it was found that it may have last encountered ten or more years earlier.

Grizzlies are also efficient carnivores with sharp teeth coupled with powerful claws and incredible strength and quickness. They can immediately react, whenever an opportunity arises to kill a prey animal. A grizzly can change instantly from a peaceful herbivore grazing in a meadow to a charging predator with teeth bared. This change happens with the speed of a reflex; as any hunter knows, to hesitate even for a second often means that the prey can escape. The claws are primarily used for digging, not for predation or defense, but they can provide quick traction when a bear attacks.

This attack behavior is often responsible for casualties to humans. In many situations a bear will 'shoot first and ask questions later' as the old cowboy saying goes. This is particularly true of mothers with offspring to defend. It is also true of any bear that has a valuable food source, like an elk carcass, to defend from other bears. And it is sometimes true when a bear is just surprised at close range; particularly if the bear cannot determine quickly what has disturbed it. In such cases, a bear will attack the human in defense. A large number of such attacks turn into bluffs when the bear gets close enough to determine that these are humans, especially if they are not running away. Running away from a charging bear will often reinforce predatory reflex behavior and the bear may complete the charge.

Subspecies and Smaller Units of Conservation

The taxonomy of this diverse bear species is still a matter of discussion among biologists. At one time, up to 56 separate subspecies were proposed to account for the range of variation found in museum specimens. Today, most taxonomists only recognize two subspecies; the 'Kodiak' bears found on the Alaskan islands of Kodiak, Afognak, and Shuyak are classified as *Ursus arctos middendorffi*. These are among the largest brown bears in the world. All other grizzly/brown bears are generally considered to be *Ursus arctos horribilis*. Two other current contenders for subspecies status are the European brown bear; *Ursus arctos arctos*, and the Hokkaido brown bear found on the Japanese island of Hokkaido; *Ursus arctos yesoensis*.

The species concept was first formally defined by Darwin and Wallace, who differentiated between populations and individuals which would not interbreed due to physical or behavioral differences. This 'biological species' concept was more clearly defined by Ernst Mayr in the 1960s; species are groups of individuals which reproduce among themselves, other species are reproductively isolated from this group by behavior, physiology, and geography.

Although this seems straightforward enough, there are many exceptions to the rule. This is because the formation of new species is a continuous process that takes place over long periods of time. Speciation is discussed in a bit more detail in the chapter 'Origins and Evolution'.

Similarly, the boundary between subspecies is even more of a blur which gradually becomes visible over tens of thousands of years. Declaring one group of animals to be sufficiently different from another (such as Kodiak bears) is a judgment made by taxonomic scientists. In the past these choices were based on the range of morphological variation known from museum specimens; differences in hair color, skull size and shape, shape of foot pads, claws, teeth, etc. Today we are developing new metrics: genetic markers and even the

Kodiak bears are considered to be a separate subspecies, Ursus arctos middendorffi, *the largest brown bears in North America.*

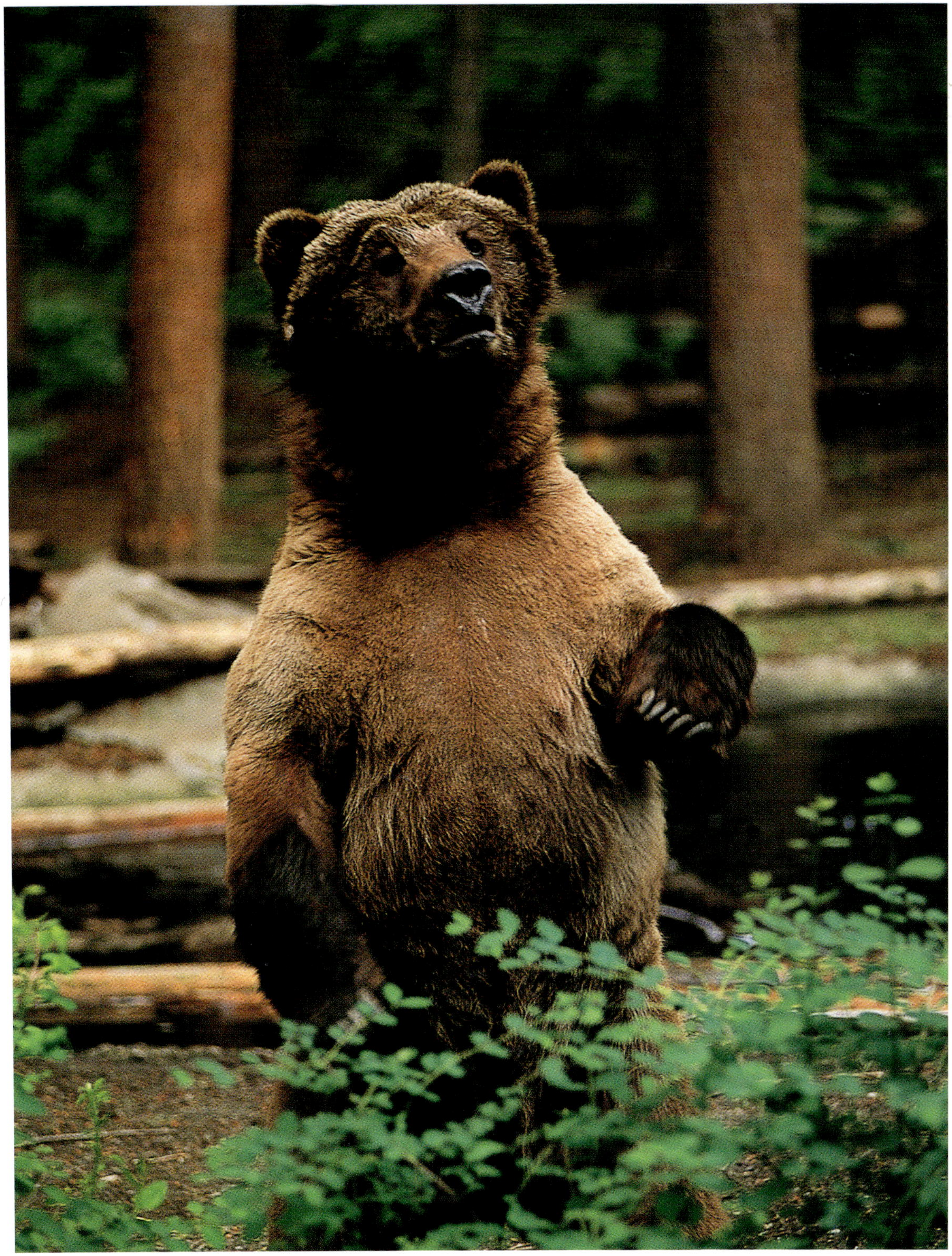

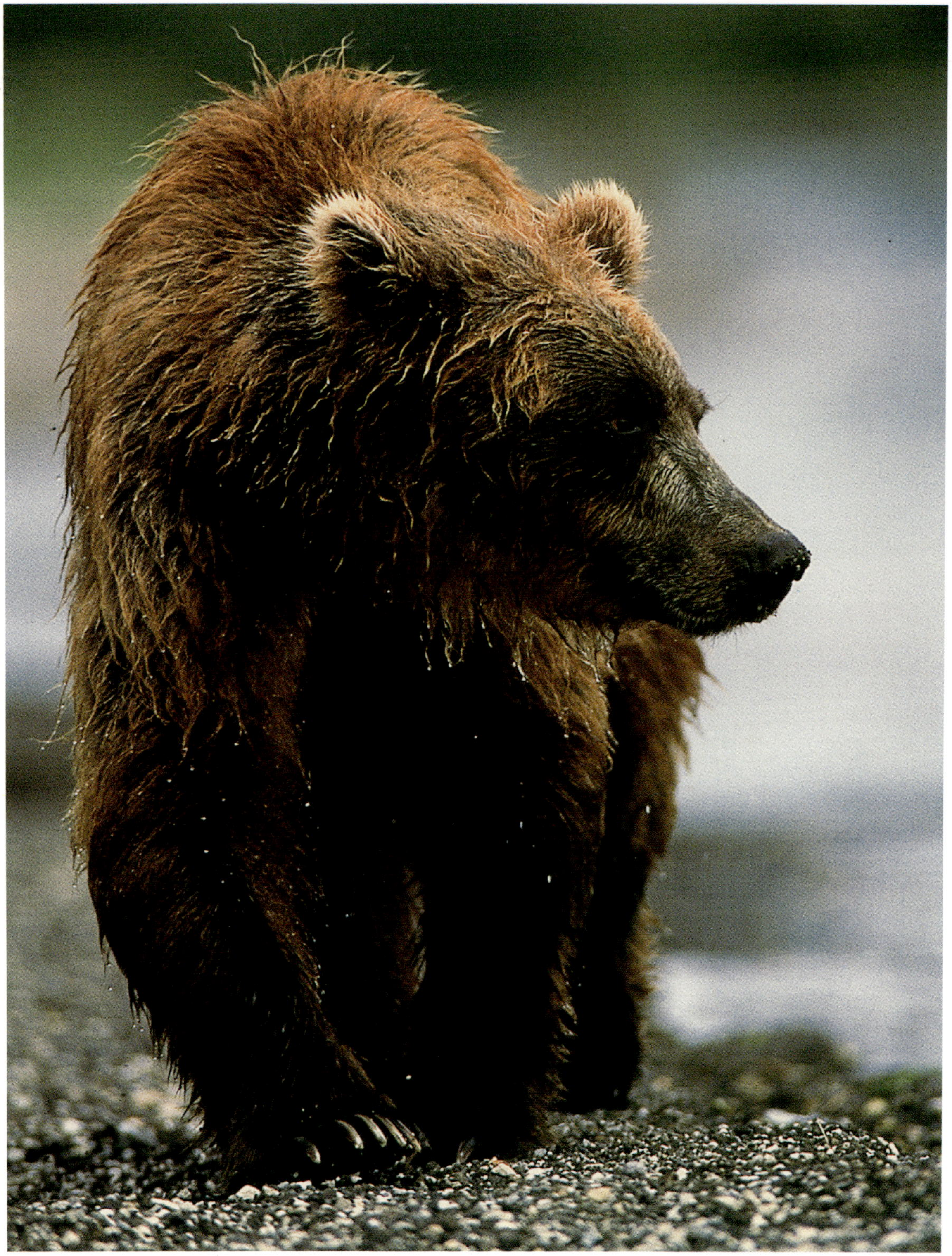

exact nucleotide sequences of DNA regions are being discovered for different species.

However, deciding how much of a genetic difference is sufficient to define a subspecies is still basically a subjective decision. The subtle differences that we find among the many populations of *Ursus arctos* reflect the genetic fine-tuning that has taken place in local environments. In the remainder of this chapter we will consider some of these differences and their importance for the species as a whole.

As our knowledge of genetic details has increased, subdivisions other than the subspecies have been proposed to identify unique groups of animals that may have relevance for conservation. Since brown bears are one of the few species other than man which have been fairly well studied from a genetic point of view, they are often the focus of discussions. Two categories which have been proposed are the Evolutionarily Significant Unit (ESU) and the Management Unit (MU). Biological definitions and genetic criteria have been proposed to identify these units. The purpose of such designations is to provide a standardized method for identifying groups of related animals which have developed local adaptations to different environments. These local adaptations represent genetic options which may be worth trying to preserve as we try to conserve bear populations.

This is an important issue for conservation. Determining what is an ESU or an MU at our present level of knowledge requires more information than just the genetic data. Preserving small groups of animals that have a slightly different genetic makeup (due to 10,000 years of divergence or less) to keep their genotypes 'pure' may or may not be a good idea. One school of thought argues that populations should not be allowed to interbreed. Another school of thought holds that interbreeding between different ESUs, subspecies, stocks, or management units will increase genetic variation and usually increase the chances that individual genes will survive. My own opinion is that humans have so greatly altered the natural environment, and shifted the forces of natural selection, that very few places in the world are the same now as they were when bears evolved to fit into them. Those places will change even more in the future until human populations reach a balance. Preserving genes and gene complexes that adapt bear populations to vanishing habitats is sort of a genetic gamble. Those habitats, or similar ones, may someday return or be recovered. On the other hand, they probably won't; as the climate warms, and human activities continue, the plant communities and other species assemblages of the future may be as different from those today as the present ones are different from the Pleistocene. Brown or grizzly bears will need to adapt to those changes. The range of their adaptability may be illustrated by the following sections.

Aggressiveness

Grizzly bear aggressiveness has two components: learned behavior and genetic predisposition. Both of these are probably influenced by the individual bear's physiological state (how hungry it is, or whether it is a female with cubs). Bears that are very well fed and do not have to fight to get food, such as coastal bears with access to abundant salmon, are generally much less aggressive towards each other and towards humans than are less fortunate bears in other areas. Grizzly populations that have had the least contact with humans, and have sparse food resources, are generally more aggressive.

There is little quantitative data to support this generalization, but experiences with grizzlies and brown bears in various parts of the world suggest that it is true. In areas where bears have been almost completely killed off by humans, we can assume that the most aggressive bears were the first ones to be killed. The bears that remained, and were able to avoid being killed, are the ones that had fewer 'aggressive genes' or the ones who learned not to be aggressive. They subsequently passed on these traits, either genetically or through learning, to their cubs. Thus the brown bears in isolated pockets of

Subadult brown bears, like most teenagers, are long-limbed and gangly; at this age they are inquisitive and adventurous.

Europe are nocturnal, secretive, and non-aggressive, and seldom seen.

Brown bear populations in many areas have been drastically reduced. Currently there are fewer than 50 brown bears in the Cantabrian Mountains of Spain, where they live in dense forest in higher elevations. There may be three remaining brown bears in the Brenta Mountains of Northern Italy, although new bears were recently introduced from Slovenia. The Brenta bears have almost never been seen, but their hair and scats have been analyzed for DNA and tracks have been observed.

In Sweden there are now over 1000 brown bears that inhabit forested areas. The areas they live in have greater densities of roads and humans than any place in North America where grizzlies are found. The Swedish people do not generally consider brown bears to be dangerous, and few people carry guns in bear country. These brown bears do not appear to be much different than similar bears farther east in Russia which are very aggressive. The difference in behavior may be due to the fact that the entire population of brown bears in Sweden was reduced to about 130 by 1930. Since then, the population has been allowed to increase and bears have been protected. There were no fatalities caused by Scandinavian bears for almost 100 years, until a single human was killed in 1999.

It is likely that many aggressive traits were lost by natural selection: in this case humans were the agents of natural selection and they removed the most aggressive bears. Any genetic basis for aggressiveness could have been removed from the population. This is a process that has been going on in Europe for over 40,000 years; brown bears that were very aggressive towards humans were killed whenever possible. It is also likely that brown bears learned to avoid humans as well, especially in recent times. How much of this change in behavior is due to genetics and how much is due to learning is something that we can only speculate upon, but both factors have contributed to produce the behavior we see today.

In coastal areas of Alaska where there are large quantities of salmon available, bears are extremely well fed and have little reason to be aggressive. We can assume that they still retain any genetic components of aggressiveness since these have not been selected against. They are often aggressive to humans when threatened by hunters or when disturbed on ungulate carcasses. Females with cubs are as aggressive as other bears in interior Alaska. Thus, the main difference in behavior here seems to be the fact that they are not hungry and have learned that they are not threatened by humans except in areas where they are hunted. Bears in viewing areas like McNeil River feed on salmon next to a small hill crowded with people and there has never been a serious injury.

Interior grizzly bears with sparse food sources appear to be more aggressive to each other as well as towards humans, although this has not been well studied. Males seem to kill cubs and even female grizzlies more frequently in the Arctic than in other areas, but it is more difficult to observe in areas with more cover. When males in the Arctic do kill cubs or females they sometimes eat them, which indicates that hunger is an important component of this behavior.

Social Behavior

Grizzly or Brown bears are often thought of as solitary animals that seldom interact, but this is a misconception. In areas with concentrated food sources, such as salmon streams, they establish intricate dominance hierarchies (pecking orders) by face-to-face encounters. In areas with sparse food sources and low densities of bears, they encounter each other rarely. In open tundra, they may rely on sight and wind-borne scent to locate each other and either avoid, or approach, other bears. In dense forests with low visibility they may communicate largely through scent marking on traditional scent-rubbing trees in order to locate each other in time and space. In many areas grizzly or brown bears will travel over well-established trails. In more open forest habitats, there are fewer marking trees. In completely open habitats, scent-marking stations are very rare.

Arctic, or barren-ground, grizzlies inhabit vast treeless expanses where scent can travel long distances on the wind. There are few if

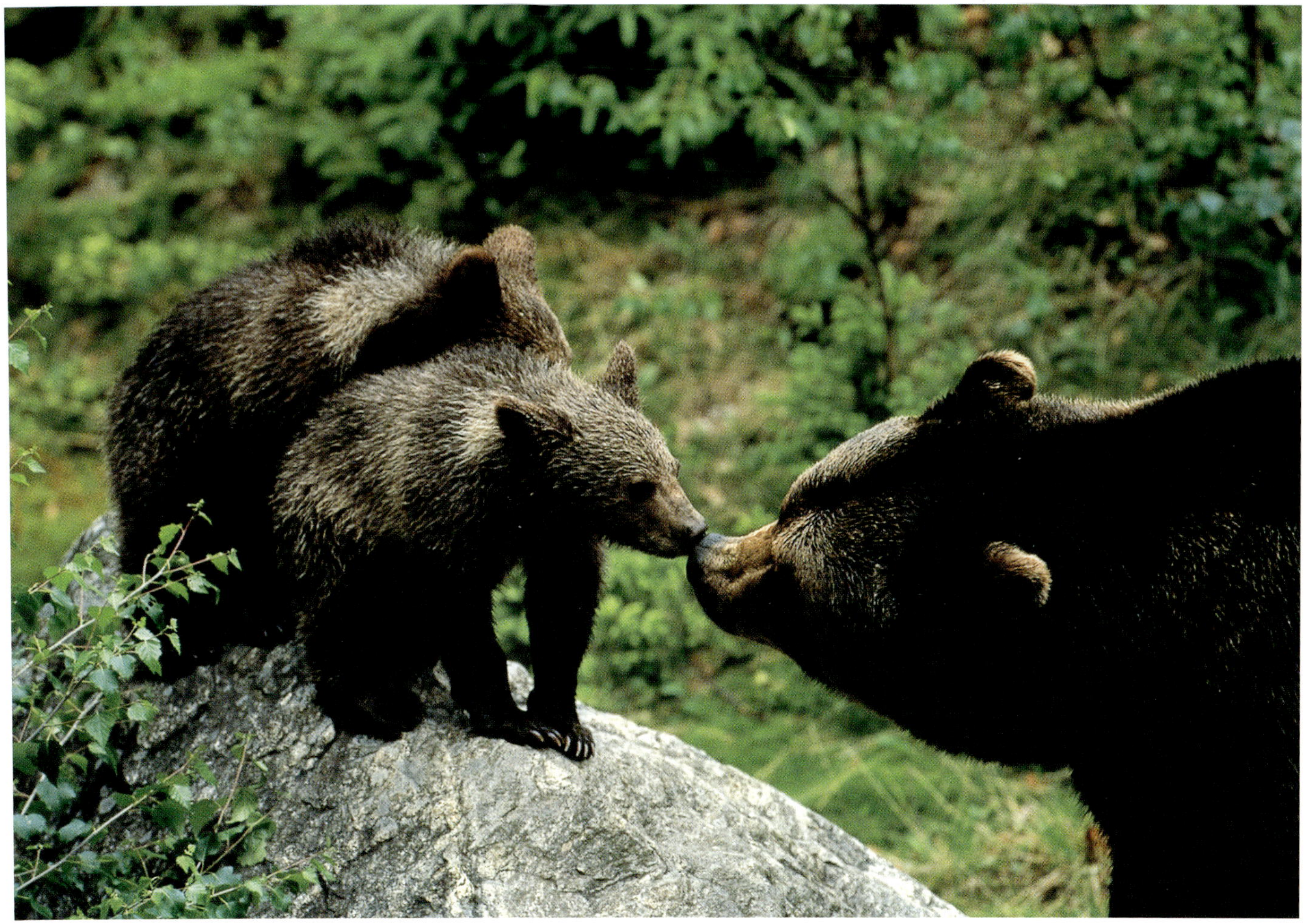

European brown bears are smaller than their Russian and American relatives. They have inhabited Europe for over 850,000 years. Today in many parts of Eastern Europe gamekeepers feed them in the fall; to help reduce depredations on agriculture and stock, and to help them store enough fat to hibernate for the winter.

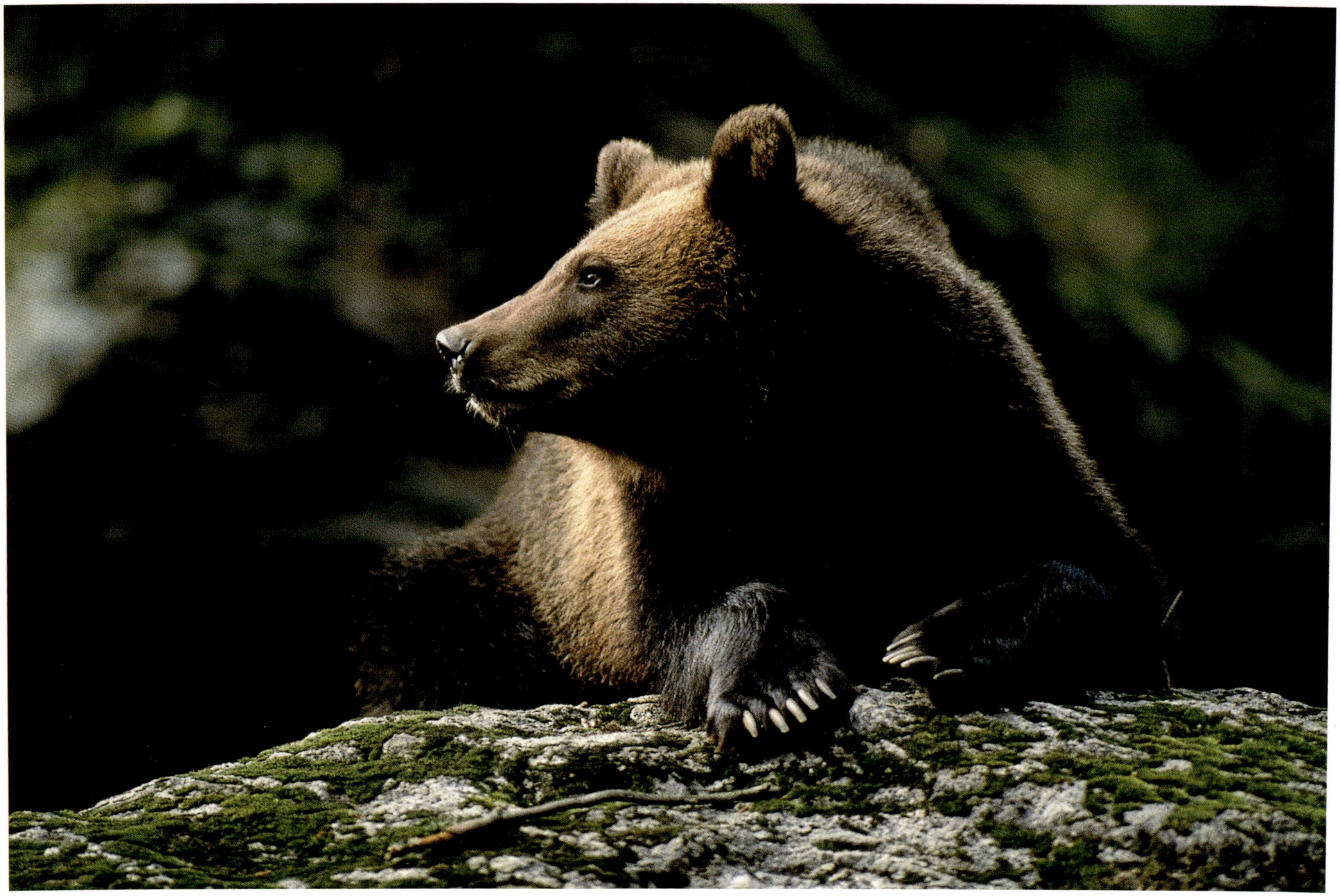

European brown bears survived the ice ages on the Iberian Peninsula and other refugia south of the glaciers. Today there are two distinct genetic lines: Iberian bears and Balkan bears. Both these lineages meet in central Sweden because their ancestors expanded north after the ice age along different routes.

any trees. Grizzly bears may occasionally use larger shrubs in sheltered places to rub against and leave scent, but again this is not well documented. To understand the diversity of adaptations exhibited by brown bears, let us look at how they live in four very different environments. A major force in determining the ecology of all bear species today is the presence and attitude of humans. The four examples below describe a range of human-bear interactions.

Brown Bears in Spain and Western Europe

Brown bears have occupied the Iberian Peninsula for at least 850,000 years, and probably longer. This date is the estimate from mitochondrial DNA studies which indicate that a population of brown bears was isolated on the Iberian Refugium during a period of glaciation. They were isolated long enough from other bear populations to diverge genetically; their descendants moved north into Western Europe during warmer periods, and retreated again to the south during cold periods. At this time they also must have shared the refugium with early humans. During the coldest periods the continental ice sheets extended south as far as France; south of that was permafrost covered in tundra. Spain itself was more hospitable. Early humans first reached Europe about 500,000 years ago, and 'modern' Cro Magnon humans about 40,000 years ago. Early humans inhabited what is now Spain for most of that period, and others farther north were forced to concentrate in the Iberian Refugium during glacial periods.

Conservation measures began in 1949 when bear hunting was prohibited in Cantabria. By 1952 hunting prohibitions spread throughout Spain. Bears continued to be killed by poachers primarily to prevent livestock depredations, until the passing of the Protected Species Law in 1973 which prohibited hunting, trapping, possessing, or commercially exploiting bears and established fines for violations. In 1990 the Spanish brown bear was formally declared to be 'in danger of extinction'.

Most of the remaining bears today live in the remote beech-oak forest of the Cantabrian Mountains, along the crest of the range. They forage on the steep ridges and valleys descending along the north coast of Spain and on the more open southern slopes. There are probably fewer than 50 bears left. In this last refuge the brown bears live with some wolves, wild hogs, roe deer, red deer, chamois, red fox, and wildcats. Their primary foods are beech nuts and acorns. They occasionally destroy domestic honey-bee hives in search of honey. In the late fall when the mast crops (beech and oak) are depleted they feed on grasses and wild apples before denning. Both wild and domestic ungulates are numerous and carrion appears to be a reliable source of food throughout the year. Food is generally most scarce in early spring as bears emerge from their dens. At this time carrion is especially important as well as emergent vegetation.

Brown bears in Cantabria are mainly crepuscular (active at dawn and dusk). Because there are so few bears, males have to travel relatively long distances during the breeding season in order to find females. Home ranges of Cantabrian bears may be 10 to 12 times as large as they are in other parts of Europe. The total number of bears is so low that they are at considerable risk of extinction. In addition the population is fragmented into two sub-populations on virtual 'islands' of habitat with little or no interchange between them. One of the consequences of small population size and isolation is that genetic diversity is inevitably reduced. For small populations like the Cantabrian bears, more habitat is needed. To effectively increase the size of habitat islands, they must be linked by habitat across which animals can move, otherwise small populations, with greatly reduced genetic options, may go extinct.

Small populations of brown bears are also found in the Pyrenees Mountains along the border between France and Spain. France probably has the most endangered population of brown bears in the world. The bears of France, Spain, and Southern Sweden represent the last of the lineage that evolved on the Iberian refugium. Italy currently has the largest brown bear population in western Europe with about 80 bears living in the central regions of Abrusso, Lazio and Molise. A feeding program has been developed, and farmers are compensated for crop losses. A small population remains in northern Greece in the oak-beech forests, and further north in Albania and Macedonia. Larger populations occur in the rest of the former Yugoslavia (Slovenia, Croatia, Bosnia-Herz, and the Yugoslav Federation), and in a fragmented region that includes Romania, the Ukraine, Slovakia, and Southern Poland.

Elsewhere, brown bears were eradicated from most western European countries by the beginning of the twentieth century. The last indigenous brown bear was killed in Austria in 1913. A source population managed to survive in Slovenia and Croatia, and in 1972 the first brown bear was recorded to disperse into central Austria where it remained. A female brown bear was captured in Slovenia and released in central Austria in 1989 where she successfully mated with the resident male and reproduced. Another pair of bears was also reintroduced and the population grew until they began to become a nuisance. There are currently about 16 bears in two Austrian sub-populations and an intensive public education and management program was initiated to maintain public support for preserving the population. Electric fences are provided to bee-keepers and shepherds, and farmers are compensated for their losses. The source population in Slovenia numbers only about 400 bears in an area that is densely settled by people.

Small bear populations and fragmented habitat are a worldwide problem. Even in remote areas, human activities can have an impact. Some possible solutions to maintain fragmented bear populations are discussed in the chapter 'Bears and Humans'. Let us take a closer look at more representative brown-bear populations in the three sections that follow.

Grizzly Bears in the Rocky Mountains

Grizzlies use a wide variety of habitats, often seasonally, in the Rocky Mountains. Bears and many other wildlife species generally follow the change of seasons upward in elevation to take advantage of plant foods at their most nutritious (growing) phase. Low-elevation meadows and wetlands are important during spring; avalanche chutes and ungulate calving areas can also be important. Mixed shrubfields, seeps, grasslands, meadow parks, and old burns may be used for foraging and resting in summer. In late summer and fall, berries at mid and high elevations can be an important food source, and whitebark pine seeds at high elevations are a preferred food item in the fall. Grizzlies also feed on carrion and may be attracted to human-provided food sources including hunting-related gut piles, hunting camps, and sources of garbage.

In the U.S. Rocky Mountains, subalpine fir communities are the most important forest type used by grizzlies. Riparian areas, mesic meadows, and grassland/forest ecotones are also important. Grizzly bears tend to inhabit remote, mountainous forested areas in Montana. Grizzlies can thrive in remote open areas, but where humans are a potential threat, they seek timber for security cover. Grizzlies may excavate their own dens or use natural caves, usually at elevations above 6500 feet, which they enter after the first heavy snowfall.

Grizzly bears have been extirpated from the lowlands that once supported much of the population and they are now generally confined to higher-elevation regions. Even within these regions, human development and activities often occur at the critical lower elevations which are used for spring habitat. Even in national parks and protected areas, their choices of habitats, foods, and their movements, are constrained by the presence of human beings.

Although grizzlies are omnivores, they are limited in their choice of foods by seasonally high calorie needs. The diet of bears in the Yellowstone ecosystem and the Canadian parks is somewhat unusual due to the absence or scarcity of berries and salmon. In many other areas, these are the consistent high-quality food sources critical to the build up of fall fat stores (hyperphagia). Berries are a large component of the bear diet in northwestern Montana and parts of southern Canada. Salmon are a critical food source for coastal bear populations.

Lacking these staple high-quality foods, grizzlies have learned to

Grizzly bears in the Rocky Mountains feed on berries to help them put on weight in preparation for hibernation.

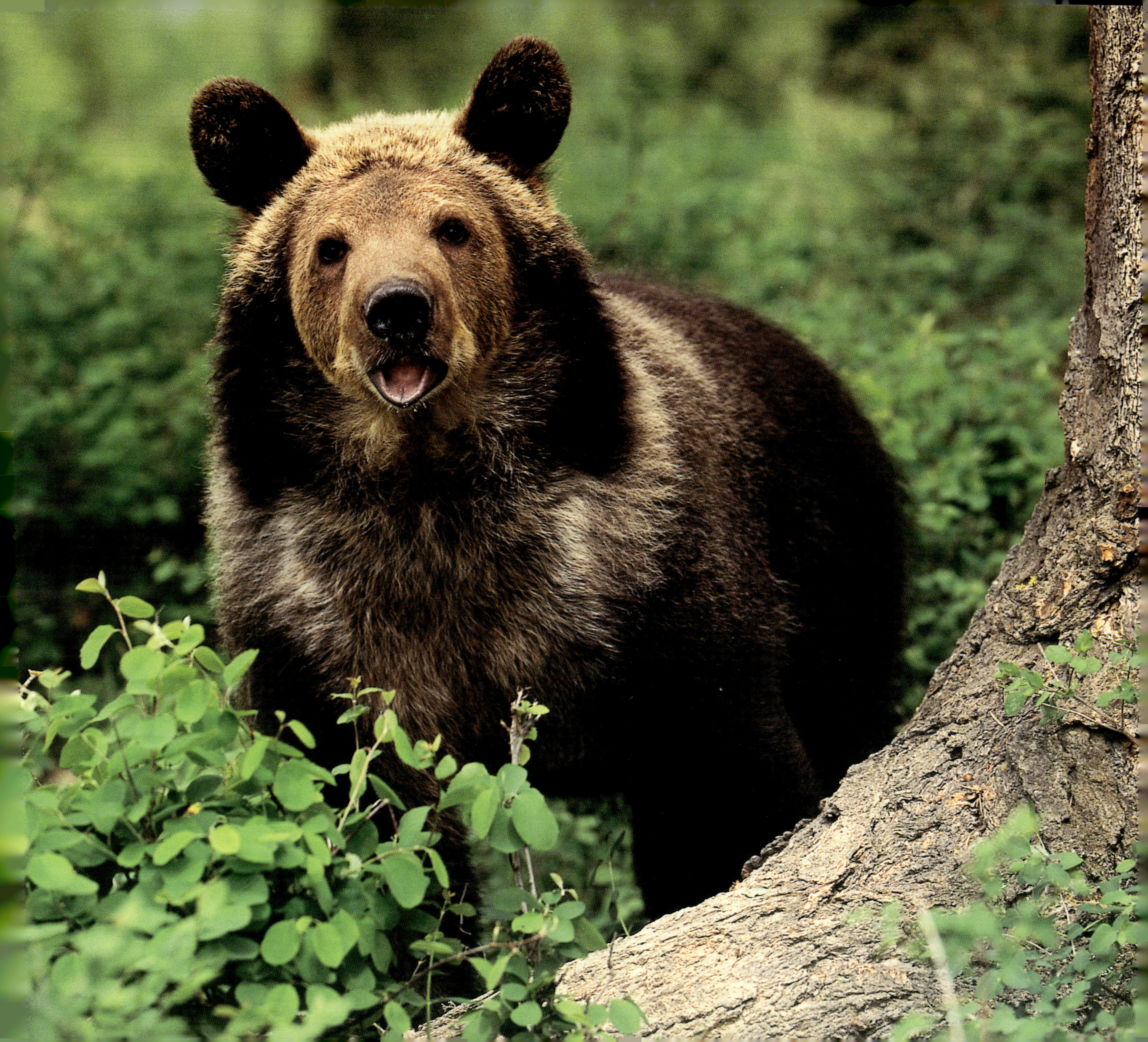

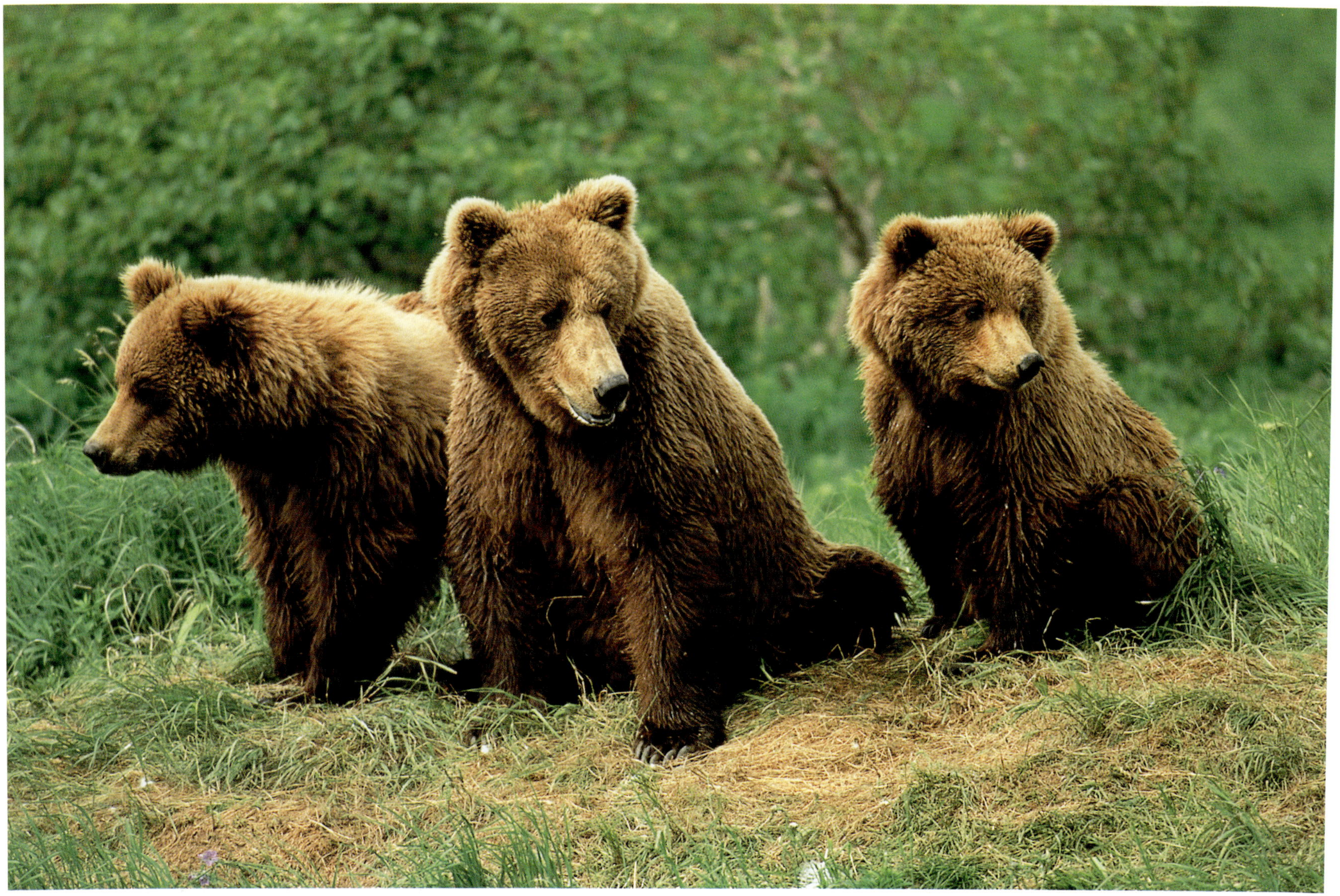

Cubs stay with their mothers for several summers until they learn to take care of themselves. These two Alaskan brown bear yearlings are nearly as large as their mother. They wait flanking her near a salmon stream until she decides it is safe to approach and look for food.

utilize other more variable food sources. Whitebark pine seeds are a critical, although inconsistent, food in the fall, and army cutworm moths provide the highest source of energy available to them. These moths lay their eggs in agricultural fields in the Great Plains states during late September and October. The larvae grow, feed, and pupate in late winter and the moths emerge and take flight in May. The adult moths migrate to high-elevation talus slopes in the Rocky Mountains where they hide during the day among the rocks. Grizzly bears move to the high country in July through September where they dig among the talus and consume moths by the thousands. A grizzly can consume enough to provide for about half of its annual energy budget by feeding on moths for 30 days.

Annual production of whitebark pine seeds, which are also high in energy, can vary greatly from year to year. The seeds become mature during the fall when they are harvested by red squirrels, Clark's nutcrackers, and other birds and mammals. Grizzly bears can locate the large caches of pine nuts that have been stored by red squirrels and feed on numbers of seeds with very little expenditure of energy. Poor years of pine seed production can greatly affect the Yellowstone bear populations by forcing them to search widely for other foods where they may experience human-caused mortality.

In early spring Eskimo potato roots are important, and other roots such as those of sweet cicely and pondweed can vary greatly in use from year to year. Spring beauty and Glacier lily roots are also important at this time of the year before much emerging vegetation is available. Winter-killed carrion often provides a bountiful supply of much-needed food, and prey animals that are weakened in spring are more easily killed. Large males will defend the kills ferociously and will often sleep on top of the carcass between bouts of feeding.

Younger animals and females with cubs generally concentrate on plant food sources; if they find a carcass they are often displaced by more aggressive bears. Later in the spring grasses, sedges, and shrubs associated with wet meadows and riparian areas are important spring foods. Common grasses and sedges are a main component of grizzly scats in the spring. Grizzly bears graze, in a fashion much like elk or bison, on the plants of open meadows. Unlike elk and bison, bears feed on both grasses and sedges. A variety of minor prey items such as rodents also contribute to their diet.

Ungulate calves are also important spring foods. Elk calves are born usually in early June. For about two weeks after birth they cannot outrun a grizzly bear. Many individual grizzlies learn to search for calves at this time. They range back and forth across calving habitat (sage and grassland) when elk are present to try and track down the unfortunate infant.

In northwestern Montana berries associated with open areas, such as globe huckleberry, buffaloberry, and mountain ash, form the bulk of grizzly bear diets. Wet meadows and riparian areas provide a source of grasses and shrubs. Although grizzlies are often associated with open habitats, this may relate to their easier observability in the open; radiolocation data indicate that they spend most of the time in the forest.

Whitebark pine nuts and several species of berries are potentially important food sources for grizzlies in the Salmon-Selway Wilderness in Idaho. Grizzlies were extirpated from this region because of competition with sheep ranching. Before the big dams were built on the Columbia River system, grizzlies in this area relied upon salmon that spawned there every fall, after a run of several hundred miles from the Pacific Ocean. It is possible that the brown bears who first reached the Yellowstone ecosystem were bears that moved inland along the salmon-bearing rivers from the coast.

Landscapes with a varied mix of forest and meadow, such as subalpine parkland, are important. Factors that affect the selection of habitat may include variation in security from humans, location relative to other bears, and feeding opportunities such as berries and ungulates. There is high variability in cover type selection by bears. Subalpine fir was the most heavily used forest type in the Scapegoat Wilderness Area in Montana, followed by riparian (streamside) areas and grassland/forest ecotones (edges between different habitat types). Most studies conclude that a wide variety of habitat types over large geographic areas are necessary for conserving grizzly bears.

Effects of human activities on grizzly bears are complex. However, there are consistent effects of human activities which have negative impacts on bears at the local level. Although bears in the Yellowstone ecosystem are fully protected, human-caused mortality comprises 86 to 91 per cent of adult bear mortality. Adult female mortality is particularly critical to the survival of a population so that even relatively small increases in mortality risk or disturbance are a threat.

Roads have been shown to be the most important variable that can be used as a reliable index to measure human influence on grizzly habitat. The two main sources of adult bear mortality in the Greater Yellowstone Ecosystem (GYE) are illegal killing and management removal of habituated bears; both are associated with roads. Road use by humans may disrupt bear behavior and social structure, reduce the availability of adjacent foraging habitats, and create barriers to movement. These effects may extend up to 2 miles (3 km) from primary roads and half to one mile (1.5 km) from secondary roads. In the GYE these buffer areas around roads represent only about one-third of the habitat. However, areas near roads account for 70 per cent of bear mortalities. Therefore the mortality risk is almost five times higher near roads. One review of relevant data concluded that road densities higher than half a mile (1km) of road for each 2½ sq miles (6.4 sq km) of habitat (which is about one third the threshold set by government agencies) are detrimental to bear survival.

Recreational development increases the risk of mortality to bears and alienates bears from preferred habitats. The effect of developments on mortality and behavior extends up to 4 miles (6 km) from the site. Even non-motorized trails may be avoided by bears to a distance of 325 yards (300 m). The impact of recreational development and associated roads reduces the ability of national parks to function as protected areas. For example, Yellowstone National Park contains 540 miles (867 km) of roads and sees more than three million visitors a year. Bears inhabiting the 'multiple-use' lands surrounding the parks face additional threats associated with roads. In contrast though, brown bears in Sweden are able to coexist with humans in areas of much greater road density than any known populations in North America. Bears in Sweden are less aggressive to humans than are bears in North America.

The historical decline of the grizzly was associated with the expansion of livestock grazing, especially of sheep, and associated predator control. Livestock depredation-associated killing remains the second most important mortality source for bears in Canada. Mineral and gas exploration forms another important disturbance source, primarily through associated road development.

It has been suggested that, by translocating bears from one population center to another, a metapopulation structure (a network of populations where some have positive growth rates while others have negative growth rates) may be artificially maintained in the Rocky Mountains. However, such an approach negates the role of natural selection in determining what bears, and what genes, migrate from one population to another; it will be expensive to maintain, and its continuation will be subject to the whims of political agendas. A far more ecologically sound method, that will be more cost-effective in the long run, will be to maintain or restore the habitat linkages and the smaller population cores between the large ecosystems, and to restore the grizzly population to the Salmon-Selway. Most of the smaller core areas in the region are roadless areas located on public lands. However, additional key habitat that increases the size of the core area, or provides a linkage for grizzly movement between cores, is located on private lands. In addition to maintaining habitat, it is necessary to minimize human impacts and increase human tolerance in order for grizzlies to persist.

Before their claws are fully developed, grizzly bear cubs have the ability to climb trees.

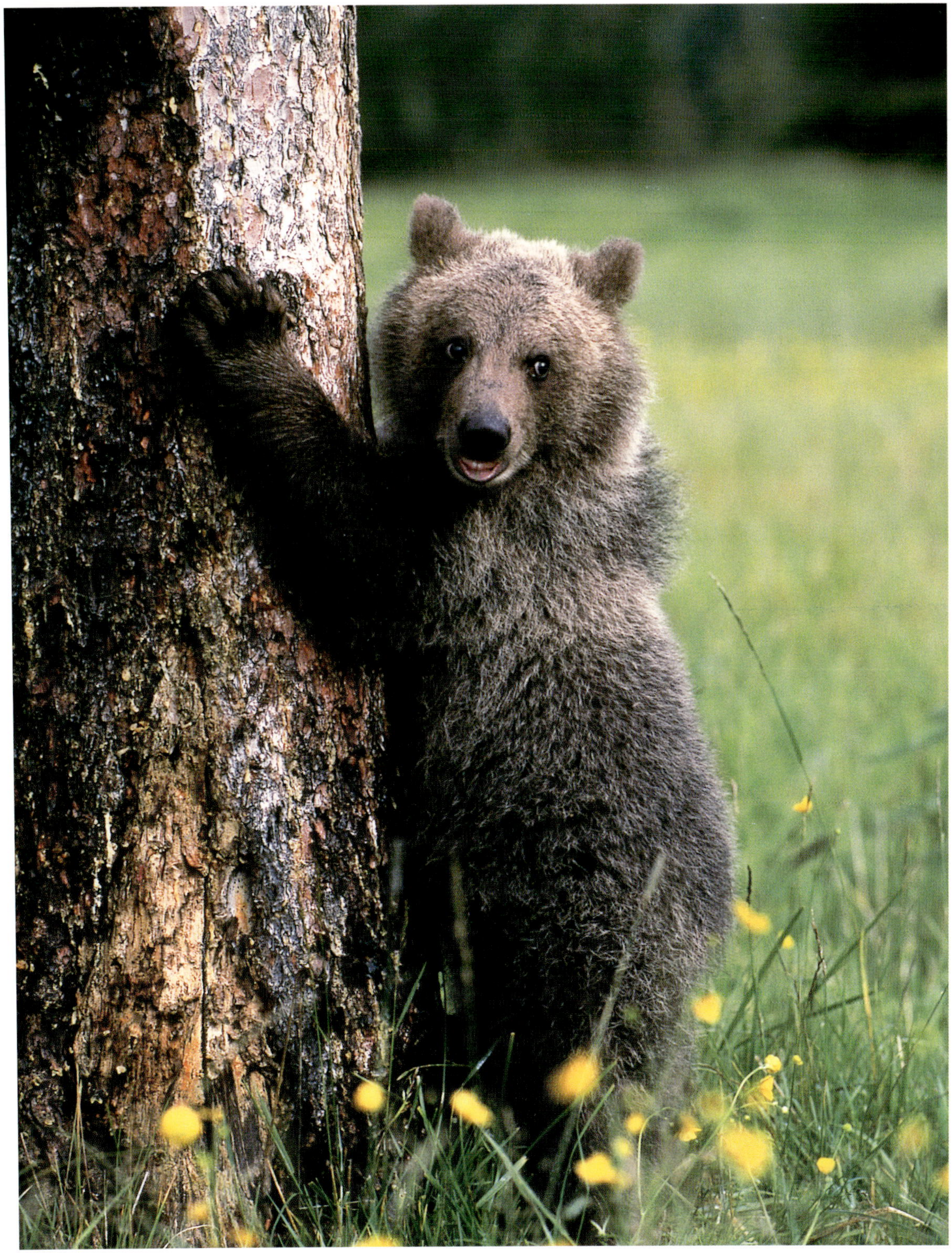

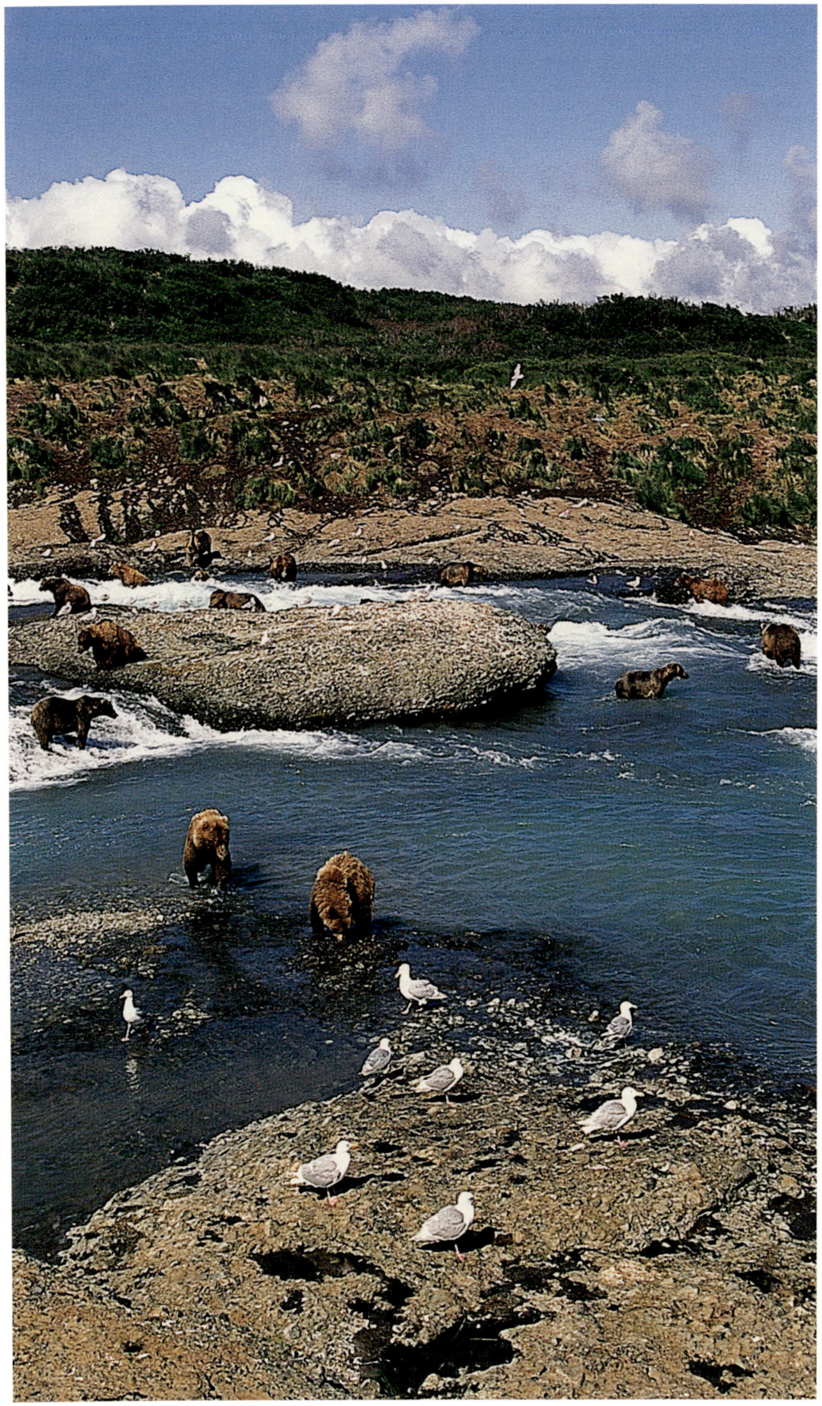

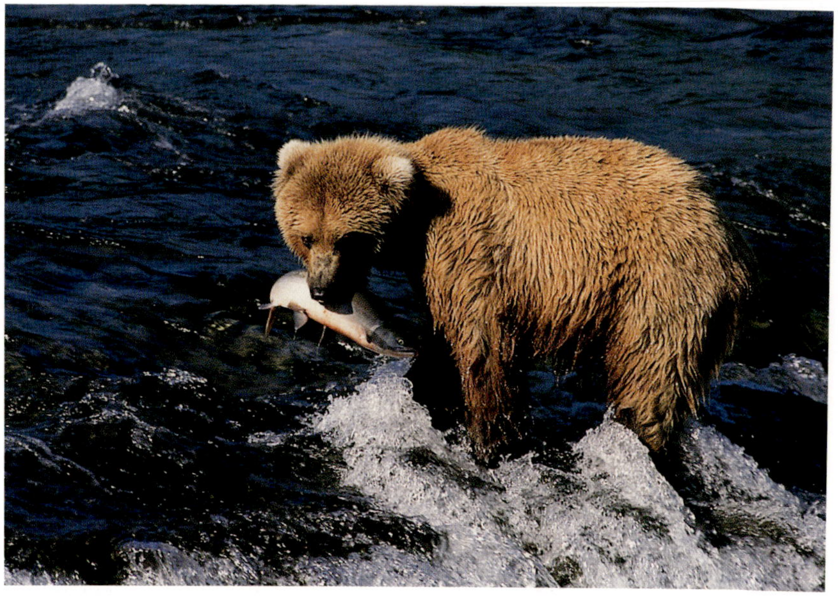

At concentrated food sources like the falls at McNeil River in Alaska, brown bears establish clear social hierarchies. Aggressive males displace other bears from the best salmon-fishing sites and from breeding females. After some initial sparring and a few serious fights to establish dominance the bears share the resources and minimize further conflict. Each bear develops his own successful strategy for catching salmon and the result is like a wonderful three-ring circus of bears: diving, swimming, waiting, pouncing, and wandering around. In areas like this humans are able to watch safely once the bears have accepted them as non-threatening and as long as they consistently remain in the same location; a viewing platform is preferable.

Brown Bears in the Temperate Coastal Rainforest

Brown bears in the coastal rainforests of British Columbia and Alaska are also constrained by human beings in their choice of habitats. In fact they have been competing with each other for over ten thousand years. Despite the large land area of forest, both bears and humans have utilized mainly the river bottoms, estuaries and coastlines. In addition to being the most productive areas for plant foods, rivers and estuaries are critical to salmon. Each species of salmon returns to spawn (a salmon 'run') at certain times of year. Each species also remains at sea for a certain period of time (1 to 3 years) before returning to spawn. Access to salmon spawning areas is of critical importance to coastal bears, not only areas with abundant salmon numbers, but also areas with numerous runs, and security for fishing.

Starting in early summer and continuing in some locations well into late fall, several species of salmon make their way up coastal inlets and enter the mid-coast river systems. Bears begin to feed on this protein- and fat-rich bounty with increasing single-mindedness that peaks during their hyperphagia stage in the late summer and early fall. At major salmon spawning streams, bear activity concentrates in these areas during late summer. Predation on spawning salmon can be intense but most salmon are eaten after they have spawned.

Because of both salmon and berries, low-elevation riparian old-growth habitat has been identified as critical brown bear habitat in coastal North America. In all seasons of activity, brown bears prefer these low-elevation riparian areas, and they select habitat in riparian old-growth forests precisely where high-volume commercially valuable timber stands occur. In the Khutzeymateen Valley of British Columbia, on Chichagof Island, and in the Tongass National Forest in Southeast Alaska, the majority of brown bear activity was concentrated at elevations lower than 328 ft (100 m) and within about 490 ft (150 m) of larger streams, due to the majority of dietary items occurring in abundance in the riparian zone. Black bears are displaced from this habitat and forage mainly on the hillsides.

Bears forage on a wide variety of plant species but are seasonally dependent on only a few. Plant foods vary greatly in nutritional value and availability to bears from year to year. Brown bears in coastal British Columbia are known to feed on at least 49 species of plants. Favorite plant food items include blueberries, devil's club berries, salmon berries, skunk cabbage and other herbaceous vegetation. Riparian areas and the dense surrounding forests also provide important security cover for bears. The high productivity along rivers allows for relatively high density bear populations. Because of the thick cover, and the large number of bears in small areas (at least historically), bears in the coastal rainforest seem to rely on scent marking on traditional rubbing trees more than bears in other areas. Bear trails are abundant throughout riparian forests, and a major trail is generally found on both sides of a river. In many areas, trails have been used by so many generations of bears that they form ruts many inches deep. In other areas a deep pattern of footsteps, one paw after another for hundreds of years, can be found. Rubbing trees and day beds are also numerous.

Brown bears also congregate in estuaries where sedges and marine invertebrates such as soft-shell clams, acorn barnacles, and blue mussels can be found. Estuaries and coastlines are critically important during spring when other food sources for hungry bears emerging from their winter dens are not available. Brown bears graze like ungulates on the wide, flat, estuary meadows. They also feed opportunistically on carrion and invertebrates and even on marine algae. Because estuaries and beaches have limited cover, bears are particularly vulnerable to hunting when foraging in these areas. Other habitats include upland old-growth forest, avalanche slopes, and sub-alpine meadows.

Bears generally avoid logging clearcuts and other areas of human activity such as inlets and rivers frequented by boats, recreational facilities, and settlements. Logging in old-growth forests in the Tongass National Forest in southeastern Alaska has been seen as a major threat to the long-term persistence of brown bears because it results in more human-bear interactions; and those interactions invariably result in dead bears. Radio-collared bears in the Tongass avoid using clearcuts in all seasons. This avoidance is likely to be caused by the low quality of clearcuts as foraging habitats. These findings seem to hold true for grizzly bear populations in other parts of North America. In coastal British Columbia, observations of brown bears feeding on salmon in a stream adjacent to a logging road dropped from 41 during a year when trucks were not hauling logs to zero in two years during hauling. In coastal areas human access is facilitated by the many inlets and rivers navigable by jet boats and conventional craft. These are the equivalent of highways in other parts of the country. They provide easy access for hunters. In coastal areas where there is both boat and road access, the impacts of human activities on brown populations can be even more severe.

Logging on the industrial scale at which it is currently practiced removes habitat for bears and greatly reduces habitat for salmon. On hillsides it greatly increases erosion and consequently increases the silt in rivers; particularly when valley bottoms have been logged and can't filter the runoff. Heavy silt loads can destroy spawning and nursery habitat. For about ten years after cutting there can be an abundance of berries and other plant foods. However, as the new trees grow they begin to crowd out the shrubs and after about 25 years all that remains is a thicket of saplings. This second-growth timber is often referred to as 'dog-hair' timber because it is so dense. It shades out the growth of understory species for 60 to 80 years or longer. It is unsuitable for use by most wildlife species including herbivores and carnivores. Thus, large-scale logging creates a desert for wildlife and fisheries that can take hundred of years to recover. The natural changes in these forests are caused by decay and wind; fire is almost non-existent because of the wet climate. Trees fall in relatively small areas, and second growth returns in patches. The result is an old-growth mosaic of different age trees and a multi-layered canopy. Enough light reaches the forest floor to allow for the growth of shrubs. Current logging practices cannot even approximately reproduce these conditions.

Hunting is also a serious threat on the coast. Contrary to the public perception that trophy hunting results primarily in the kill of large, older bears, data from British Columbia found that the majority of females killed were under 7 years of age (with the single largest group being 3- to 4-year-olds) and the majority of males killed were under 9 years of age. This indicates that vulnerability is a more important factor in determining which bears die than is selection by hunters and guides. Young inexperienced bears, particularly female bears, are consistently more vulnerable to human-caused mortality.

Many other bears are killed when they come into conflict with humans. Once brown bears become habituated to humans and to human sources of food, they are eventually killed. Poaching, particularly for bear parts and trophies, is an increasing threat to both brown and black bears along the coast.

Grizzly Bears in the Arctic

Until the last decade or two, many Arctic grizzly populations were undisturbed by man. Near the northern limit of grizzly bear range in Alaska and Canada the landscape is open, treeless, Arctic tundra, and the climate is dominated by long severe winters, with short cool summers. The predominant vegetation is tussock tundra with cottongrass and sedges. Wet sedge meadows are found in poorly drained areas. Willow communities, usually stunted, are found along river channels. Topography varies from rugged mountains to rolling hills, ridges and buttes, to tundra which exists on a thin layer of soil over permafrost. Similar conditions exist all across northern Eurasia as well. Grizzlies in this harsh environment use the tundra for some foods, particularly during caribou calving, but need higher, well-drained slopes for denning and for most of their food.

This general type of habitat has persisted in western Alaska for

Brown bears learn to exploit a variety of local food sources; this one is searching for clams.

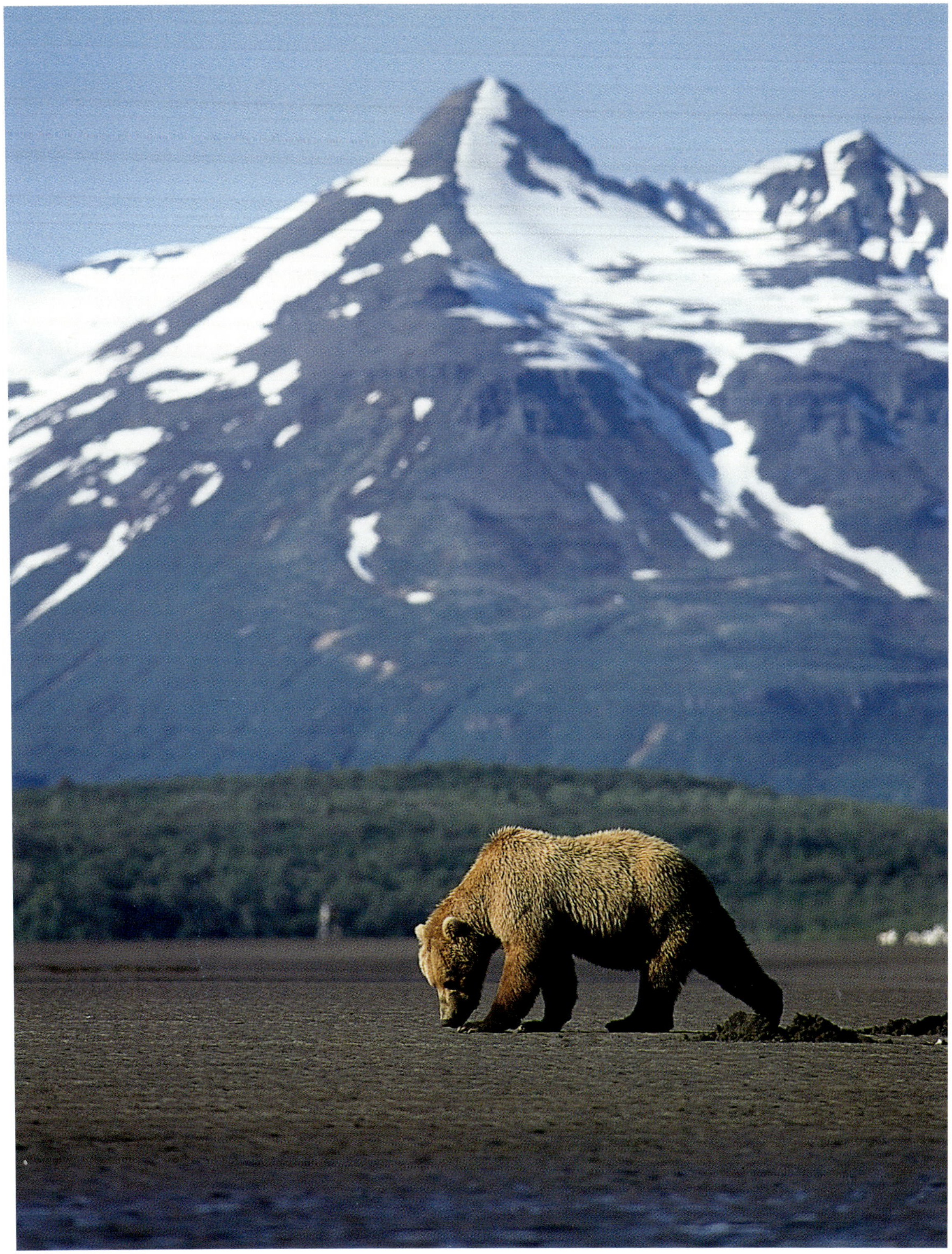

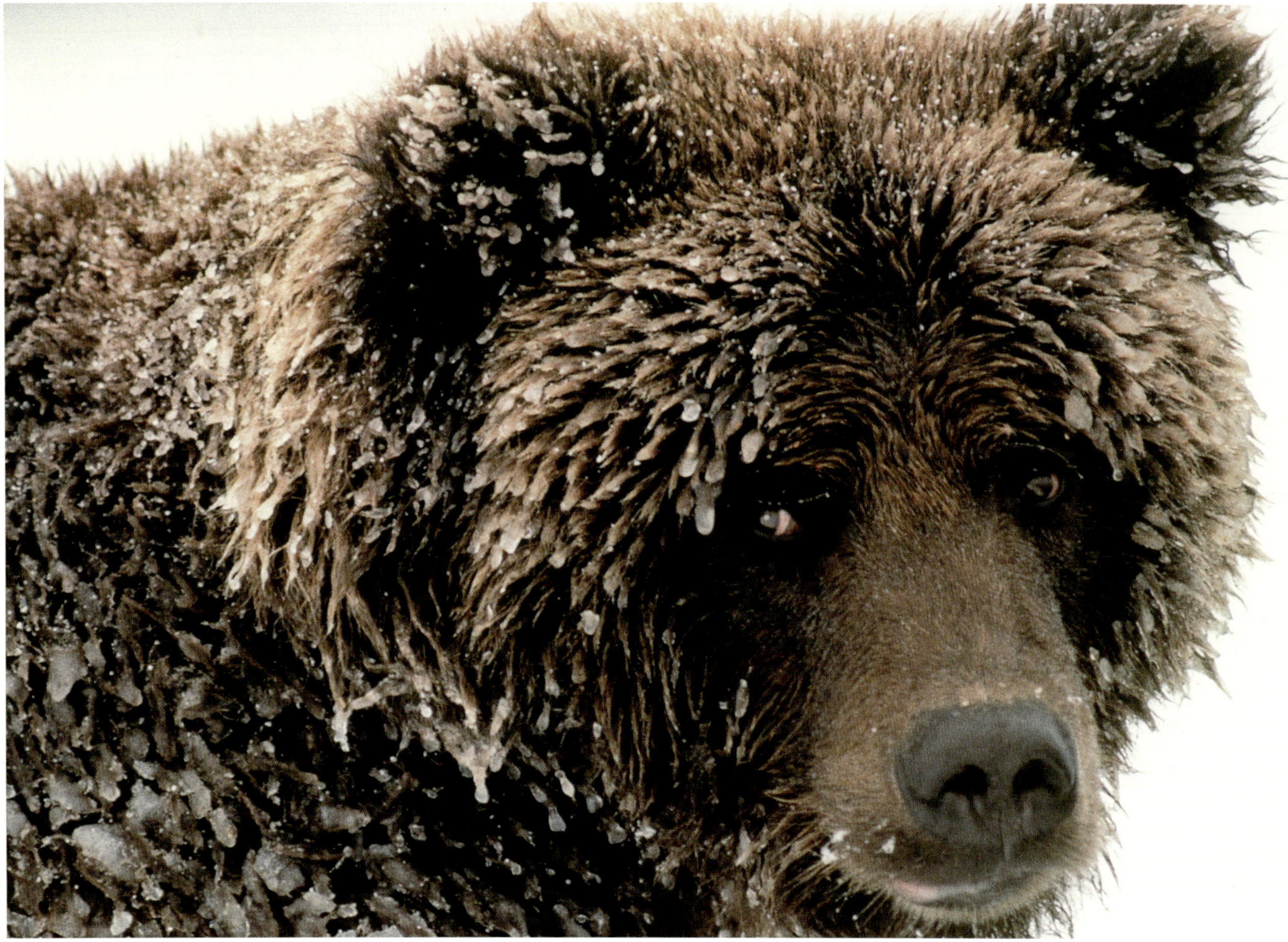

Brown bears adapted to cold northern climates and now occupy the largest range of any land mammal except wolves and man. Their coat consists of warm soft underfur and a longer layer of guard hairs, which are covered with ice on this bear in Katmai National Park, Alaska.

hundreds of thousands of years with some changes in the relative abundance of different species. It has probably been occupied by grizzly bears for almost 70,000 years.

After emerging from the den in the spring bears find that food is scarce before greenup, or the time that plant foods emerge and begin their rapid growth. During this time, grizzlies rely on roots such as Eskimo potato, dried berries that have lasted through the winter such as bear-berry, fresh shoots of emerging plants, and early flowers. Dry tundra, floodplain plant communities, and tussock tundra are the most important habitat types.

Caribou migrate to the coastal plain for calving in May and June. These remote areas are generally free of predators, but in some areas such as the Arctic National Wildlife Refuge the coastal plain is close enough to the foothills where the bears den that they have an opportunity to prey on caribou calves. Brown bears of all sexes and ages may travel out over the tundra to the calving areas. Caribou calves are only vulnerable for a week or less; after that they can easily outrun a bear across the tussock tundra. Since calving times vary greatly among the caribou in a herd, calves are available for a much longer period. During the calving season some bears can feed well on calves, often catching a couple a day.

Bears that remain further inland, farther from the calving grounds, are much less successful in feeding on caribou. However, some caribou will calve later in the season after the herds have begun to move back inland, and in some years the weather will keep the caribou herds inland until they calve. Some bears take advantage of this fortunate situation and begin preying on calves.

As summer progresses there is a much greater variety of plant foods. As the snow cover melts and plants proliferate, bears begin to graze on the highly nutritious shoots and leaves of the growing plants. Horsetail and a wide variety of grasses and sedges are important foods. Grizzly bears in the Arctic graze on these tundra plants much as bears on the coast graze on grass and sedge in estuaries and bears in the interior graze on grass and sedge in mountain meadows. Wet sedge meadows, the ecotones (or edges) between wet meadows and the drier tundra, and areas of late snowmelt are the preferred habitats. The areas just below melting snowbanks provide highly nutritious emergent shoots; these are micro-climates with early spring conditions and they are important to grizzlies everywhere.

Plants are the basis of the Arctic grizzlies' diet, they are a reliable, stable food source. During the short growing season, it is light for most of the 24 hours, and plants grow rapidly. In years when conditions are poor for some plants, conditions are usually better for other plants. However, animal prey are much richer in fat and protein, and grizzlies are constantly ready to take advantage of them. Some bears learn to ambush caribou in river bottoms, and all bears are capable of instantly charging a calf or an adult in a sudden encounter. Once a caribou gets ahead of the bear and has space to run, the bear doesn't have a chance. In the late summer and fall, the bulk of the diet shifts to roots, berries, and ground squirrels. Dry tundra, riparian areas, and wet sites are the habitats that are most used. In some years when populations of ground squirrels are high, they become the primary food item, particularly during the fall. With their incredible strength, grizzlies will dig them out of their burrows, sometimes to depths of a few feet. The bears dig rapidly, tossing boulders the size of basketballs out of their way with scarcely a shrug. At times it seems that they must have expended more energy catching the squirrel than they could possibly have gained from the meal; on average however, ground squirrels provide an important source of nutrition at times when other foods are less available.

These tundra, or barren-ground, grizzly bears hibernate for 7 to 8 months and have only 4 to 5 months to accumulate fat reserves. Development times are slow compared with more temperate bear populations; offspring are generally weaned at 2 to 4 years of age compared with 1 to 3 years of age in Montana. In the Arctic, breeding behavior has been observed in males as young as 5 years old. Genetic studies have shown, however, that the youngest males that successfully bred were 9 years old, and in the western Arctic it was estimated that only about half of the males over 9 years of age are successful breeders. Virtually all females breed successfully.

There is much flexibility in reproductive strategy; but investing effort in a single female appears to be favored over searching for additional breeding opportunities which can be scarce in the Arctic where the density of bears is very low. In general, dominant males would stay with a single female during the entire time that she was receptive. They would often sequester her; attempt to keep her in one place and away from other males. Fighting frequently occurs between rival males, but sometimes two or more males would tolerate each other as they accompanied a receptive female. It seems likely that when there is a good breeding year, males may spend less time with individual females in estrous in order to breed with other females.

Other grizzly populations, particularly coastal ones, congregate during the breeding season at concentrated food sources. At these feeding aggregations a more structured dominance hierarchy is established particularly among males. Dominant males appear to spend less time with individual females in estrous, often encountering additional receptive females and subsequently breeding with them. As dominant males change partners, subordinate males have an opportunity to breed with the females that have been abandoned.

Environmental conditions in the Arctic, including the availability of mobile prey such as caribou, are highly variable from year to year. When there is sufficient food, more females are able to successfully give birth and raise cubs. Male aggression in some cases can limit a female's access to sources of food. If food is scarce, male aggression towards both juveniles and other adults may increase. When there is a good food year, however, it is good over a large area in the Arctic and males are not as likely to restrict females from food sources.

Behavioral observations indicate that female bears are strongly philopatric (loyal to their place of birth), and that their female offspring tend to establish home ranges adjacent to, or overlapping, their mother's. Thus, over time groups (or demes) of related females tend to form. The genetic evidence demonstrates that although females may cluster in groups of relatively stationary, related individuals, there are still high levels of gene flow throughout contiguous grizzly habitat. All of northern Alaska, and perhaps Canada, is effectively one large interbreeding (panmictic) population. This is due to the long-range dispersals of the male segment of the population.

Grizzly bears have probably inhabited the Arctic foothills for over 18,000 years with little conflict from humans. The high Arctic was the last environment that humans colonized, about 4000 years ago, but then, as now, the Inupiat live and hunt primarily on the coast. Arctic bears had little appeal to trophy hunters from overseas or further south; they were much smaller than the impressive Kodiak or coastal bears. So the barren-ground grizzlies were left alone to move freely across the tundra until the beginning of oil, gas, and mineral development, which is still restricted to relatively small areas in the Arctic, and occurs mostly on the coastal plain rather than the foothills. It has had some surprising effects. Prudhoe Bay was established in the 1970s on the Arctic coast of Alaska. A pipeline and a road were constructed to the south. Grizzlies frequently came into conflict with construction crews because of the attraction of open garbage areas. Eventually a few bears, including at least one female, found their way along the road from the foothills to the main camps on the coast, where they found a bonanza of garbage. They quickly gained weight and learned where to find leftovers; in the central dump and in the dumpsters outside of mess halls.

To date there have been no fatalities to oil field workers from bears, but there have been some close calls. In the last two decades, the bear population has steadily grown. Females residing in Prudhoe have had cubs and their cubs have remained. Additional bears have migrated in from the foothills. Presumably, these bears will remain as long as the oilfield operates and they can continue to find food.

By the time that ice forms on the rivers, grizzly bears need to have stored enough fat to survive through the winter.

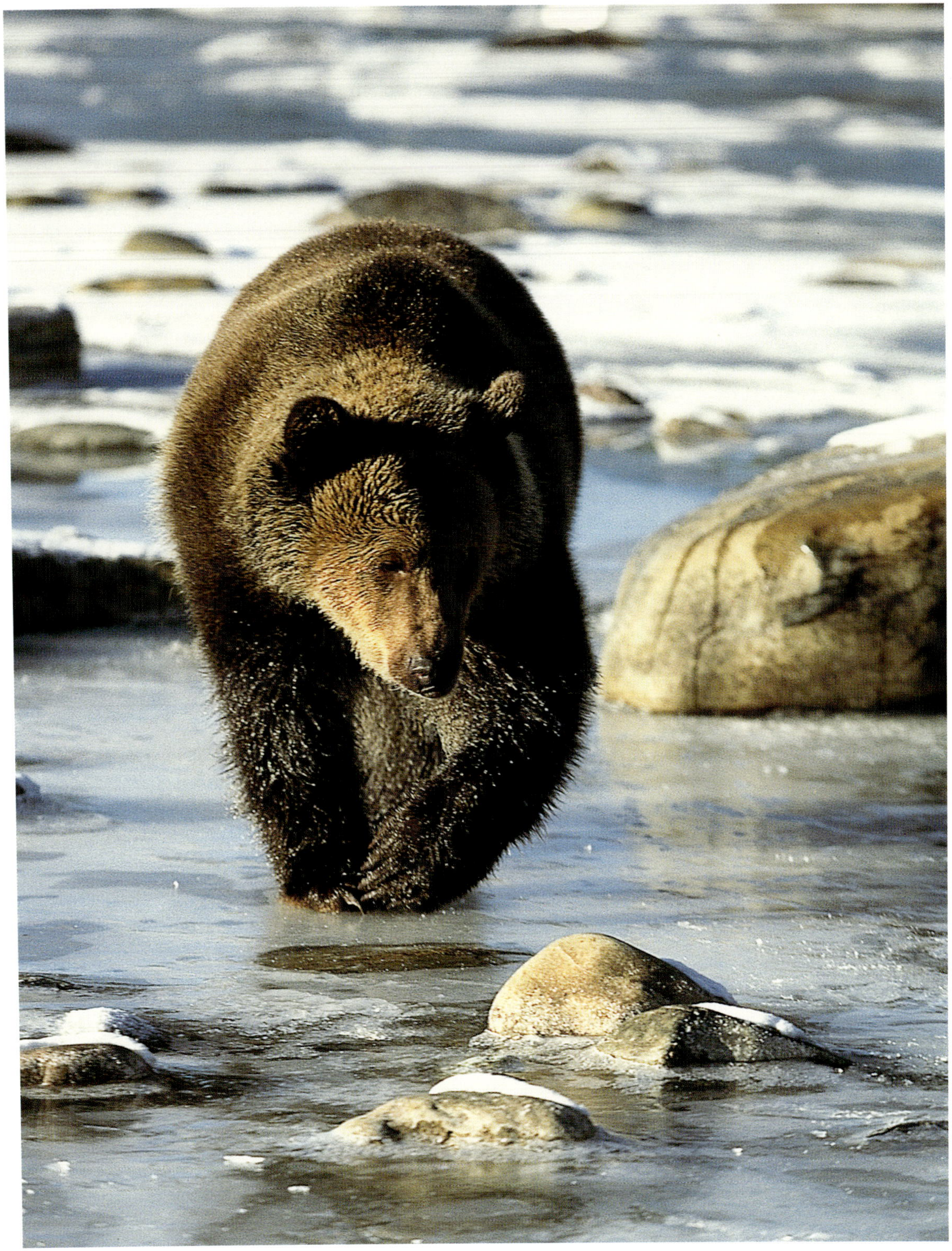

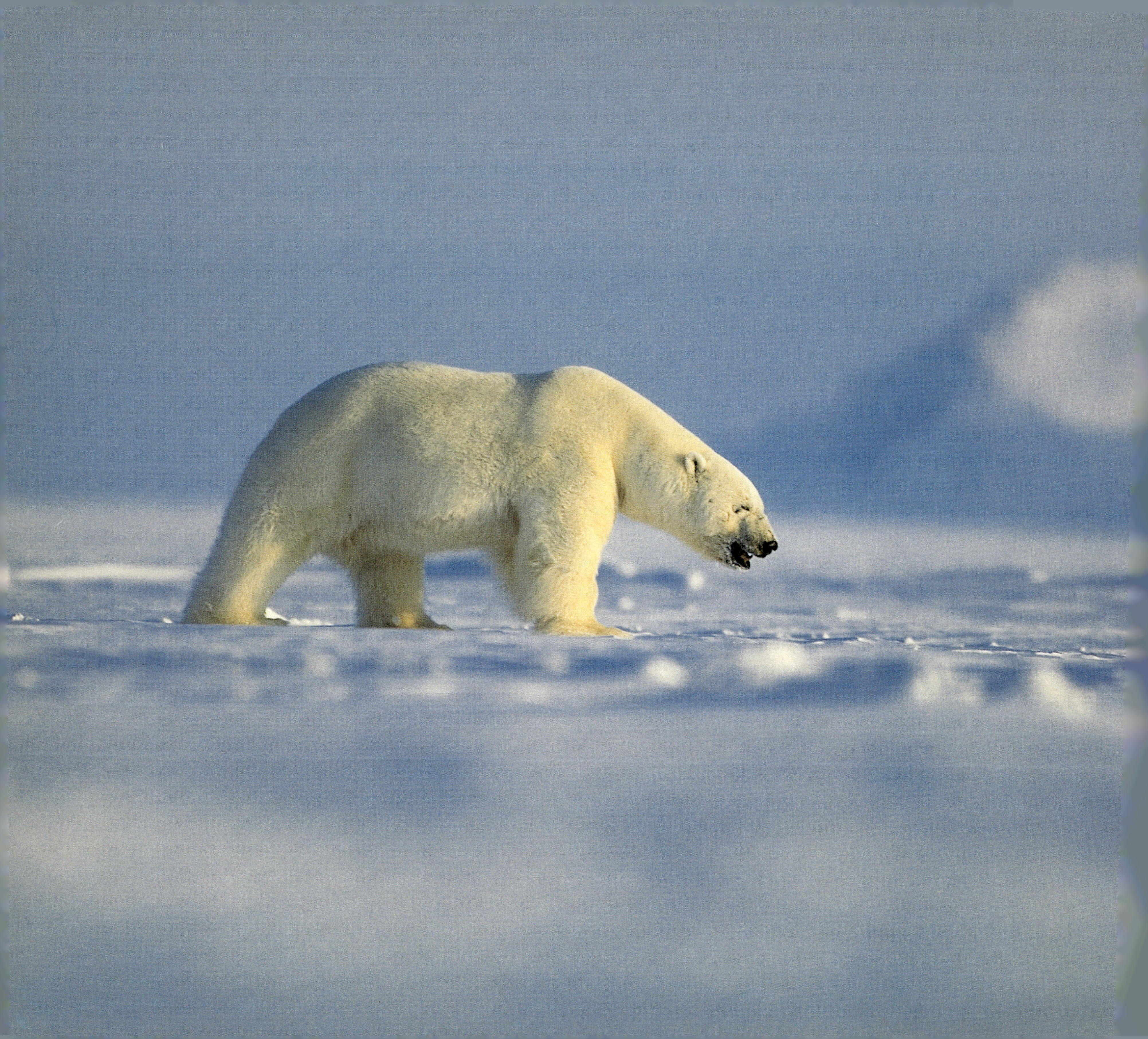

The Polar Bear

Polar bears are the closest relatives of brown bears. They must have diverged from an ancestral population of brown bears that became isolated away from the mainland, and other brown bears, about one million years ago. We can imagine that the ancestral polar bears were brown bears that lived in northern Siberia, perhaps along the coast of the Arctic Ocean or on Wrangell Island. They discovered an abundant source of food in the form of marine mammals; seals, walruses, and even whales, and learned to prey upon them. As they were doing this, one group of bears became isolated. It may have been a relatively small group to begin with, and they may even have been stranded on the ice when it receded away from shore during a period of warm climate. We will probably never know the whole story. Somehow, perhaps improbably, they managed to survive and reproduce. Adaptations that favored their new environment would have been rapidly selected for, and they developed white coats and thick layers of fat. In a relatively short period of evolutionary time, they became the polar bears that we know today.

Polar bears are marine carnivores. They feed exclusively on a diet of meat, primarily seals, and many polar bears spend their lives on the ice without ever setting foot on land. The southern limit of their distribution is determined by the extent that the pack ice moves south in winter. To survive, and thrive, on the polar ice pack requires many extreme adaptations. To provide camouflage on the ice their fur appears white. It is more than white, however, each hair is translucent and it conducts sunlight down to the skin where heat is absorbed. The skin is black to absorb the maximum amount of heat from sunlight. The thick fur then acts as an insulating blanket to preserve the heat.

Polar bears rely, perhaps more than any other bear species, on their sense of smell. They live in a world that can be two-dimensional for sight, and even one-dimensional for long periods of time. They live in a world where the air is almost always moving, and scent molecules can travel almost endlessly without settling down or bumping into obstacles. Sights and sounds are secondary. They can detect the breath of a seal that surfaces for seconds in a small hole through the ice which is several miles away. That is, as long as it is upwind. Whenever possible, polar bears face into the wind as they travel and they know what is ahead of them long before it ever comes into sight. Animal handlers working for a marine park once captured several beluga whales near Churchill, Manitoba. They stored the small, white whales in a warehouse overnight, keeping their skin moist. The whales were undoubtedly uncomfortable, but alive and healthy. However, during the night several polar bears followed their scent into town from miles away, broke into the warehouse, and killed and ate the unfortunate belugas. Other scents from the town provided a strong and constant stream of information for the bears on the shores of Hudson's Bay, but they were immediately aware of the belugas and were so attracted by this rarely encountered source of food that they disregarded their learned avoidance of the town and all its dangers.

The only part of the polar bear's skin that is generally visible is the nose. When stalking prey, polar bears are reputed to hold one front paw over their nose and creep forward on three legs so that they are almost invisible. Native hunters have observed this behavior but it is not often seen, and scientists have never reported it. In one story, an old Inuit, and a young boy, who worked at the Naval Arctic Research Lab in Barrow, Alaska, were in a large enclosure which housed an adult polar bear one day. The polar bear had been put into a smaller cage, but the latch had not been properly fastened. The older eskimo turned to see the bear, about 20 feet away, crouching with his paw in front of his face. He froze in position; he had raised the bear from a cub, but the bear still apparently considered him (or the boy) to be

Bears are finely adapted to their environment. This is most evident in the exquisite symmetry of the polar bear.

prey. The bear also stopped. The young boy, however, panicked and ran. This elicited an attack response from the bear who charged after him. As the huge bear passed, the old man shouted at him to stop and slapped him on the nose. Amazingly the bear stopped; turned submissively; and backed away. Not wishing to push his luck, the old eskimo backed off too, and he and the boy got safely out of the enclosure.

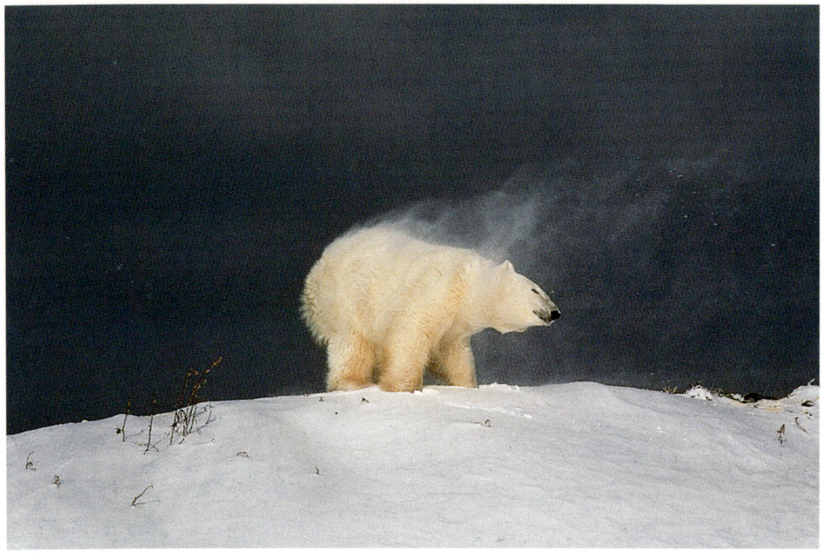

The polar bear is well insulated, even against drifting snow.

This story illustrates several things about polar bears. Being predatory, polar bears tend to look upon all animals they encounter as potential prey; unless they learn otherwise. They are, however, able to learn enough to override their instinctive behavior. There are many stories of humans being attacked by polar bears. There are also stories of seeming friendships between polar bears and other animals that could have been prey. One of the most interesting was the time that a polar bear approached an eskimo sled dog that was chained and could not flee. The young bear, many times larger than the dog, played and snuggled with his captive playmate. Perhaps if the dog had tried to run away, rather than eliciting a play response, he would have been quickly killed.

Polar bears have developed many interesting ways of moving across the ice. When stalking seals they will sometimes lay their chest and neck on the ice and push themselves forward with their rear legs. Sliding along like this keeps their eyes and nose close to the surface and out of sight until they work their way close enough to attack. Sometimes they extend their forelegs in front of them and put their head between their legs as they push themselves. They move with equal ease across ice or water. A thick layer of fat beneath the skin minimizes any loss of heat, even in arctic waters near the freezing point of salt water. Water conducts heat away much faster than air so polar bears will avoid the water when the weather is cold. They can swim for long distances, even going underwater between ice holes while hunting. They have been clocked swimming at speeds up to 4 miles (6.5 km) per hour and have been recorded traveling as far as 65 km across open water, and can climb out onto ice, even nearly vertical ice blocks, using their sharp claws. On very thin ice they spreadeagle their legs to distribute the weight over a larger area and inch their way along until they reach thicker ice.

The distance an individual bear travels varies tremendously. In areas where ice is stable throughout the year, a polar bear's home range may be only a few thousand square kilometers. In other areas where they stay near the edge of the pack ice they have been known to range over areas larger than 116,000 sq miles (300,000 sq km). In the Bering Sea, for example, the pack ice itself can move 620 miles (1000 km) from summer to winter. Polar bears follow the ice edge and range widely across the pack ice searching for seals.

Because of the uncertainty of prey availability, polar bear metabolism can shut down quickly in times of food stress. If a polar bear does not eat for about 10 to 14 days, he will go into a state of winter sleep similar to the state that other bears go into during hibernation. The polar bear waits in this dormant state with little movement, surviving on stored fat, until prey becomes available again. He doesn't urinate or even drink water; body wastes are recycled without the use of the kidneys and water is produced from the metabolism of fat. This state can occur regardless of the time of year. Polar bears in Hudson Bay come ashore in late July and live on their stored fat for several months until the ice freezes and they can return to hunt seals.

Seals are not their only food, but they are the major prey of most polar bears. Ringed seals are the most important species and bearded seals are second. Other food items can include narwhals, beluga whales, walrus, seabirds, and vegetation. Polar bears have been observed attacking seabirds that were swimming on the surface, by diving and then surfacing underneath them. They have also been observed diving for kelp and swimming up to seals that were basking on the edge of the ice. Carrion is also an important food source.

Groups of polar bears as large as 44 animals have been observed feeding on the remains of a bowhead whale carcass after the whale had been hauled onto the ice and divided up by native hunters. Since eskimos have been hunting whales in the arctic for more than 4000 years, this has probably been an important food source, particularly in the spring when migrating bowheads are often restricted to narrow openings (leads) in the ice and are more vulnerable to hunting. The smaller beluga whales are also an occasional prey item.

Pack ice is a mosaic of various pieces of ice; it is patched together from old ice of various ages up to several years old, and newer, usually thinner ice. It is a dynamic environment that is constantly moving with the currents and the winds. Pressure ridges of stacked and jumbled ice are pushed up when large plates of ice collide, and leads of open water are formed when plates of ice pull apart. Throughout the ice pack there are numerous open water openings called polynyas. Polynyas are like watering holes in the desert for many species; they provide feeding opportunities for birds, and they provide breathing holes for marine mammals. Seals can often dig their own breathing holes in the thinner ice, but belugas and other whales must often rely on open areas in order to breathe.

Sometimes the ice conditions greatly restrict the number of polynyas. At times, a number of whales may all be forced to breathe from a single opening for days at a time because there are no other polynyas that they can swim to before running out of breath. In times like these, the whales circle beneath the opening, taking turns to surface and breathe before submerging again. Occasionally, polar bears will discover these breathing holes; they can smell them from long distances and in fact they may also be able to hear them as the whales repeatedly surface and exhale rapidly. Polar bears have been observed

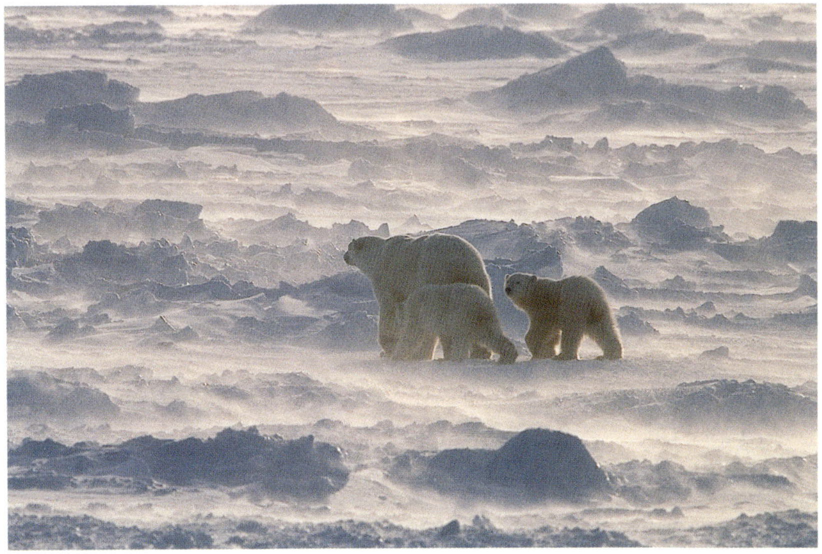

Polar bear cubs follow their mother and learn to survive.

preying on beluga whales in these situations. They wait by the open hole and attempt to grab the beluga by the top of the head or the snout. If they get a good grip they are sometimes able to haul the whale out onto the ice like they would a seal or a walrus. As long as the whales continue to surface, the bears can catch them and feed. By the time the ice shifts enough to open more polynyas and the whales can escape, there may be several dead belugas, and many more with deep tooth marks on their heads which will rapidly heal.

Polar bears mate in the spring, from late March through late May. The fertilized egg remains in the blastocyst stage for about four months until it is implanted in the uterus and begins to develop around late September. The gestation period lasts about three months and the young are born between late November and early January while their mother rests comfortably in a den dug into a snowdrift. Many male polar bears will never set foot on land during their lifetimes. Females generally come onto shore to give birth; they dig maternity dens in deep snowdrifts near the coast in late October or early November. Some areas are more favorable than others; concentrations of denning females occur on Wrangel Island off northern Siberia, on Kong Karl's Land in the Svalbard Archipelago near Spitzbergen, and south of Churchill, Manitoba, in Canada. Polar winds tend to circulate from the north and they form drifts on south-facing slopes where the sun warms them in late winter and spring.

Two cubs are common, but occasionally three are born. In extremely favorable conditions of nutrition, four may be born. The cubs are helpless and sightless at birth, like all other bears, and are covered with a very fine layer of hair. Inside the den they rely on their mother's warmth and the insulation of densely packed snow to keep them warm. Although the temperature outside is often well below zero (either Centigrade or Fahrenheit) they are never in any danger of freezing. When they first venture outside the temperature is often still below zero. Den emergence depends on local conditions as well as the latitude; bears that den further south are able to come out as early as late February while those further north may not emerge until April. Cubs and mother stay near the den for less than two weeks before moving out onto the ice. The cubs will travel with their mother and learn to hunt for two-and-a-half years. This is longer than most bear species, but they have more demanding tasks to learn in order to survive. Catching seals requires stealth, patience, and critical knowledge of where seals can be found. The early eskimos undoubtedly learned the same skills by observing polar bears.

Humans in the Arctic had to adopt the hunting techniques of polar bears as well as devising many of their own, such as harpooning whales. The bear however, was a primary teacher. Eskimos also hunted the bear, and used polar bear hides for clothing, especially pants, which were critical for waiting immobile for long periods of time at seal breathing holes, just as the bears do. Polar bears were treated with great reverence; Inupiat legends say they are 'people inside a bear hide'. When a polar bear has been killed the hunter must treat it as a guest. Eskimos still hunt polar bears today, as they have for thousands of years, but with modern weapons. There are, however, a few old men today who killed polar bears with spears and knives in their youth.

Polar bears are legally hunted throughout most of their range today. They are not considered rare or endangered at present by the Convention on International Trade in Endangered Species (CITES). Hunting quotas are enforced by law in Alaska, and by agreement in parts of Canada. There are no legal limits for eskimos in Quebec, Greenland, and Alaska. Hunting is prohibited in Russia and the Svalbard Archipelago, but enforcement is difficult. In Russia especially, the current economic conditions have encouraged poaching and the extent of it is unknown. An international Agreement on the Conservation of Polar Bears was signed in 1973 by Canada, Denmark, Norway, the United States, and the former USSR which regulates hunting and guides the management of polar bear populations. Overharvesting and illegal killing are considered to be the greatest threat to polar bear populations today. However, human activities are becoming more of a threat as oil and gas development in particular begins to encroach on the Arctic. Human developments displace polar bears from important habitat, create conflicts that result in bear deaths, create disturbance and stress that affects their behavior and survival, and can introduce toxic substances that impact polar bears and their prey in direct and indirect ways. Polar bears that encounter oil spills will probably die either by ingestion or through loss of insulation and associated stresses. Because polar bears have low reproductive rates, human-caused mortality can greatly affect the stability of their populations.

Polar bears are equally at home on the ice or in the water.

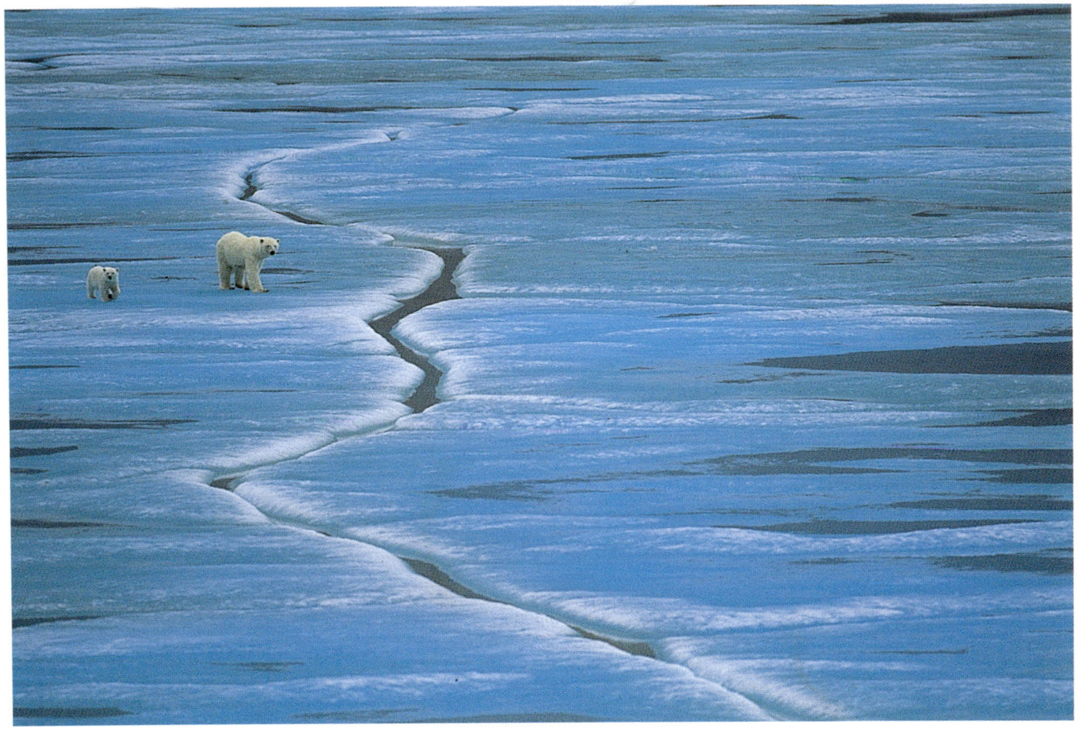

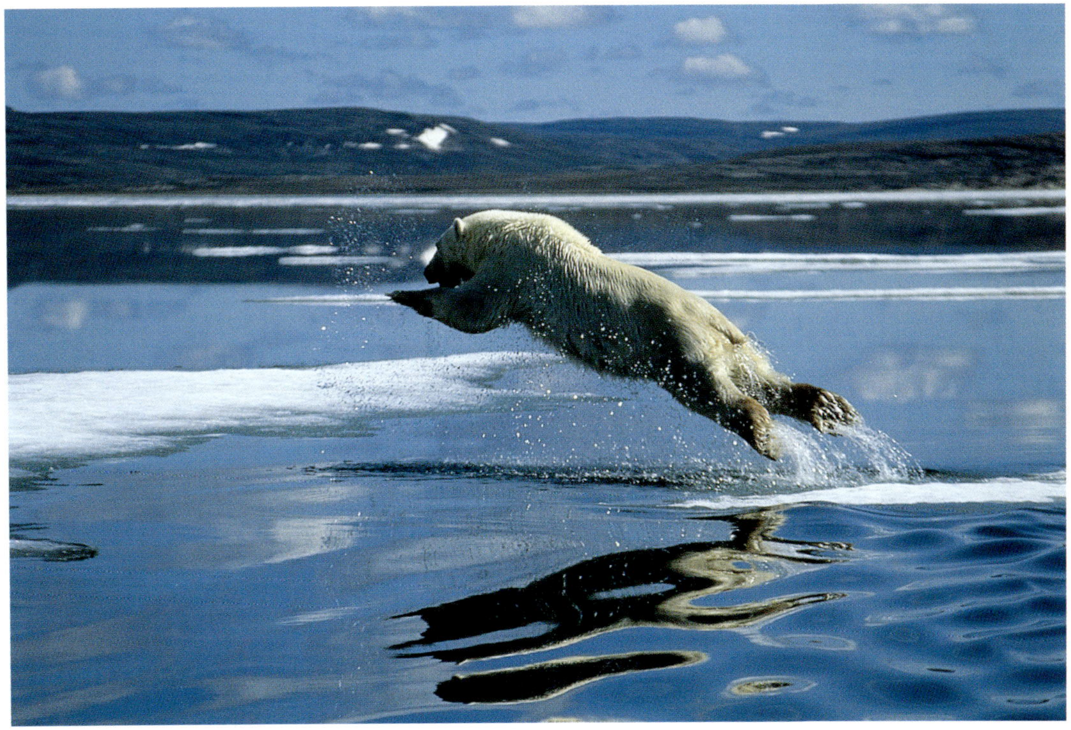

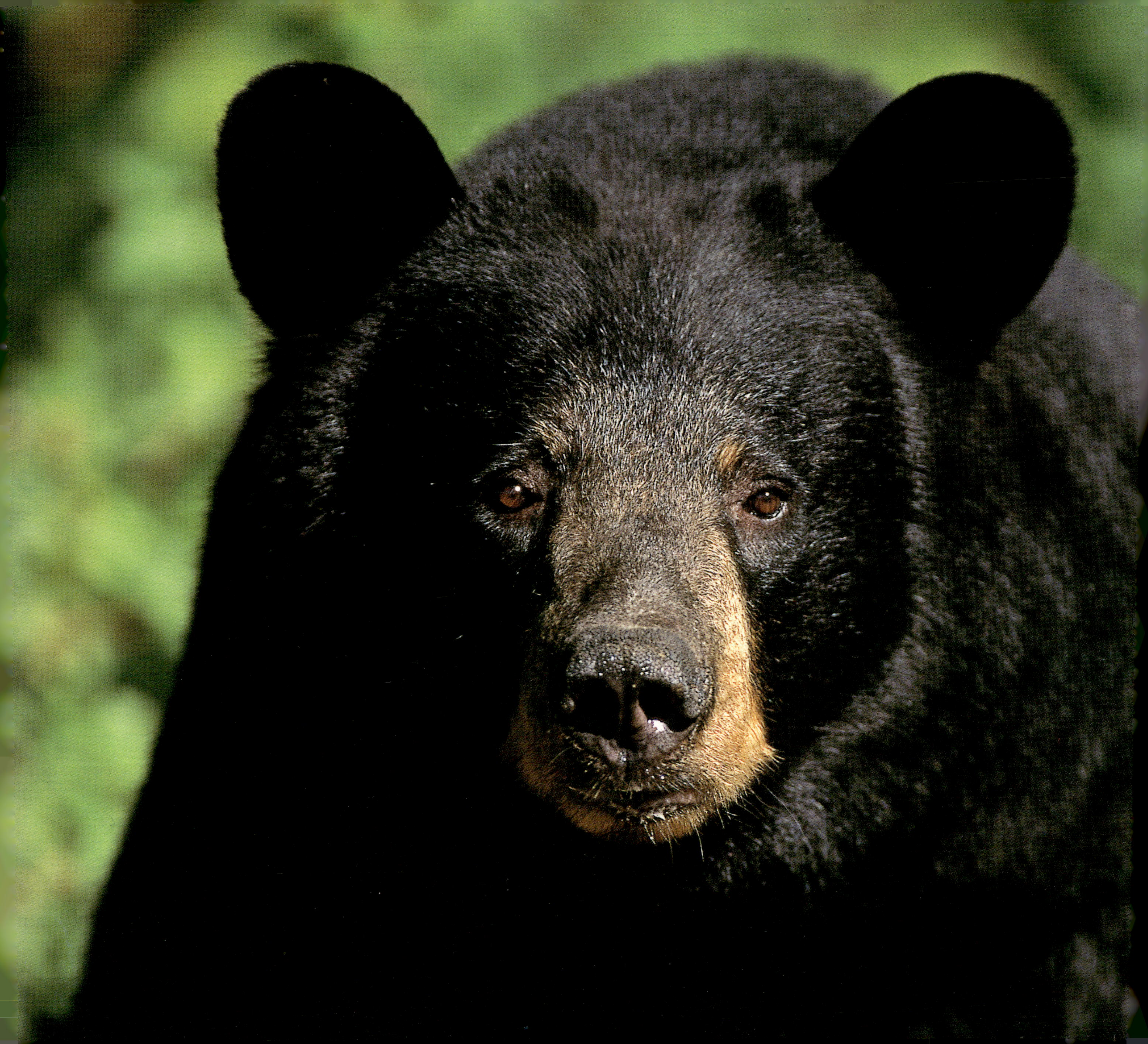

The American Black Bear

American black bears, *Ursus americanus*, are the quintessential generalists. Their ancestors colonized the New World about 3.5 million years ago, following the Bering Land Bridge route that the Tremarctine (short-faced) bears had followed about 12 million years earlier. These early black bears found themselves in a world already well populated with large, dangerous predators. In addition to at least two species of very large short-faced bears, there were cats; big cats. The first cats arrived in North America about 36 million years ago and had evolved into many species, some of which were larger than any living lions and tigers. At the time the black bears arrived there were three main groups of cats, the saber-toothed cats, the scimitar-toothed cats, and the true cats which included mountain lions, cheetahs, and jaguars. Some of these cats evolved in North America, but others such as the lion arrived from Asia. Coyotes probably arrived at about the same time as black bears, and wolves may have arrived slightly later. From the beginning, black bears could not compete with these specialists for large prey species and they were not large and strong enough to drive them away from their kills. However, there was a wide variety of other food sources available, and like their cousins in southern Asia, black bears were able to utilize fruits, insects, honey, plants, carrion, and small prey successfully. They climbed trees to escape some predators. They survived, reproduced, adapted, and spread out across North America.

During the last few ice ages, black bears and many other species of the Pleistocene fauna were forced south by the expanding ice sheets. As less habitat became available, the competition for resources intensified. In times like these, generalists often have an advantage, and this proved true for the black bear. The race against extinction goes not always to the swift or the strong. During the glacial periods, and afterwards as humans and other new species invaded from the Old World, many of the larger mammals disappeared. The Pleistocene lion, the saber-toothed cat, the Florida short-faced bear, the giant short-faced bear, and other species winked out of existence in North America along with their prey: mammoths, mastodons, giant sloths, horses, camels and others. For a brief period the black bear was probably the only bear left in what is now the contiguous United States. They shared this land with dire wolves, cheetahs and coyotes about a million years ago. Wolves arrived about 700,000 years ago. Mountain lions and Pleistocene lions arrived a few hundred thousand years after that. The black bear's monopoly of the bear niche was short-lived, however, for as the ice sheets receded at the end of the Pleistocene about 10,000 years ago, two new and formidable predators arrived on the scene: grizzly bears, and humans.

The black bear, however, was already well equipped to coexist with dangerous predators and they not only survived, but managed to expand their range northward after the ice age into lands already occupied by both grizzlies and humans. They avoided grizzlies, animals that recently evolved in open habitats, by staying in the forest. Only in Northern Labrador, where there are no grizzly bears, do black bears now inhabit the open tundra. They are currently found all across Canada except for Prince Edward Island, throughout the U.S. in at least 32 of the states, and in Northern Mexico. There are 16 currently recognized subspecies, several of which are declining and one, the Louisiana subspecies, which is considered threatened. As a whole, though, the species is increasing in numbers after reaching a low point caused by human persecution.

Black bears are generally considered to inhabit forests; primarily deciduous hardwoods or coniferous boreal forests. It is likely that they adapted to these major habitat types during the Pleistocene, moving south with the forests as the ice advanced and then genera-

American black bears can often be identified by their distinctive brown muzzle.

tions later moving north again as the ice receded. Their tree-climbing ability had evolved millions of years earlier, but it probably became more developed as they spread out across North America. Tree-climbing may have provided security from some of the larger predators of that time such as the giant short-faced bear and the Pleistocene lion. Black bears may have adapted to exploit the resources of forests in part because those and other carnivore species dominated the open grasslands.

Black bears have been living in North America as a distinct species for at least 2.5 million years. During this time they have colonized a wide range of habitats, and have had time to adapt to local conditions. They have begun to evolve; in some cases where they have been more isolated, they have become more different than in other areas with more gene flow from other populations. No populations have been isolated long enough to evolve into a new species, but they have begun to diverge from each other; this is reflected in the fact that they are considered to have so many subspecies. Subspecies are generally separated by differences in physical characteristics such as skull shape and size that vary consistently between different populations. There are other differences that are not diagnostic; one of the most striking variations is in color.

Black bears are found in a variety of colors. Color phases do not correspond to subspecies or other units of conservation in most cases, but they probably represent variations that arose in one locale and then spread to others. One of the most striking color phases is the white, Kermode or spirit, bear that is found in an area of coastal British Columbia. Another regional color phase is seen in the blue, or glacier, bears that inhabit parts of Alaska, northwestern British Columbia, and the Yukon Territories. They get their color from a deep blue-black undercoat with white or yellow guard hairs. These color phases may have arisen on isolated island refuges during glacial periods. Other populations are often a mix of color phases; the black phase seems to be more common east of the Mississippi River. In the western states, brown and cinnamon phases are more common in some areas. The lighter shades have been described as brown, chocolate, chestnut, cinnamon, honey and blonde as well as other terms.

Black bears inhabit forested areas throughout their range. They have adapted to open forests such as chapparal in the Southwest and spruce bogs in the north, to dense rainforests in the Pacific Northwest, to swamps in the Southeast, to the thick expanses of the boreal forest across Canada. One of the major components of black bear habitat is a heavy understory of shrubs. The understory provides food and cover. Although they are very adept at climbing, they seldom forage in trees. They use trees primarily for security; to climb away from danger and to leave their cubs while foraging.

Black bears have not lost the ability to survive on the tundra, however. In northeastern Canada there is a population of black bears which have recently immigrated (within the memory of Inuit hunters) and which may still be expanding. Brown bears long ago occupied this part of the Arctic, the Ungava peninsula of Labrador and Quebec, but were probably extirpated by humans by about 1927. With the brown bears gone, black bears have been able to exploit the resources of the tundra, which are quite different from the boreal forests that they emigrated from.

Their reliance on forested habitat has greatly influenced their evolution; there is some evidence that black bears became separated into two lineages about two million years ago when the vast continental forest of North America became fragmented into a western and an eastern forest. Later, at the beginning of the Pleistocene, the western lineage became separated into a coastal group and an interior group about 350,000 years ago. The coastal group subsequently diverged into the four coastal subspecies: *Ursus Americanus kermodei, carlottae, vancouveri* and *altifrontalis*. The interior group split to form *cinnamomum* and *americanus*.

Subadult American black bears look like awkward teenagers; they are at the bottom of the social hierarchy.

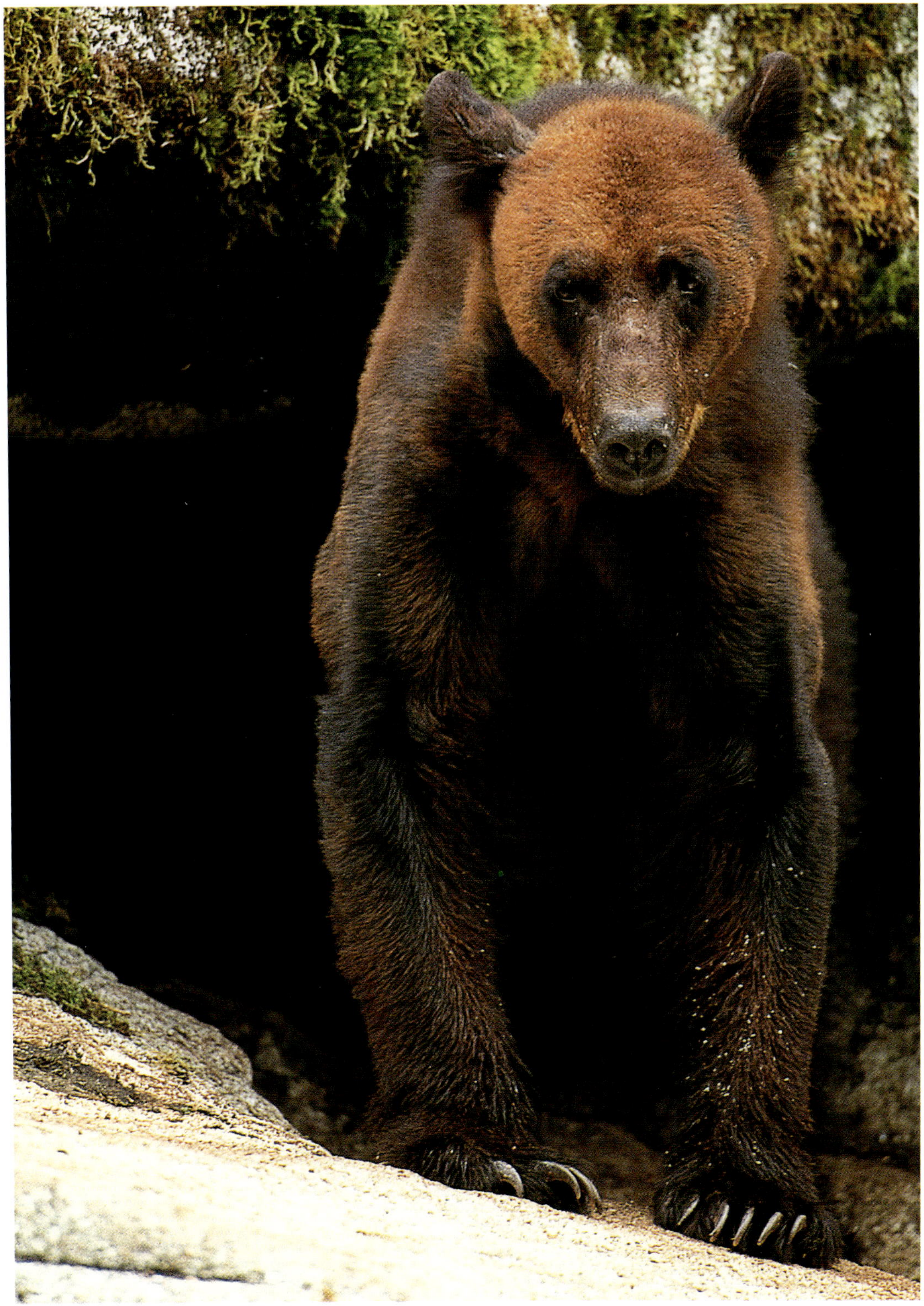

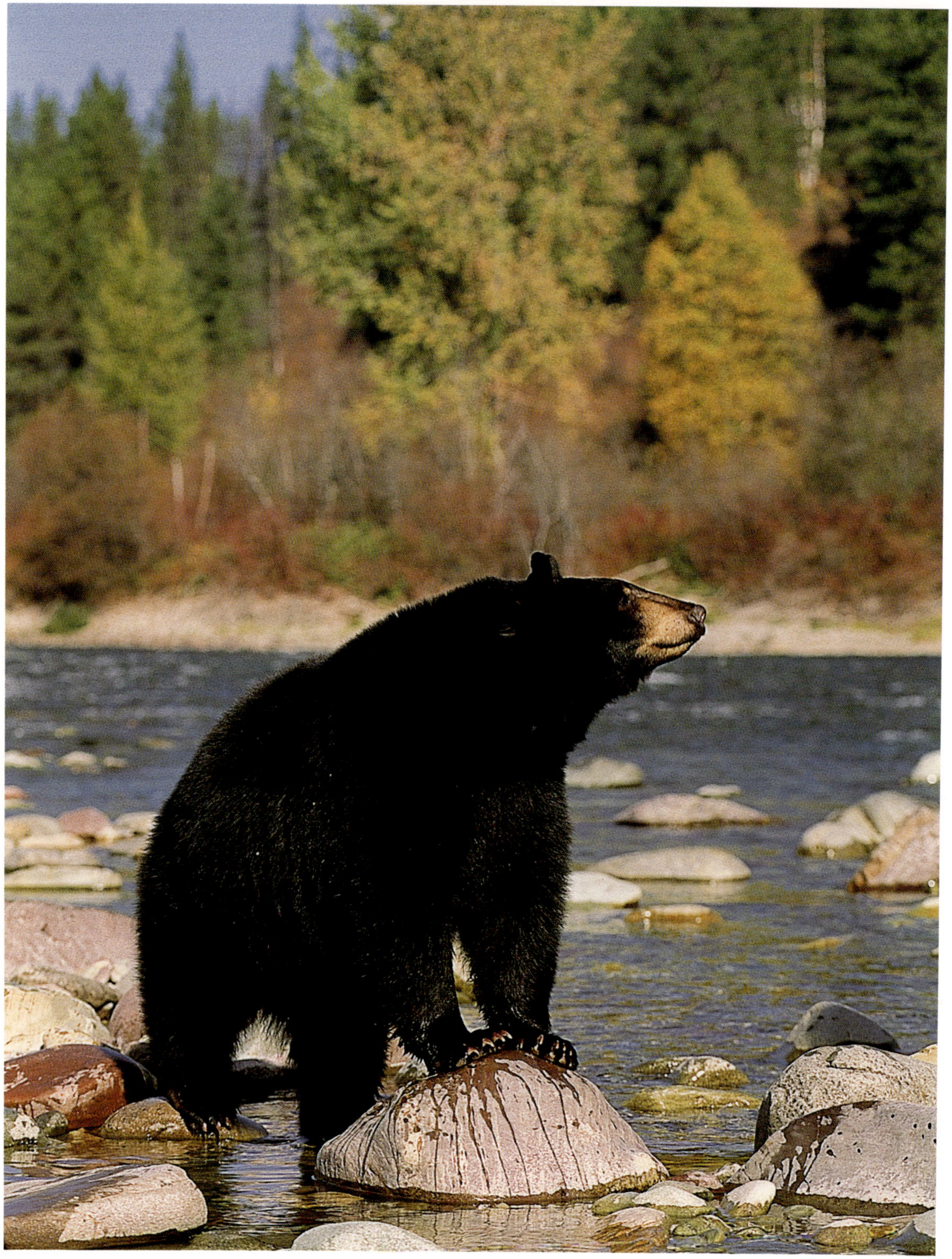

The coastal subspecies may have been isolated on separate island refugia during the last Pleistocene glaciation. The subspecies *carlottae* is found on the Queen Charlotte Islands (Haida Gwai), while *vancouveri* is found on Vancouver Island. The subspecies *kermodei*, or the spirit bear, is found primarily on Princess Royal Island (see below) and may have survived the ice age on the westernmost part of this island in the Hecate Strait lowlands. Other possible refugia on the Northwest Pacific coast include the islands of Southeast Alaska (see the brown bear chapter), the Queen Charlotte Strait lowlands, the coastal fringe of mainland British Columbia, and western Washington. Of the 16 current black bear subspecies, eight are likely to be found in British Columbia. This suggests that conditions during the Pleistocene isolated black bears in this region into many 'islands' of habitat. On the coast they were probably islands surrounded by water and ice; in the interior they may have been islands of forest surrounded by open grasslands. The present-day variation in black bear populations represents local adaptations to climate and food sources in these various 'islands'.

Black bears feed primarily on plants although in some areas they prey on mammals such as deer fawns or moose calves, and in others they rely on salmon. Like the brown bears, they require large amounts of food during the period of hyperphagia in the fall when they need to put on fat for hibernation. At this time of year, high energy mast crops such as acorns or berries can be critical foods. They can gain up to 3 lb (1.3 kg) per day feeding on plant foods. In coastal areas they feed on salmon in the fall. In areas where there are few brown bears, large concentrations of black bears will congregate to feed at salmon spawning sites or at falls where the salmon are concentrated. In areas where brown bears are dominant, black bears are more dispersed and secretive. They tend to feed on salmon only where and when they can avoid brown bears. The presence of brown bears greatly influences the behavior and distribution of black bears wherever the two species coexist. To understand the diversity of adaptations exhibited by black bears, let us look at how they live in four very different North American environments.

Black Bears in the Great Smoky Mountains

The last, or Wisconsinan, ice age reached its maximum extent about 18,000 years ago. At that point the North American (Laurentide) ice sheet extended well south of the Great Lakes into what is now Illinois, Ohio, and Kentucky. Immediately south of the ice sheet, the land was covered in tundra. The tundra probably extended into the Great Smoky Mountains of Tennessee. South of the tundra was a belt of spruce forest, unlike the forest at the northern tree line today, that must have stretched clear across the continent. South of the spruce forest were grasslands and deciduous trees; however, none of the plant communities we recognize today would necessarily have been present then. The same plant species existed, they just grouped themselves into different assemblages in response to environmental variables such as light, precipitation, soil moisture and temperature, which were very different than they are now. The hardwoods, beech, ash, oak, elm, aspen, and birch were present, but in very different proportions. The spruce forest itself contained a varied mixture of hardwoods; particularly ash, elm, and oak.

At that time, black bears probably did not venture onto the tundra or the grasslands very often. Just south of the ice lived musk ox and caribou, and further south lived camels, llamas, deer, elk, pronghorn antelope, and horses, which black bears might have been able to prey upon. There were also large mammals like mammoths, mastodons, bison, and ground sloths that would have provided huge amounts of carrion. However there were also fearsome predators. As mentioned before, the open habitats were dominated by the American (or Pleistocene) lion, the giant short-faced bear, the American cheetah, the dire wolf, and the saber-tooth cats. Not only were black bears unable

As fall approaches American black bears develop a well-rounded physique through intensive feeding, termed hyperphagia.

to compete with them for prey or carrion; black bears would have been prey themselves. For this reason, black bears stayed within the forest where they could exploit an abundance of rich food sources, and could climb trees to escape predators.

As the ice sheet receded, the tundra moved north, colonizing the bare cold ground that was exposed, and the forests followed. The climate warmed to a maximum which has often been called the hypsithermal, which lasted for several thousand years beginning about 11,000 years ago. During this period, plants migrated much farther north than they are found today. Black bears moved north with the forests, and may have begun to inhabit the Great Smoky Mountains in Eastern Tennessee around 13,000 years ago. They are still there today.

Many of their same food plants remained in the Smokies too; oaks, beeches, chestnuts and berries. Forest-dwelling prey have changed greatly, but the white-tailed deer remain, as well as mice, voles, shrews, rabbits, and a host of other small mammals. Black bears still capture them opportunistically. They also respond to danger in the same fashion. Mothers with cubs will send them up a tree and then move away, often climbing a tree themselves if necessary, to divert attention from the location of the cub. The giant predators have all gone extinct now though, and the only real danger for black bears is humans. Red wolves have been re-introduced but are very few in number. Mountain lions were eliminated and haven't made it back. The grizzly bear never made it east of the Mississippi.

Although humans are the only threat to black bears, they are more than enough. Black bears are not considered to be threatened or endangered, but their range has been greatly reduced as humans have expanded. From the Great Smokies north, black bears are still found along the spine of the Appalachians into Canada. To the south and west though, populations are increasingly fragmented. The rich valleys to the west of Great Smoky Mountain National Park near Gatlinburg, Tennessee, which once were bottomlands where bears thrived, are now neon and pavement. Elm and oak have been replaced by Elvis museums, theme parks, gas stations, motels, and tourist traps. Acorns and beech nuts have been replaced by jelly doughnuts, French fries, and bacon burgers. When bears do venture out of the mountains and down to the strip developments in search of food, this is what they find, and they come into conflict with people. If they venture out of the Park in other directions they may find cornfields or casinos. Some bears have learned to feed in agricultural fields and others have learned to raid farms, beehives, and orchards.

Black bears on the margins of the forest often become conditioned to human foods, and are eventually eliminated. When the International Bear Association held its meetings at the edge of the Park in 1998, they extracted an agreement from the hotel they chose that the garbage dumpsters would be bear-proofed as a condition for patronage. Up to that point, those dumpsters had been a sort of local tourist attraction where bears could be routinely observed. Places such as this are what biologists call 'population sinks'. These are areas where the death rate exceeds the birth rate and the population declines.

Optimal black bear habitat is found where the terrain is rugged and difficult for humans to gain access. The forest has thick understory vegetation, and abundant natural foods such as nuts and berries. They prefer to den in tree cavities, but also use caves and shallow depressions. They choose den sites that are away from roads and other human activities whenever possible. These areas are termed 'population sources' where the birth rate exceeds the death rate and the population increases. As the population increases, as it has done in the Great Smoky Mountain National Park, the younger animals disperse away from their mothers. Like all bears, the males disperse farther and the females remain close to their mother's home range.

When the population has grown enough to reach the carrying capacity of the environment (all available space is occupied by older bears), the dispersing subadults end up on the margins. They eventually get in trouble there. Sometimes they will den under porches or beneath summer cabins that are unoccupied. Population sinks are not always human-caused; low productivity of habitat or other sources of mortality can cause populations to decline, but humans are probably

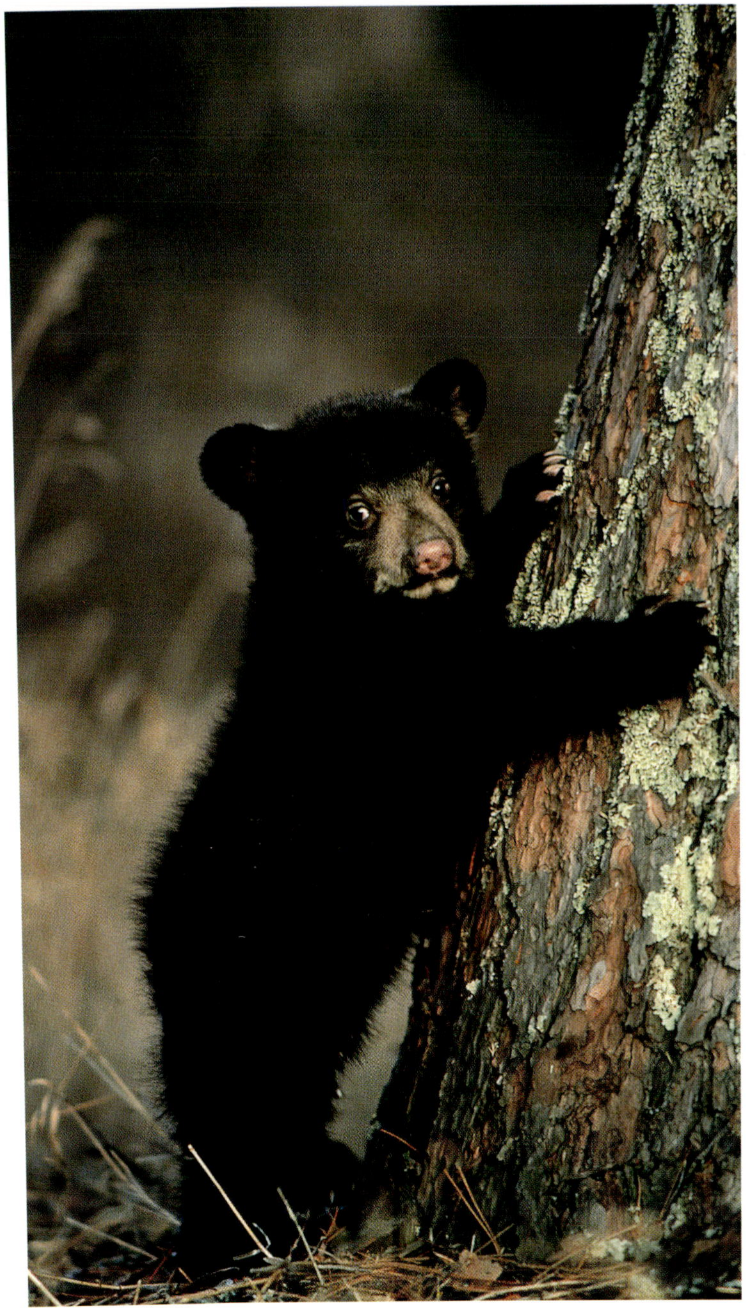

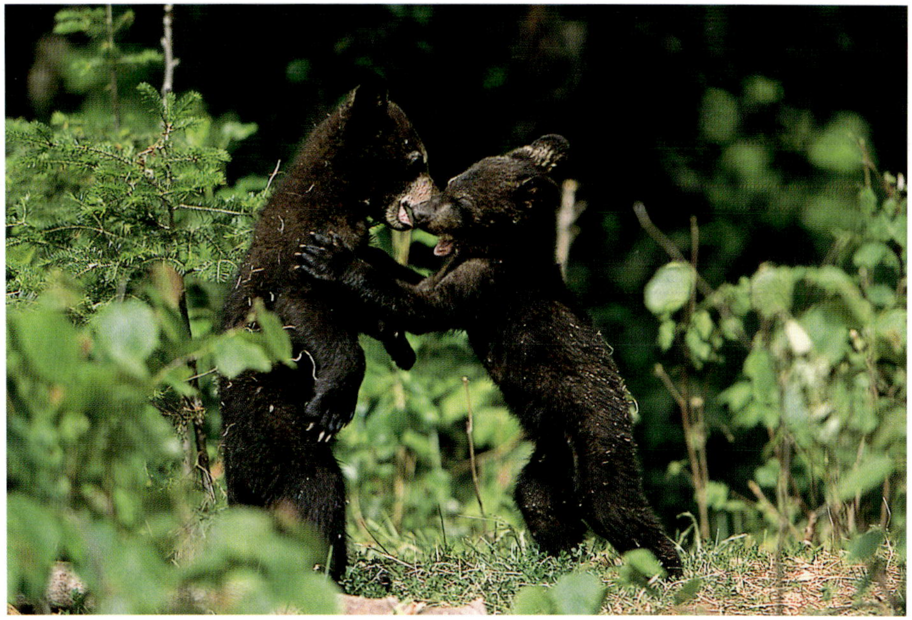

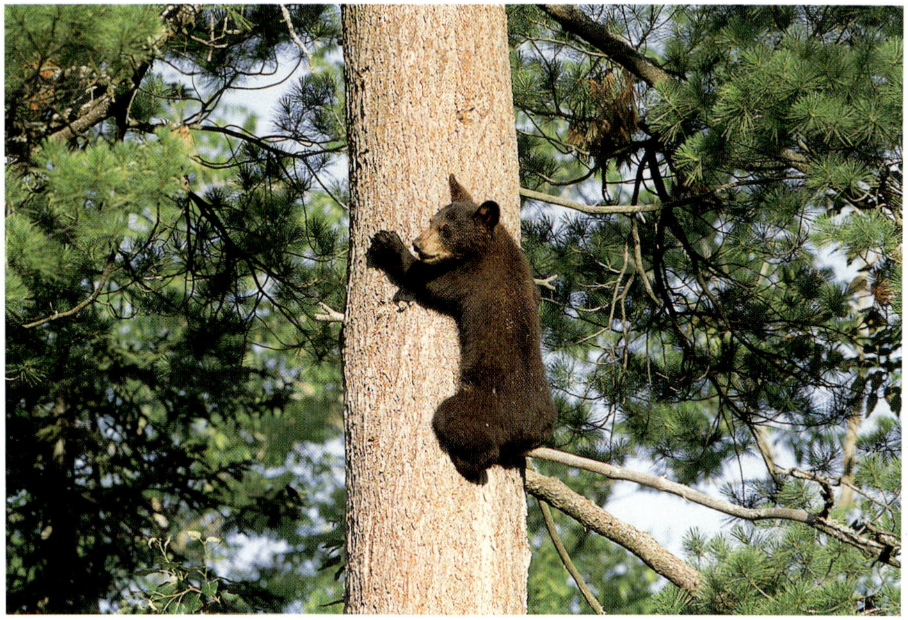

American black bear cubs wrestle and climb trees as they play; these activities develop skills they will need to survive. Cubs learn to climb at an early age and their mother will send them up trees while she feeds or when danger may be present.

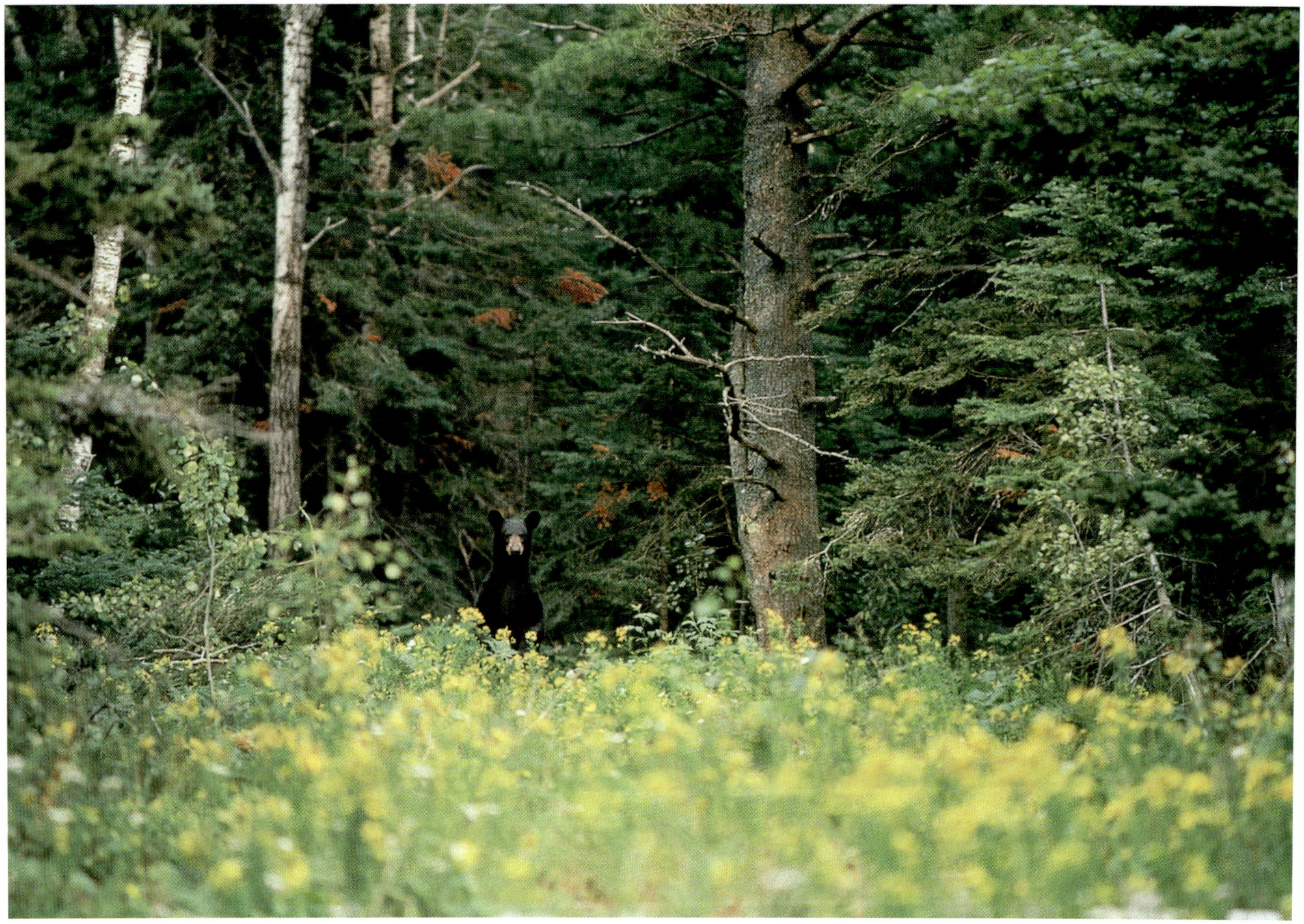

American black bears adapted to life in the forest, probably because more dangerous predators such as the large cats and the short-faced bears occupied the open habitats. Their distribution today is primarily dependent upon large forested areas with little human disturbance.

the main reason today for population sinks of black bears. Worldwide, humans are probably the main reason for population sinks for all bear species.

Black Bears in the Greater Yellowstone Ecosystem

Greater Yellowstone is the name that conservationists have given to the mosaic of forests and mountains that surround and include Yellowstone National Park in Wyoming, Montana, and Idaho. In this high-elevation habitat, American black bears are second-class citizens. Grizzlies are clearly in charge. Grizzlies have only been here for about 11,000 years however. Black bears were here long before that; perhaps for 3 million years.

During the last 3 million years, the glaciers have descended from the north six times. During those cold periods, the large continental ice sheets did not extend quite as far as the Yellowstone ecosystem. However, because of the high altitude of Yellowstone, glaciers formed in the higher mountains and descended into the valleys. Like a smaller version of the continental ice sheets, snow and rain fell on the peaks and added to the size of the glaciers that formed there. The weight of the ice caused it to flow slowly downhill, scouring everything in its path down to the bare rock. In the cold soil near the margins of the glacier, the plants formed tundra. Below the tundra there was forest; the mix of conifers and deciduous trees that reached across the continent in varying compositions.

Like elsewhere south of the continental ice sheets, the black bears lived in the forest and avoided the larger predators. During the warm interglacial periods the forest covered the entire Yellowstone plateau and black bears thrived. When grizzly bears, and humans, arrived the black bears were well adapted. In fact, things may have improved for them since so many other competitors disappeared at about the same time. Black bears and grizzlies have shared this region ever since. Grizzlies will kill black bears readily and often eat them. Black bears and grizzlies will sometimes share the same food sources, but it is an uneasy banquet and the black bears are constantly alert. Generally, only the large male black bears will hang out with grizzlies. When there were open pit dumps in Yellowstone Park in the 1960s, black bears would often feed at the Rabbit Creek dump near Old Faithful geyser. No black bears were ever seen at the Trout Creek dump in Hayden Valley. The Rabbit Creek dump was surrounded by trees. The nearest tree to the Trout Creek dump was about 2 miles away.

Grizzlies are well adapted to digging; long claws and powerful shoulder muscles. Black bears have claws primarily adapted for climbing. They can also dig for roots and tubers, but are not as efficient as grizzly bears. They are very good at tearing apart decaying logs for insect larvae, and will dig up ant hills to get at ant eggs and larvae. Black bears also utilize honey when they can find it. It was fairly scarce in the Rocky Mountains for millions of years. Think about this. The honey bee that we know today evolved in Eurasia and was brought to the U.S.A. by humans. There are native bees, wasps, and hornets in North America, but none of them are particularly good honey producers. It may have been that the ancestors of the black bear fed often on honey in Eurasia. After they crossed the Bering Land Bridge, they did without it, more or less, until millions of years later when humans brought the bees across on boats.

Black Bears, and other bears that feed on ants, bees, and other biting insects have probably developed some sort of resistance to insect venom and a higher threshold of pain, especially in the less hairy areas around the muzzle. When feeding on beehives, black bears seem to regard the swarms of angry bees attacking them as minor irritations. Grizzly bears may have similar adaptations, but there is some indication that bear deterrent sprays (which utilize concentrated capsicum from chilli peppers) are less effective on black bears than on grizzly bears. These sprays sting the eyes and burn the skin; they can cause people to collapse in pain on the ground. They have been very effective on grizzly bears when the bear is blasted directly in the face. Their effects on black bears may be somewhat less certain.

In general, black bears learn to avoid grizzlies, and then look for food. Both species feed on most of the same plants but black bears may utilize less desirable and nutritious ones when grizzlies are nearby. Grizzlies dig up the roots and tubers of plants as well. In the spring both species graze on emerging grasses. Occasionally they can be found on lawns. Carrion from winter-killed elk, deer, and bison is also important. Again, black bears can feed on carcasses only until a grizzly arrives and usurps it from them. Sometimes, a large black bear and a small grizzly may share a carcass, or a black bear and a wolf, or a wolf and a grizzly. Coyotes and ravens may hang around and grab small pieces when they get the opportunity. The animals must be able to assess the state-of-mind of the other species, and somehow communicate their own attitude, as they negotiate for the carcass. This is done mostly by body language; the posture and actions. If a grizzly is hungry and aggressive, though, no one else gets any food until he leaves.

In the late summer and fall, berries are the black bear's primary food item. Black bear, and grizzly, scats at this time often look like the filling for a blueberry pie (but much less appetizing and aromatic). If there were no grizzlies, black bears would quickly learn to feed on whitebark pine nuts and perhaps moths, but those food sources are pre-empted by grizzlies in the fall.

Black bears are more tolerant of human disturbance; perhaps because humans are more tolerant of black bears than they are of grizzlies. Black bears are generally not as threatening. For various reasons, black bears live closer to areas occupied by humans, and often come into conflict with humans when they search for food in populated areas. Attractants such as bee hives, bird feeders, humming-bird food, compost piles, orchards, barbecue grills, and garbage cans will often lure bears into yards and gardens. On two occasions I have been awakened by black bears while sleeping outside in back yards but each of us emerged unscathed by the encounter.

Black bears, of course, became famous as the roadside bears of Yellowstone. For decades they were permitted to beg by the side of the road where they were fed by tourists. Park regulations prohibited this, but enforcement was extremely difficult. Few serious incidents occurred, so bears were generally chased away by park rangers only when they began to cause problems. If a bear continued to be a nuisance, or if it acted aggressively toward tourists, it was simply removed from the population; taken to a zoo or shot. Grizzlies rarely begged along the roads. This may be because grizzlies dominated whatever natural foods were available. Black bears, especially younger animals, were forced to forage in the least desirable and most risky habitat; the roadside. In years of poor whitebark pine production in Yellowstone, large male grizzlies dominate whitebark pine and berry habitat and other grizzlies move into areas closer to humans such as roadsides. The same dynamics apply to black bears. Since they are even lower on the pecking order, they move into areas that are even closer to humans during poor food years.

Black bears quickly learn where food is available. To discourage them from obtaining food along roads, they are now chased away whenever they are seen near roads. For both grizzlies and black bears it is sadly true that 'a fed bear is a dead bear'. Once bears learn to obtain foods from humans it is extremely difficult to teach them otherwise. They can be chased away with anti-riot bullets made of rubber, loud noises, or shouting people. However, even if they are repeatedly chased away it only takes one incident where they obtain food again (and don't get hurt), to reinforce their food-getting behavior. Currently, groups of highly trained people with aggressive Karelian bear dogs have had the best success in re-training nuisance bears. When bears approach human areas they are chased away with rubber bullets, charging dogs, loud noises, etc. They learn to associate danger and pain with human beings instead of food. After a few encounters like that, they are much less likely to return.

The Spirit Bears in the Great Bear Rainforest

Conservationists along the Pacific coast of Canada in British Columbia have named this region the Great Bear Rainforest. It is an apt description of a unique place; in fact coastal temperate rainforest is one of the most endangered ecosystems on earth. Similar ecosystems (or biogeographic realms) are found only in Northwestern North

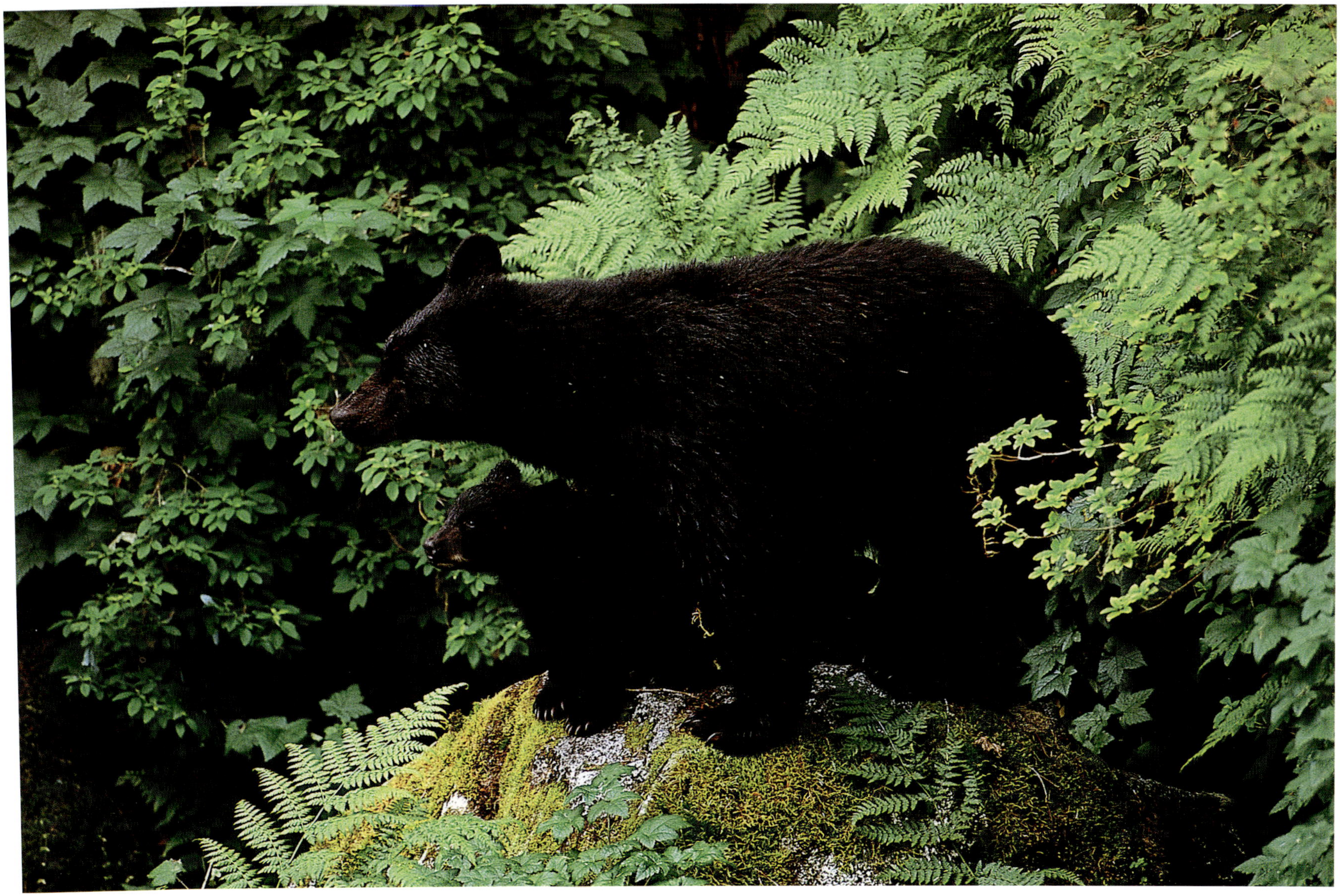

In southeast Alaska and coastal British Columbia black bears occupy many of the large islands and brown bears are effectively excluded. Both species of bears feed on the same foods. Female black bears with cubs are often displaced to higher elevations where they avoid conflicts.

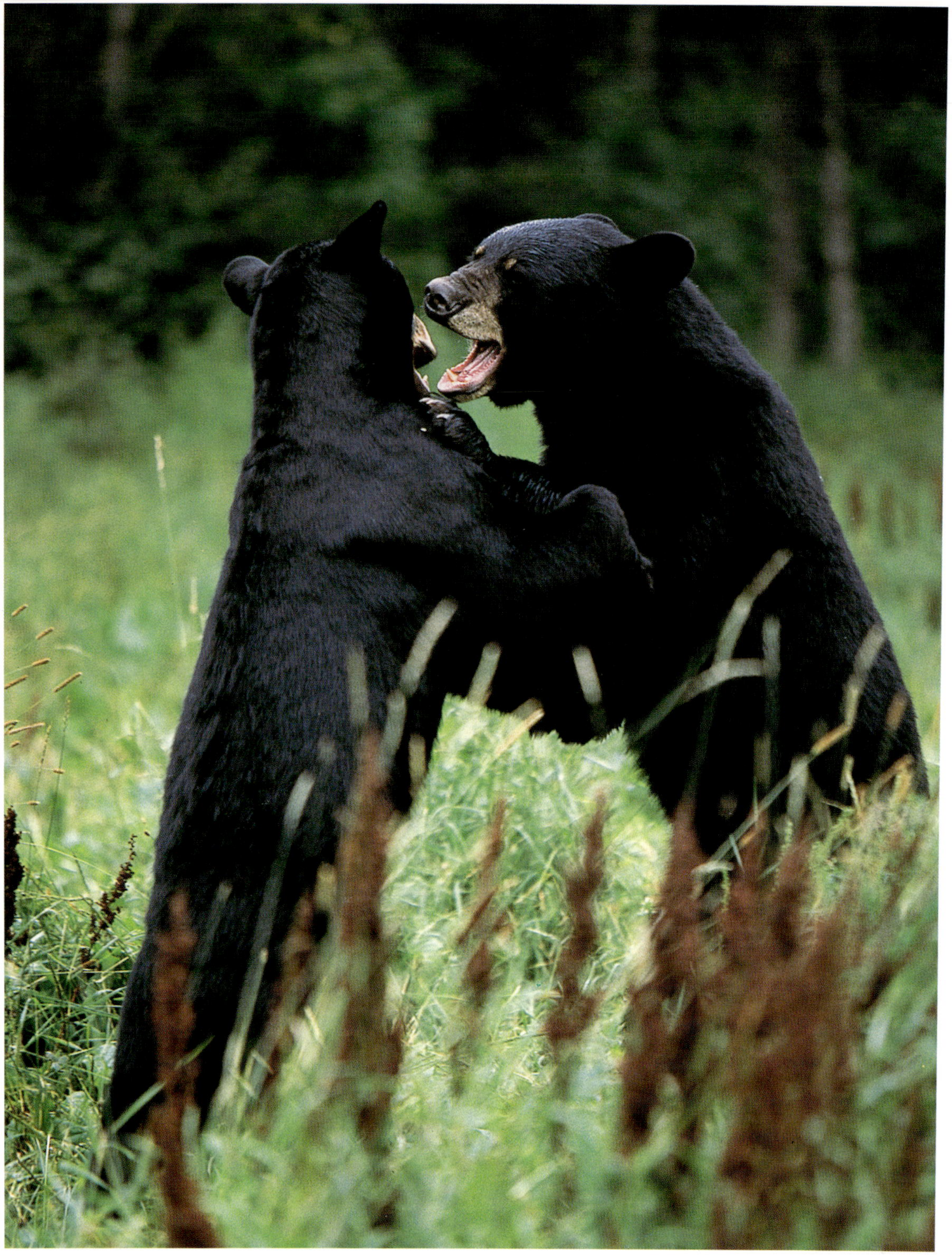

America, southern Japan and Korea, and on the Australian island of Tasmania. In British Columbia it is the home of great bears; both black bears and brown bears. Some of the black bears are white.

Conservationists have given the white black bears the name 'spirit bears'; in part because of their ghostly appearance and their importance in the spiritual world of the coastal Indians. Taxonomists have named them *Ursus americanus kermodei* after Frances Kermode, who was a director of the Royal British Columbia Museum. Although the white bears were originally thought to be perhaps a separate subspecies from the black bears, they had been scientifically studied only from museum skins. As they were observed in the wild, scientists soon learned what the coastal Indians had long known; black and white bears were color phases of the same species. White-colored female bears gave birth to black cubs and white cubs. Black-colored females do the same. The white hair color is apparently determined by a recessive gene, not unlike humans with blue eyes. The greatest concentration of spirit bears is on Princess Royal Island and on the adjacent mainland. There are brown bears (or grizzlies) inhabiting this part of the coast and some brown bears live on the islands, but the majority of bears in the area today are black bears. About 10 per cent of the black bears near Princess Royal Island are white. These black (and white) bears feed on most of the same foods as brown bears do, but they seem to partition the food resources in time and space. For the most part, black bears feed in places and at times when brown bears are not present. They do not dig for roots and tubers as much as brown bears do. A more complete description of foods can be found in the section of the brown bear chapter that describes coastal bears.

Black bears rely primarily on plants and carrion in the spring after they emerge from their dens. They forage on the marine sedge, and a variety of grasses and sedges in estuary meadows and along the shore. In general, habitats below 1600 ft (500 m) in elevation are preferred. The coastal western hemlock zone from 1600 to 3000 ft (500 to 900 m) and the mountain hemlock zone from about 3000 to 3900 ft (900 to 1200 m) receives low to moderate use, but is important for denning. The alpine tundra parkland above 3900 ft (1200 m) receives almost no use at all; it is primarily rock and ice, but bears travel across this habitat on mountain passes when they travel between valleys. At least 34 different plant species are utilized. As berries become ripe and salmon arrive, black bears shift their diet to concentrate almost exclusively on these food sources.

Salmon are vulnerable to bears when they pool up below obstacles in streams. If the water levels of creeks are low (due to lack of rainfall), large concentrations of salmon can build up at the mouths of streams where small waterfalls and rocky cascades are often found. Bears can often catch fish as they attempt to leap up the falls, or they can corner them in pools and shallow water. When it rains, and the creeks rise, the salmon swim upstream to the spawning beds. Bears follow the salmon upstream, catching them at any opportunity when they leave the security of the deeper water. After spawning, as the salmon weaken and then die, they become easy pickings for all ages of bears, and cubs learn from their mothers how to catch them. Every bear develops its own unique fishing style as it learns to catch fish in different locations and conditions. Some bears might submerge their heads to lunge after salmon in one pool and then wait patiently beside a waterfall in another spot to snap at salmon in mid-air. Some bears may try to herd salmon into shallow dead-end pockets while others may leap into the middle of streams and land among them.

It is usually the larger, dominant, and more aggressive male bears that pre-empt others from the good fishing spots, or steal the salmon that others have caught. Radio-location studies indicate that subadults and females with cubs are forced to forage at higher elevations than adult males. The big males feed along the streams and in the rich valley bottoms. In coastal areas with both brown and black bears, the black bears forage high up on the hillsides most of the time. This is

Play fighting, without teeth bared, is a social interaction that siblings often engage in even when they are adults.

done to avoid brown bears and also to find preferred berry patches.

Both species of bears require large, older trees for den sites. Virtually all black bear den sites are in large tree cavities, logs, root wads (the tangle of roots that is exposed when a tree topples over), or in stumps. Red cedar seems to decay into suitable den cavities more frequently than hemlock, spruce, or fir, and black bears tend to use this tree species more often when it is available. Trees that are old enough to decay, or fall over, and provide denning habitat are almost all over 250 years old. Den sites are generally located on slopes steeper than 15 degrees and in areas that are well-drained. Neither species of bear likes to den below about 600 ft (200 m) in elevation. They both prefer to den between about 1600 and 3000 ft (500 and 900 m). These elevations offer den sites provided by large old trees, have little risk of flooding, and may provide thermal insulation from snow with less chance of rain. When brown bears are present, they choose the higher elevations and the black bears are displaced into den sites on the lower hillsides. The picture which emerges from this data is that bears carefully pick their den sites and show strong preference for particular habitats when choosing these sites. The lack of suitable den sites (old-growth forest and large trees) could reduce the population density.

Studies of black bears on Haida Gwai (the Queen Charlotte Islands) have found the remains of salmon up to several hundred feet from the streams where they were caught. Some of the salmon are carried away whole to a more secluded place where the bear can eat safely; the largest fish are carried the farthest away from the stream. Pieces of fish are often dropped to decompose. Bear scat is also high in nitrogen-rich fish remains as well as the seeds from berries and other plants. Black bears eat an average of 3½ lb (1.6 kg) from each salmon carcass. The jaws are not eaten and give a record of consumption; about 13 salmon per day per bear for the 45 days of the spawning period. This is a total of about 585 salmon per bear which is converted into fat for winter sleep. Although bears consume about 75 per cent of all salmon in the stream, over 70 per cent of them are captured after they have spawned so the effect on the salmon population is insignificant.

On Haida Gwai and elsewhere black bears feed on salmon mostly after dark. Researchers have spent many long nights using night-vision scopes watching the black bears feed, watching the places they carry the fish, and even watching the places they defecate. Scientists have counted the number of trips of individual bears, counted the number of seeds in scat samples, estimated the amount of salmon biomass that is left on the ground to enrich the soil, and estimated the number of times that bears relieve themselves. There is no scientific doubt that bears do defecate in the woods; and their fertilization activities help to make the immense tree growth of the old-growth forest possible.

Without salmon to feed on, both black and brown bears would be hard pressed to put on enough fat for hibernation and reproduction. Bear populations would decline and the forest would support only a few bears, scattered over much larger areas. As discussed also in the chapter on brown bears, there are really three groups of species forming the keystone of the temperate rainforest in the Pacific Northwest. The loss of any of them can greatly affect the structure and function of the rainforest.

These keystones are bears, salmon, and old-growth trees. Without large trees to shade the streams and without fallen limbs and trunks to provide fish-rearing habitat and a rich forest understory, both salmon and bears would suffer. Erosion of soil begins to cover the vital spawning gravel, and the increasing volume of flood runoff washes away the sheltered places that young fish need. The interplay of these three groups of species is much richer and more complex than this simple outline, and the rich tapestry of species is now beginning to unravel because of man's activities; a discussion of the effects of logging, fishing, and hunting can be found in the chapter 'Bears and Humans'.

This yearling is a rich cinnamon color; these color phases are common in black bears.

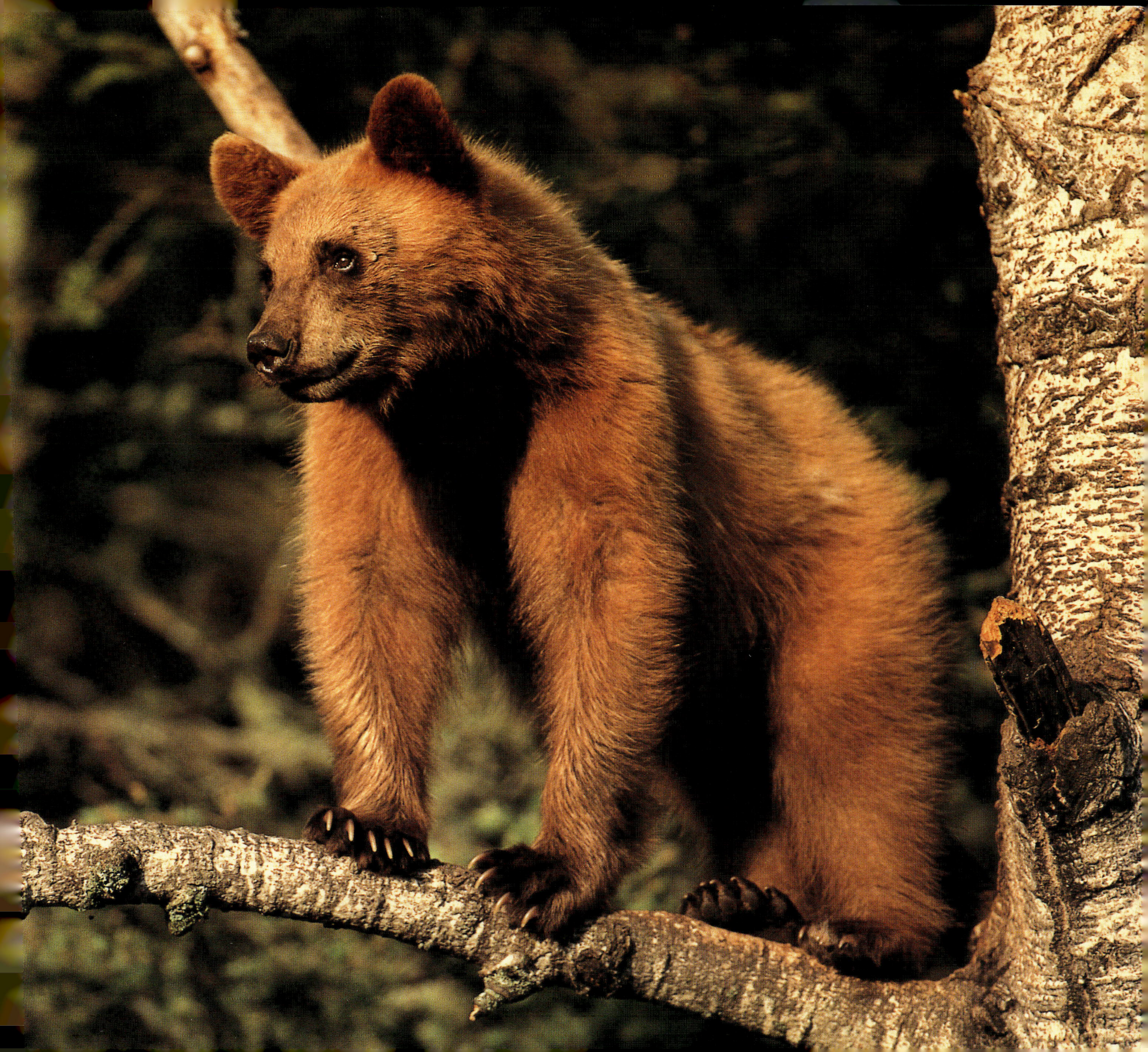

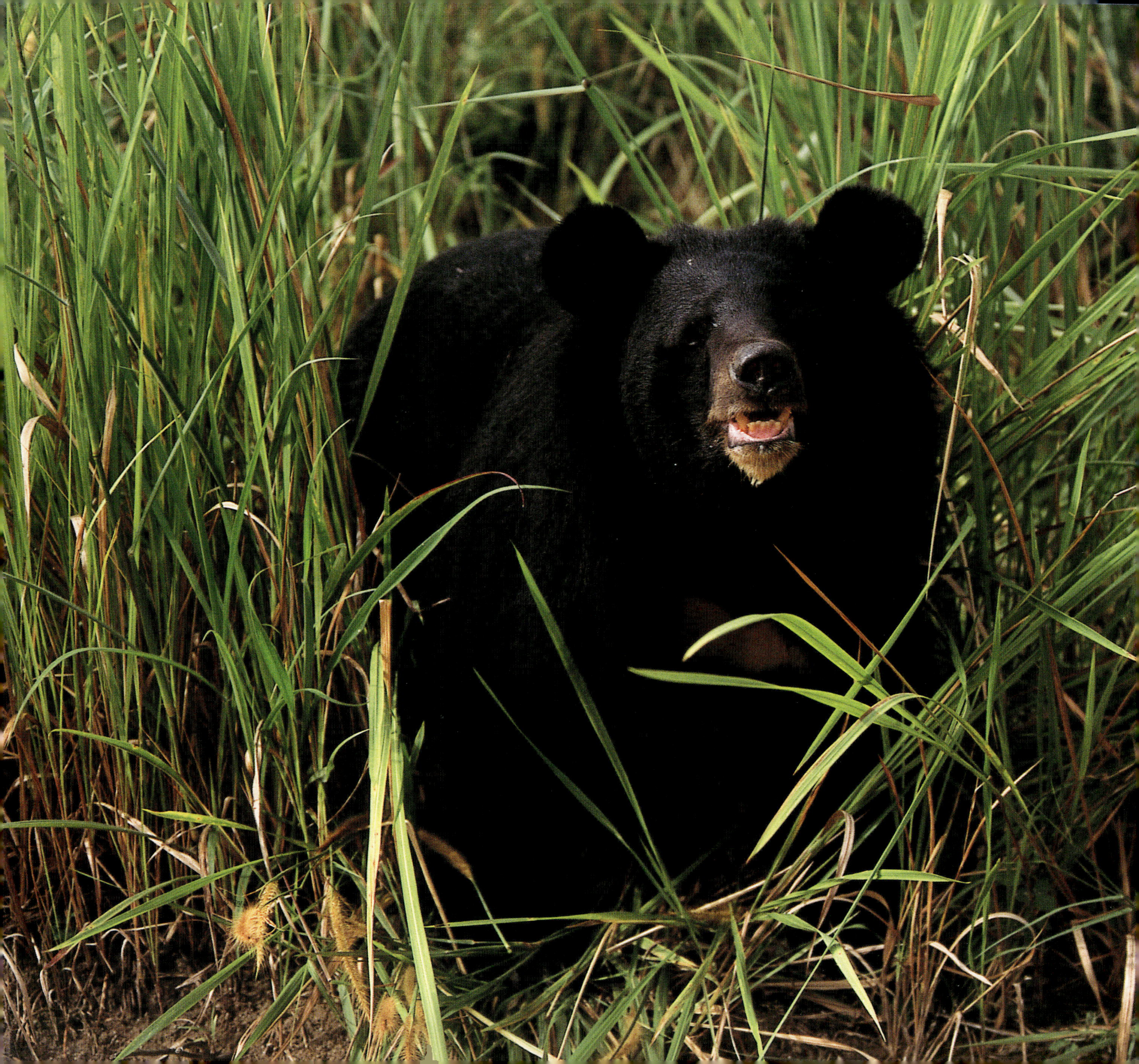

The Asiatic Black Bear

The Asiatic, or Tibetan, black bear, *Ursus thibetanus*, is in many ways very similar to its cousin, the American black bear, even though the two species have evolved separately for over 3 million years. At that time their common ancestors lived in western Asia, perhaps in the area of the Russian far east and further south. During a glacial period over three million years ago when sea levels were low, bears from the northernmost population must have expanded across the Bering Land Bridge to the New World and occupied the areas above the ice sheets.

During these interglacial periods, the Land Bridge and the area that it connected (also referred to as Beringia) was a fairly flat area, rising gradually to meet what are now the edges of the continents. Depending upon the climate, the vegetation varied from grasslands to tundra. In a few places there were even pockets of spruce forest, where fossilized spruce pollen has been found. It was probably during one of the cold periods, when the climate was mild enough to support spruce, grasses, and grazing mammals, that the early black bears moved into Beringia and beyond. These conditions must have lasted for many thousands of years.

As the sea levels rose, the group of bears in the New World became isolated and were probably stranded in eastern Beringia for some time, just as brown bears were at the end of the Pleistocene era. As continental glaciers receded, the ancestral American black bears began expanding southward. The black bears in Asia probably expanded their range southward and eastward as the climate changed. What happened after that is difficult to know for certain. American black bears and Asiatic black bears are considered to be sister taxa; they are more closely related to each other than to any other living bear species. At some point, about 5 million years ago, they had a common ancestor.

At about that time, Asiatic black bears must have occupied the western coast of Asia from what is now the Russian Far East, to what is now Malaysia. They may have also occupied areas eastward, at least to the south of what is now the Gobi Desert. During warm periods, this vast desert must have been as dry, or drier, than it is now. During one or more cold periods, the Asiatic black bears colonized the islands of Japan. They probably first reached the Japanese islands at approximately the same time that they crossed over to the New World. During subsequent cold periods, bears may have migrated back and forth between the Japanese islands and the Asian mainland.

As a result of this frequent (on an evolutionary time scale) intermixing, the Asiatic black bears on the Japanese islands are still considered to be the same species as the mainland bears; including bears as far west as the Himalayas. There are slight genetic differences, but the most recent land connections to Japan probably occurred during the late Pleistocene only 18,000 to 13,000 years ago. Little genetic change has accumulated in the short time since then and even this change may be dampened by occasional dispersing males from the mainland that may swim between the islands and mainland and pass on their genes. The Japanese black bears are now considered a subspecies of the continental species.

The current distribution of Asiatic black bears is divided into two large areas. One group in southeast Asia extends from Malaysia, through the Himalayas as far as Pakistan, Iran, and Iraq. The easternmost point of their range is in the Makran range of the Sarbaz mountains of southwestern Iran. By the late 1960s they were considered extinct in Iran, but some were seen there in the 1980s. The other black bear group is found along the western Asia coast and includes Japan, Korea, and the Russian Far East. Asiatic black bears

The Asiatic black bear may be most closely related to the American black bear but the genetic data are inconclusive.

are found as far north as southern Siberia. These two groups may have become divided only recently by the spread of human populations. Bears have probably been excluded from the central portion of their historic range, western China, only since the rise of agriculture about 8,000 years ago. Since that time, most black bear habitat has become fragmented by human occupation and conversion to agriculture, and humans have increased greatly in numbers.

Asiatic black bears are found throughout the southern slopes of the Himalayas through northern India, Nepal, Sikkim, and Bhutan. East of the Himalayas they continue on into Myanmar (Burma), Bangladesh, Laos, Thailand, Cambodia, Malaysia, and China. The group of Asiatic black bears in southeast Asia overlaps some of the range of the sun bear and also the sloth bear. The Asiatic black bear probably moved into these regions long after the sloth bears were established, but it is less certain whether black bears or sun bears came next. Competition for resources between these three species helped to shape their recent evolution. It is possible that early sloth bears were more widespread before the arrival of the Asiatic black bear, and they have since become more specialized and restricted to a smaller range.

Asiatic black bears, like their American black bear cousins, are generalists. At the eastern edge of their distribution, in Iran, they feed on olives, figs, insects, and the buds of the date palm. They come into conflict with farmers when they climb the palm trees, and have been so reduced in numbers that they are almost never seen. Only 30 or less may remain in Iran.

Their preferred habitat is forest; including tropical rainforests and oak forests in China, Vietnam, Laos, and Cambodia; rhododendron forests in the Himalaya; oak and bamboo forests in Japan; pine and broad-leaf mixed forests in the Russian Far East. Most of the forest, and the black bear habitat, is at higher elevations. They inhabit a wide variety of broad-leaved forests from tropical rainforests to deciduous oak forests. There are old records of Asiatic black bears occupying lower elevation habitats in the past, but they have been displaced from those areas by human occupation and the removal of forest. Asiatic black bears travel through tree plantations, scrublands, agricultural land, orchards, and even near villages when traveling between forested areas. In Russia, where human populations are relatively low, the major habitat threat of today is the timber harvest. Russian forests are the last remaining in most of Asia and multinational logging companies are rapidly removing them. In other parts of their range they face the usual threats associated with large human populations.

Asiatic black bears are distinguishable by a crescent-shaped white patch on the chest. They are found in forested areas from sea level to well above 9800 ft (3000 m) throughout their range and further north. Asiatic black bears are good tree climbers. They forage for fruits from trees as well as a wide variety of leaves, flowers, honey, and insects. Occasionally, Asiatic black bears will attack goats or other livestock. They often come into conflict with farmers while crop raiding. Maize (corn) is a particular favorite. Attempts by farmers, who generally do not have firearms, to protect their crops often lead to injuries and deaths on both sides. As with the other tropical bear species, it is critical to protect the habitat that is remaining and to try to provide larger areas of forest in many places.

In China Asiatic black bears prefer tropical rainforests and oak forests. They are found primarily in southwest China in the mountainous regions and in the Himalayan forest regions of southern and eastern Tibet. Black bears in China come into conflict with crops, orchards, and beehives and many are killed as nuisance bears and for food and medicinal uses. Bear farms are popular in China where black bears and other species are raised for the milking of gall bile; often in inhumane conditions.

In India, Asiatic black bears are found in the Himalayan foothills where remnants of native forests remain. Bears forage and travel through developed landscapes where orchards, plantations, cultivated areas and small patches of brush or riparian cover are found. They are generally found below 12,300 ft (3750 m) in

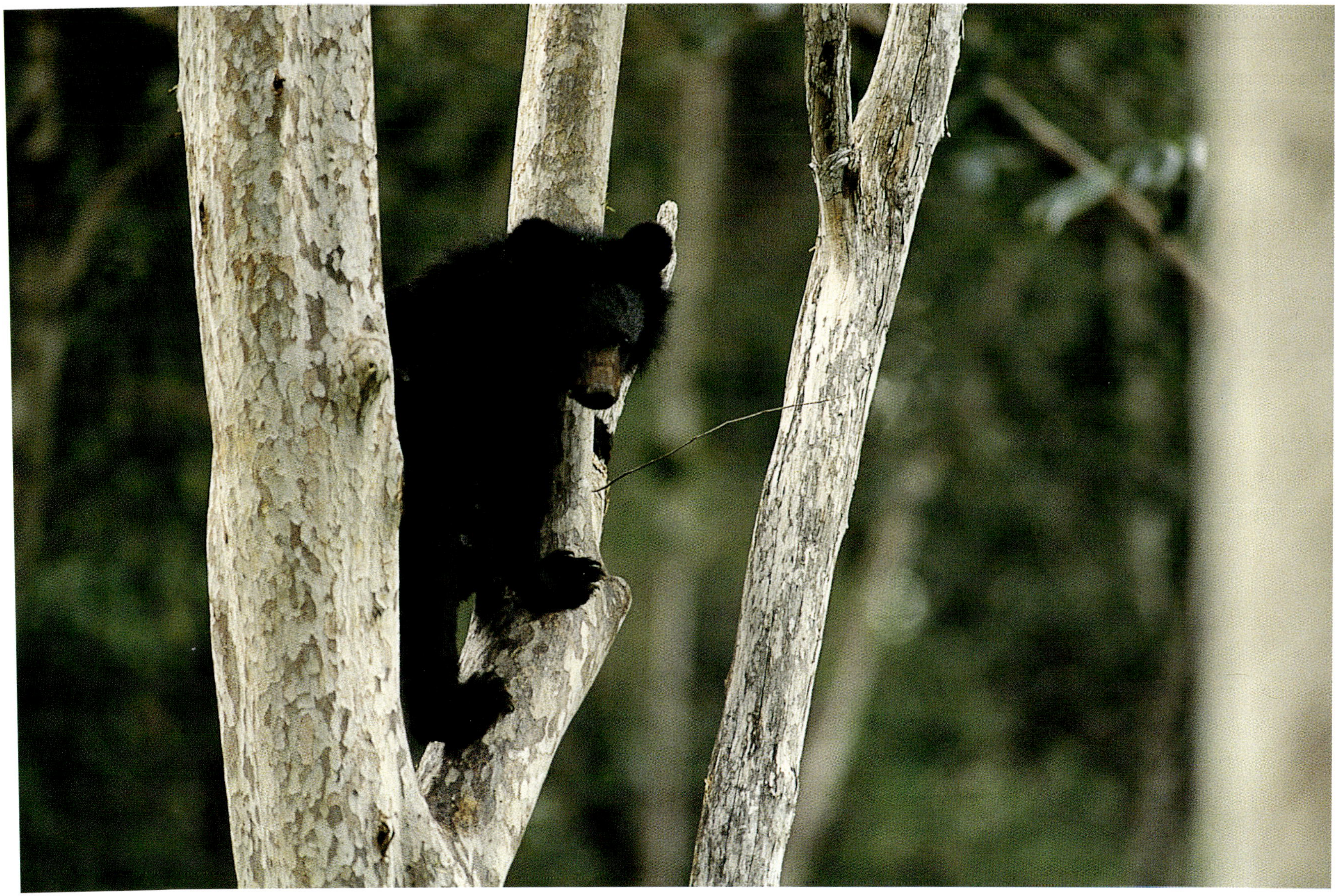

Asiatic black bears have a wide distribution from the Russian Far East to Iran. Most of their habitat is heavily fragmented and modified by human activities. In Japan they have been able to coexist with humans even in densely populated areas.

elevation. In the upper elevations, above 9800 ft (3000 m), their range overlaps with the Himalayan brown bear. In lower elevations, below about 3900 ft (1200 m), their range overlaps with the sloth bear. In India there has been intense pressure from human populations for centuries. Clearing of land for agriculture, and firewood gathering, have reduced the native forests. Most of the protected natural areas that remain today were the former hunting preserves of Indian royalty; as the power of the maharajahs declined, many of their forested reserves later became national parks and wildlife sanctuaries.

In Russia the black bears are found mainly in mixed forests of pine and broadleaved species. In the southern part of this range they coexist with brown bears, tigers, and leopards. In Japan, Asiatic black bears are found on the islands of Honshu, Kyushu and Shikoku; there are no records of them on Hokkaido, which is populated by brown bears. The nearest of the 'Japanese' islands, Russian Sakhalin, is only about 6 miles (10 km) from the mainland, and the next large island, Hokkaido, is only about 25 miles (40 km) from Sakhalin.

Land bridges between these areas would have occurred with a much smaller drop in sea levels than the Bering Land Bridge requires; and the Kurile Islands to the north may have formed an almost continuous land bridge between northern Japan and the Kamchatka Peninsula in Russia. In addition, bears could occasionally swim to and from Sakhalin, and even between the other islands. Asiatic black bears are very good swimmers. It is likely that Asiatic black bears occupied all of these islands at one time or another until they were displaced by brown bears on Sakhalin and Hokkaido. They live today even on the outskirts of Tokyo. They are also found on the heavily populated island of Taiwan which they probably reached during an ice age in the Pliocene or before. In these urbanized areas they are secretive and largely nocturnal, living in fairly small patches of rugged terrain and foraging at night in croplands and orchards as well as on native berries and nuts.

In Japan, bears do not come under the jurisdiction of any government agency, and therefore management and protection is loosely organized. In some areas they are being studied using radio-telemetry, but in others they are quickly removed when they begin to cause trouble with crops. Asiatic black bears are considered to be game animals as well as pest species. Over 1000 black bears are killed annually; most of these are nuisance bears that are trapped in cages and then shot. In Nagano prefecture, where over 100 bears are killed annually, aversive conditioning techniques are being applied (trapped bears are given unpleasant stimuli before being released) and electric fences have been installed to keep bears away from crops. In areas near forests, where bears are at risk, farmers are encouraged to plant crops that will not attract bears.

Asiatic black bears are primarily found in broad-leaf forests where acorns are one of their principal fall foods. These native broad-leaf forests have been increasingly cleared and evergreen plantations have been planted, thus removing large areas of habitat for black bears. Conservation efforts in Japan are critically important; if bears can coexist with such high densities of human populations, there may be hope for the rest of Asia.

Japanese black bears have small home ranges; a male home range may be as large as 70 sq miles (180 sq km) but most are smaller. In spring they feed on emergent vegetation such as grasses, sedges, tree buds and shrub shoots. In the fall they feed on berries and nuts. They build 'nests' in trees and bamboo forests using branches that they often break while feeding in the tree canopy.

Their optimal habitat, like all other bear species, is remote, rugged, and inaccessible terrain where human disturbance is minimal. In Japan such areas are often found in steep ravines. They den in hollow trees, in holes dug under large boulders, or in hillsides, and generally hibernate from November until April on a schedule similar to the American black bears which are found at the same latitude in North America.

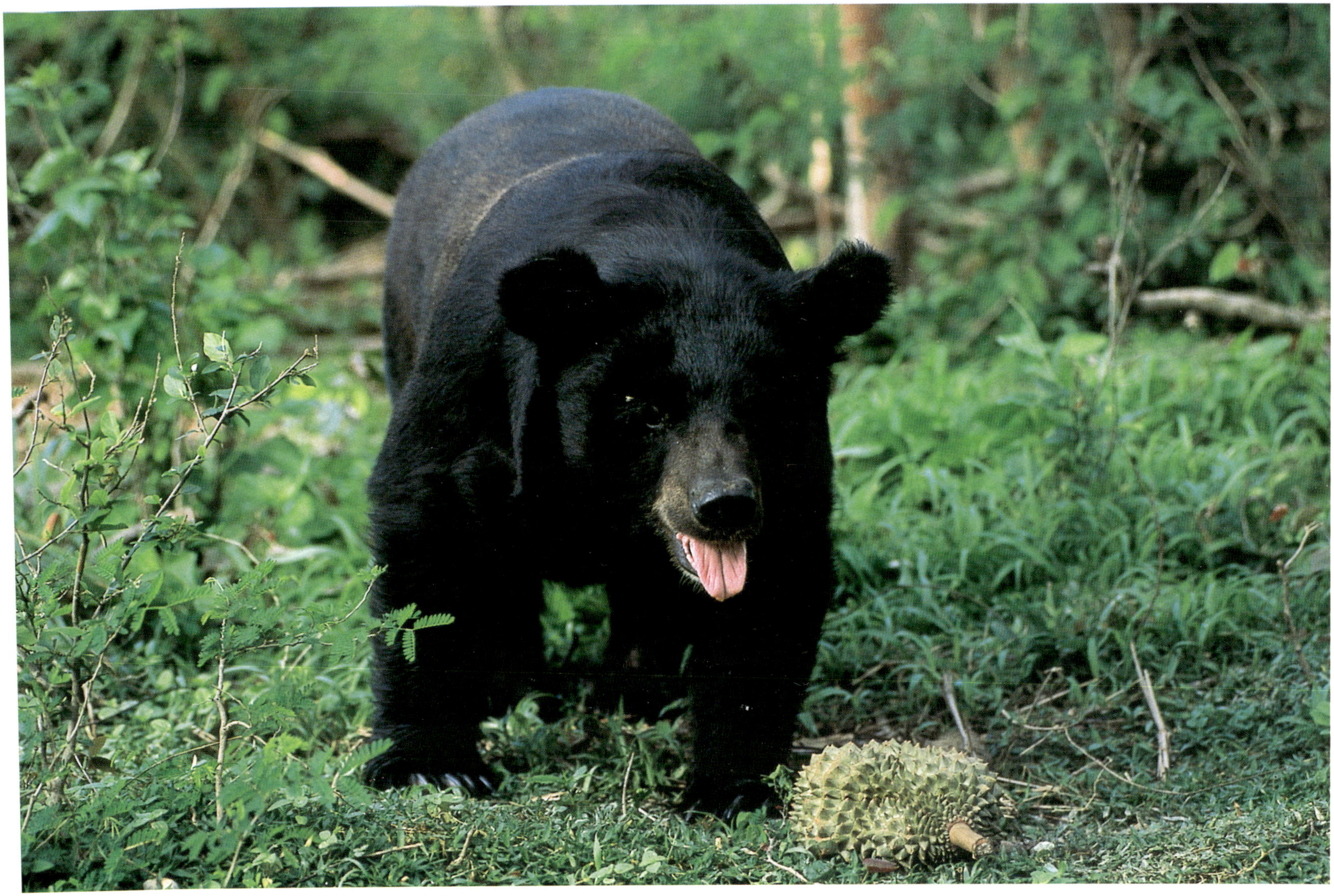

Asiatic black bears are primarily found in forested habitats ranging from tropical rainforests to oak to bamboo. They also feed and travel in developed landscapes. Fruit is a favorite food item, and there are often conflicts with farmers in plantations.

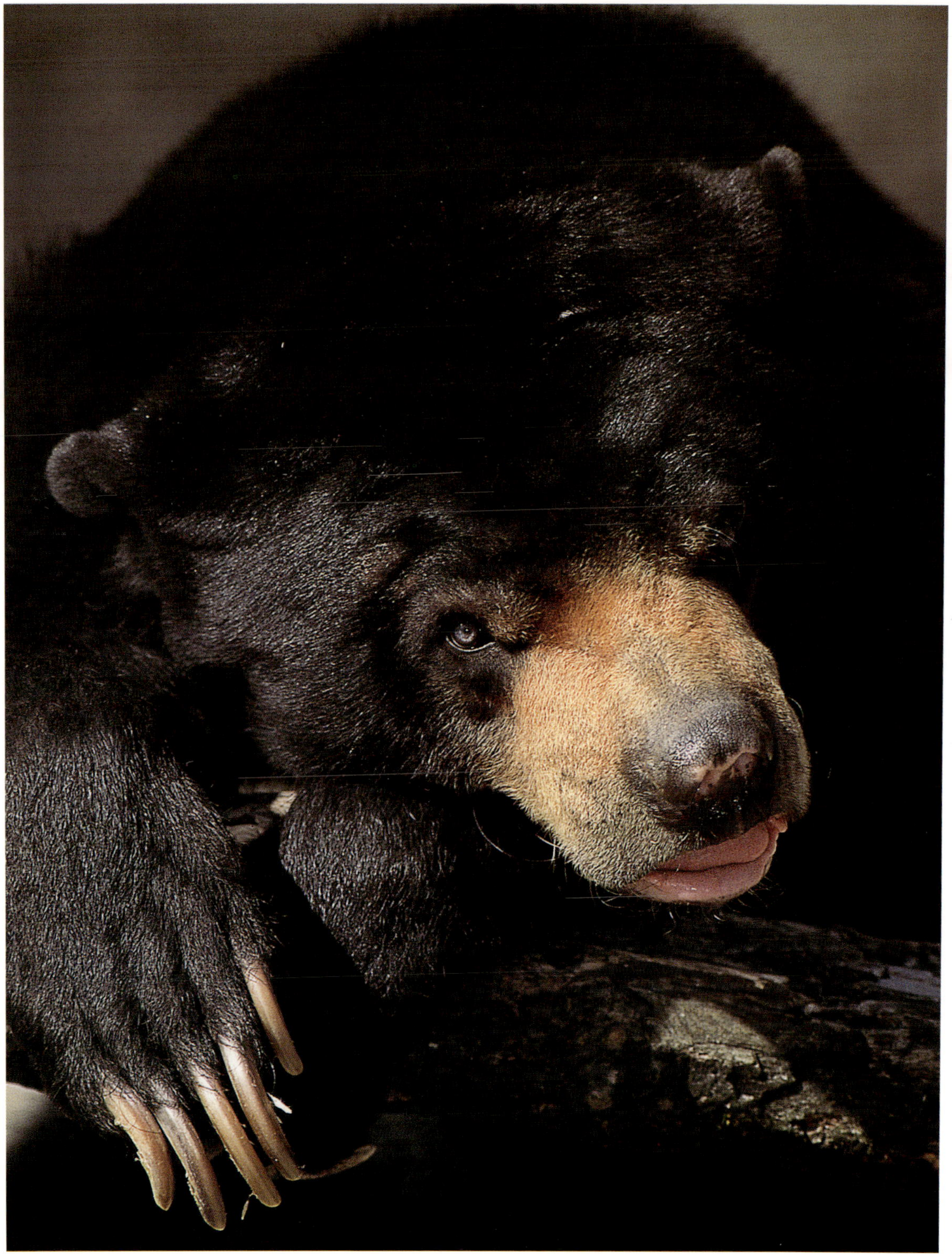

The Sun Bear

Sun bears are the smallest of the bear species. There are two scientific names currently in use *Ursus malayanus* and *Helarctos malayanus*. They probably evolved in Southeast Asia from the main lineage of bears about one million years after the sloth bear line branched off. It is likely that ancestral populations became isolated on the Malay Peninsula or perhaps on one of the larger islands such as Sumatra or Borneo during periods of higher sea levels during the Pliocene epoch about 5 million years ago. The ancestors of all the Ursine bears were relatively small. The lineage that produced the sun bear produced a larger ancestor, and then the modern sun bear became small again. The ancestral sun bears were able to exploit an environment that contained a number of larger, more efficient predators such as tigers and leopards, by climbing trees and specializing on plant foods, particularly fruit, and insects. These adaptations became more specialized as the sun bear evolved.

At the height of their distribution sun bears ranged throughout most of southeast Asia, and may have inhabited most of the islands west of Wallace's Line at one time or another. Wallace's Line lies between the islands of Bali and Lombok, separates Borneo from Sulawesi (Celebes), and divides the Philippines; it marks the edge of the continental shelf. East of the continental shelf the ocean becomes deep; so deep that even during the coldest ice ages (and the lowest sea levels) there was no dry land connection. On the continental shelf itself, many of the islands became connected to each other and to the mainland during periods of low sea level. Sun bears were evidently able to colonize some of the islands of the continental shelf and survive there, but as far as we know they never made it across the 18 or so miles (30 km) of deep water to the oceanic islands There are no fossil records of sun bears from the oceanic islands but that could just be due to limited opportunities to search for them. It is more likely that sun bears never were able to colonize them. Sun bears can swim, like other bears, but even if a few somehow made it to the oceanic islands they did not establish successful populations. This could be either because the islands they reached were too small to support a population over time, or the initial number of bears was too small to reproduce and grow, or maybe there was too much competition from the very different fauna found there.

Historically sun bears were found in eastern Tibet, and Sichuan China, and Pleistocene fossils were found on the island of Java. They are no longer found on the island of Java. Large areas of sun bear habitat are found on the Indonesian island of Sumatra, the island of Borneo (divided between the nations of Indonesia, Brunei and Malaysia), and the Malaysian peninsula. Other isolated populations are found in Myanmar (Burma), Cambodia (Kampuchea), China, Thailand, Laos, Vietnam and perhaps India. Presumably, these mainland populations were once all connected by contiguous habitat. The largest current blocks of habitat, and perhaps the largest sun bear populations, are found in the Indonesian provinces of Sumatra and Kalimantan (on Borneo). Many of the recent records of sun bear occurrences have been from these areas; particularly in the larger protected areas such as the Leuser Ecosystem, and Kerinci National Park. International scientific teams have recently begun studies here. There are also many recent records from Malaysian Borneo and the mainland. Very little is known about the extent of occupied habitat or population estimates in any of these places.

Sun bears inhabit lowland tropical rainforest and their ranges overlap with Asiatic black bears at the lower elevations of that bear's range. These tropical hardwood forests are rapidly being logged and converted into plantations and settlements which remove large areas of bear habitat. Regenerating forest is undoubtedly of much less value

The sun bear is the smallest of the eight species of bear. They have a sleek coat of short hair.

to sun bears than the mature forests that were logged, and continued logging and fragmentation of lowland rainforest poses a great threat. Sun bears are listed as endangered under CITES (The Convention on International Trade in Endangered Species) and are protected in Indonesia and Laos. They have no protection in Vietnam and legal hunting is allowed in Sarawak and Malaysia. Despite their legal protection, live sun bears, and sun bear parts, can be found for sale in most areas where they exist.

Sun bears are the least well known of all bear species. They feed primarily on plants, especially fruits, and are particularly fond of honey. They face competition for fruits from a variety of other species including primates, birds and bats. They are very adept at climbing trees to reach fruit and wild honey, and they will often climb tall thin trees to reach the upper branches of very large neighboring trees which are more difficult to climb. On smaller diameter trees they employ a technique that is similar to the way that some Polynesian islanders climb coconut trees (or telephone linemen climb poles): they hook their fore legs around the trunk and push upward, using their hind legs alternately, which are wedged against the trunk. They appear to almost waddle up the trunk. Their front feet are turned inward and the front claws are long and heavy as adaptations for climbing. For their size, the head is relatively large, broad and heavy and they have massive teeth. The canines are particularly heavy and they have a very long tongue, which is extended while feeding enabling them to extract food such as honey from cavities.

They also feed on insects, especially ants and termites. Ants are found in the trees and on the ground; termites are found in underground colonies, above ground where they build large mounds that the sun bears dig apart, and in trees. One of the sun bear's major competitors for termites is the bearded pig. Sun bears frequently tear apart decaying logs on the forest floor in search of insect larvae and other foods; they may be important contributors to soil formation because of this log-shredding activity. They occupy a variety of habitats including upper elevation mountainous regions. The lowland tropical rainforests which are their principal habitat have a dense canopy and often a dark, but somewhat open understory. Their small size may have evolved as an adaptation to climbing trees, but along with their dark coloration it makes them inconspicuous and difficult to see. The name 'sun bear' probably refers to a characteristic yellowish chest marking. However this marking is often crescent-shaped like a moon and in some places they have been called moon bears. In their preferred habitat they are seldom exposed to the direct sun because the tree canopy obscures it.

Sun bears are active, and they also rest, both during the day and at night. It may be that they become more nocturnal in areas of human disturbance. Their major wild predators today are snakes, leopards and tigers. There were formerly tigers on Java and on Bali, but today there are tigers and sun bears coexisting only on Sumatra and on the mainland. As a result, tigers pose less of a threat to sun bears now, but they must have been a powerful force in sun bear evolution. Sun bears could escape tigers by climbing trees. However, since leopards can climb trees easily, there is no effective escape for them there. It may be that these small but tenacious bears rely on their camouflage to some extent and when cornered they can defend themselves well with sharp claws and teeth. Confronted with a defensive sun bear, a leopard may look elsewhere for prey rather than risk an injury.

Sun bears have been known to act aggressively toward humans, their other major predator, when cornered or threatened. When approached closely they will often rush without warning and give loud growls or barking vocalizations. The sun bears' sleek coat of short hair may be an adaptation to the warm climate, although sloth bears and Asiatic black bears share much of the same area and have long hair. The sun bears' coloration may be an adaptation for camouflage except for the yellow chest patch. This patch may be a secondary sexual characteristic for attracting the opposite sex, or it may be an important part of a threat display.

They have a very long tongue which is probably an adaptation for extracting honey and insects from deep crevices in trees. Sun bears

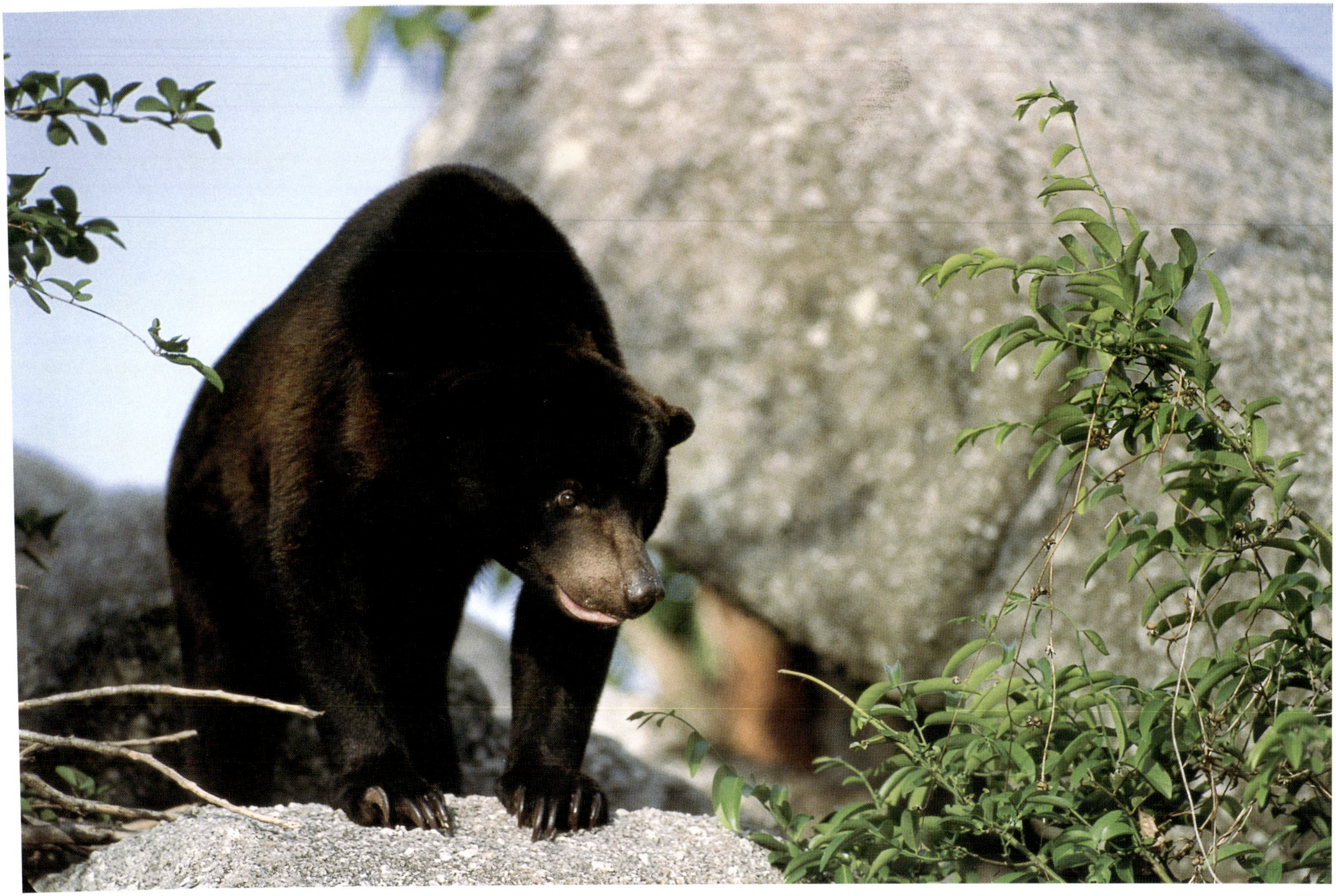

Today the sun bear's distribution is limited to the larger areas of native forests, and the surviving populations are mainly small in size. They learn to avoid gardens and fruit plantations, but often come into conflict with humans in those areas when natural foods become scarce.

climb high into the rainforest canopy. In so doing, they leave a lot of conspicuous markings. They often dig their claws deep into the bark like climbing spurs or crampons while ascending, or grasp around the entire trunk as described above, but will often slide down the trunk dragging their claws. Sharp little holes reveal the route up, while long parallel scratches reveal the route down.

Sun bears do not appear to use scent-marking stations for communication to the extent that the northern bears do; some sun bear researchers have reported them rubbing against trees, but no mention has been made of traditional marking sites. However, their presence can be readily determined by the signs they leave while feeding; claw marks on trees, termite diggings, and torn bark on trees and logs. They may also leave other scent signals such as urination, but little is known of such behavior.

The ability to hibernate, or to enter a dormant state, evolved fairly early in the ancestral bears. Delayed implantation, one of the adaptations associated with hibernation, is also widespread. To date, little is known about the physiology of sun bears, but they have given birth at different times of the year in zoos. Because they have less of a seasonal imperative in the wild for giving birth at a certain time they may implant the embryo sooner than the northern bears do. They have not been known to hibernate and there is no information on whether they can enter a state of dormancy when food is scarce, but females give birth in dens and remain much less active during the early weeks of the cub's life.

Sun bears today face their greatest threats from habitat loss and poaching. They have traditionally been hunted by indigenous peoples, and most longhouses in the Borneo rainforest contain a bear hide, but there was no significant impact on populations from traditional uses. Poaching has become a growing threat. The increase throughout Asia in trade of bear parts for medicinal purposes, and the high monetary value of those parts, has greatly reduced sun bear populations. They are also captured and sold as pets throughout southeast Asia. Wild pets are a prized status symbol in many Asian cultures where rich and poor alike may wish to display a wild animal. As the bears grow large and more difficult to manage they are often sold to restaurants, traders, wildlife markets, bear farms or to the bear equivalent of the glue factory where they are killed for their valuable parts; paws for food, gall bladders for medicine, etc.

Asian businessmen are the primary consumers in the parts trade, which is widespread in southeast Asia. Evidence suggests that sun bears in Indonesian Kalimantan on the island of Borneo suffer some of the greatest poaching near the border with Malaysian Borneo, and there are undoubtedly many such areas where bears in protected areas can be accessed by poachers and transported away fairly easily. Sun bears are also frequently killed when they invade fruit plantations and gardens. They are particularly fond of coconut palms and will climb the trees to eat the soft, sweet heart at the growing tip of the tree. Humans also prize this food for heart-of-palm salads. In eating the palm hearts, sun bears kill the entire tree which is valuable for producing coconuts, so the bears are killed whenever possible near coconut plantations.

Although there may be a few exceptions, the primary factor limiting the distribution of sun bears is the presence of human beings. Proliferating human settlements, an increase in logging activity, the development of plantations, and oil and gas activity with accompanying roads are all reducing the amount of habitat that bears can use. Military conflicts in many parts of the sun bear's range have undoubtedly had an impact and increased the availability of firearms. It is important to determine their status and distribution more accurately and to protect critical habitat. In many instances it may be possible to re-connect some of the fragmented habitat that remains and some efforts are currently underway (to maintain biodiversity, not just sun bears) in places like Vietnam.

Sun bears, even cubs, have extremely sharp claws and well-developed tree-climbing muscles.

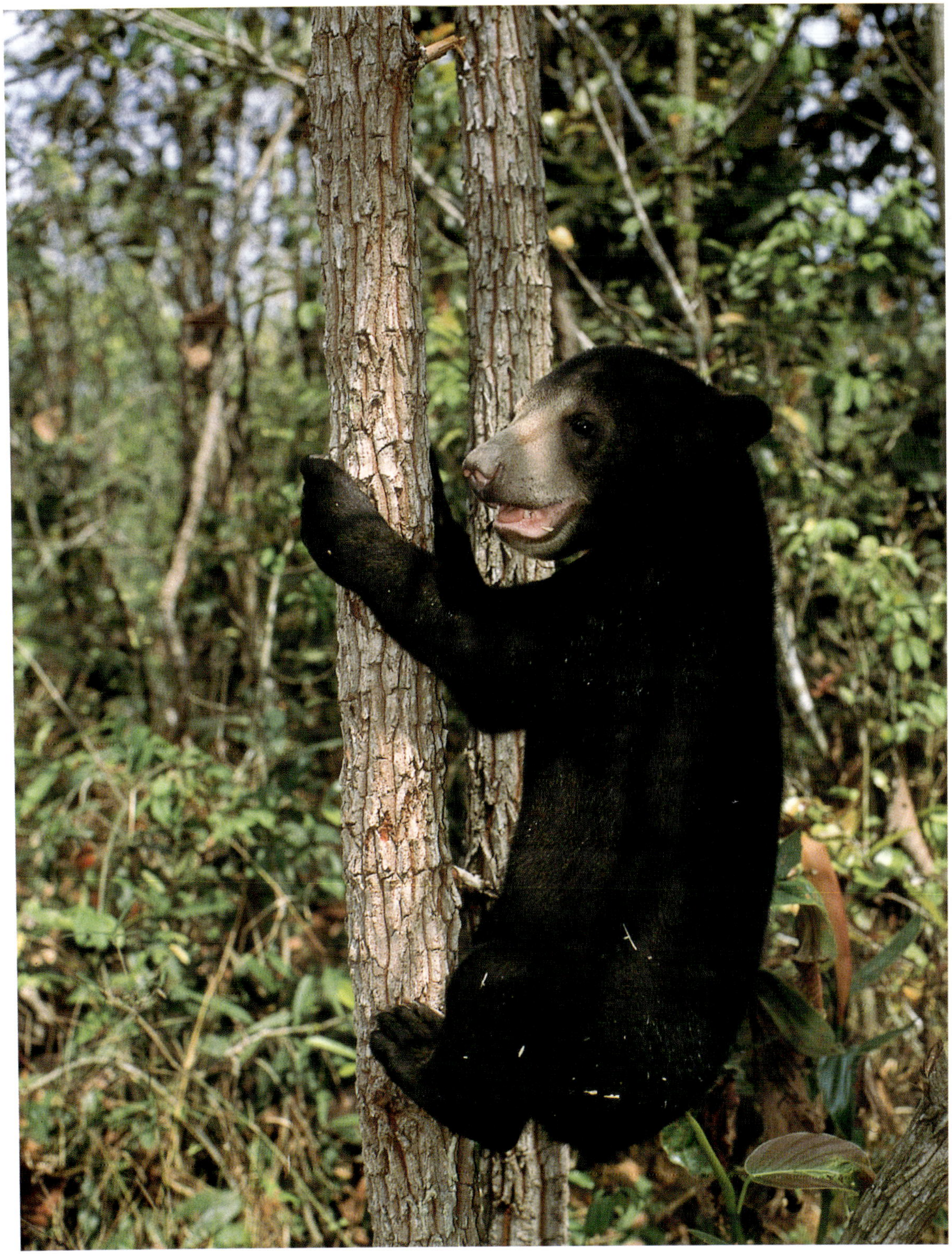

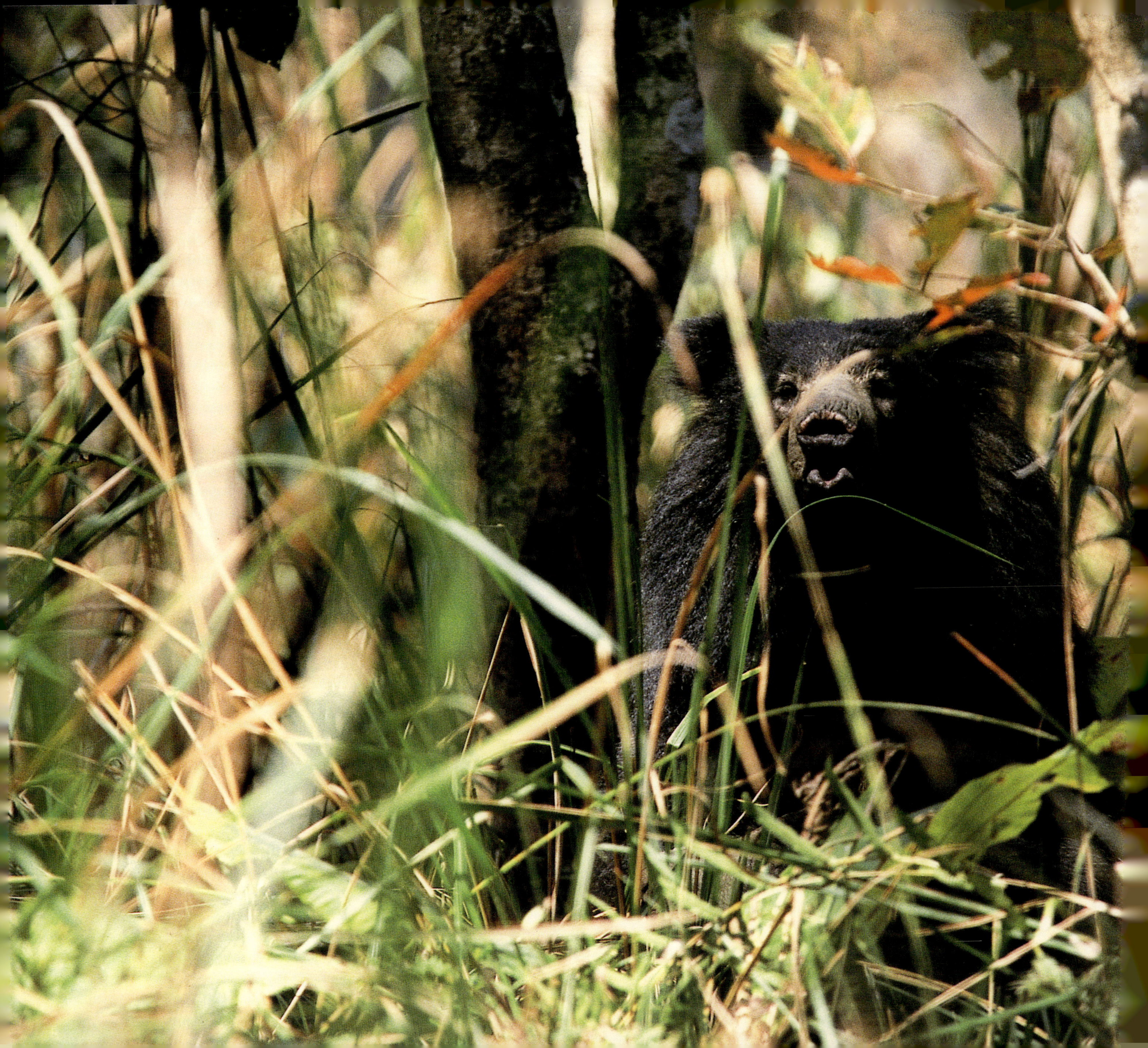

The Sloth Bear

The sloth bear arose from the oldest lineage of the true bears. The scientific name has recently been either *Melursus ursinus* or *Ursus ursinus*. They diverged from the main lineage of bears about 6 million years ago. Like the giant panda, it is likely that climatic fluctuations were important in isolating ancestral sloth bears in the south of Asia long enough for them to diverge as a separate species. It is possible that a group of bears managed to colonize the Indian subcontinent either during a warm, interglacial period in the late Miocene era, or during one of the cold periods. Cold periods occurred at that time about every 100,000 years.

In one scenario, we could imagine that after the ancestral sloth bears had occupied India, the climate cooled again and a wall of glaciers descended from the Himalayas that may have blocked any movement of bears in or out of India. Another possibility is that their ancestors moved south across eastern Asia during a cold period, perhaps as far as the edge of the Himalayas. Then, as the climate warmed, one group moved into the mountain foothills and became isolated there.

Such a group could have evolved around the margins of the Himalayas and perhaps expanded into lowland areas at a later period; maybe when Asiatic black bears arrived to compete with them. Whatever happened way back then, the sloth bears were left alone to evolve in isolation, somewhere in southern Asia, and to acquire the unique characteristics that enabled them to survive. During historic times they once occupied all of India and southern Nepal except for the very mountainous regions in the north.

Sloth bears are the insectivores of the bear world. They have a number of interesting adaptations that enable them to exploit ants and termites as primary food sources. Like the other bears in southern Asia, the sloth bear evolved from omnivorous, tree-climbing ancestors that avoided predation from the large cats and other carnivores. Early sloth bears could not successfully compete with more efficient carnivores in capturing prey, and were probably not large enough to drive the large predators from kills. Carrion is occasionally used, but carrion decomposes too rapidly in the tropics to supply a reliable source of food.

As the sloth bear evolved it adapted to feeding on fruits and insects which were abundant. Ants and termites in particular are widespread and represent a large and stable food source. As early sloth bears utilized this resource, natural selection favored the development of large, mobile lips. The bear's snout is also much more mobile than that of other species and the hair is greatly reduced. In addition, the first pair of upper incisor teeth have disappeared, providing an opening for effectively sucking insects into the mouth. In some individuals, only one upper incisor is present.

A sloth bear feeds on termite or ant mounds by digging with its long front claws to expose the nest full of insects. The front feet are turned inward, which may be an adaptation for digging and throwing soil out on either side of their bodies. After exposing an insect mound they proceed to vacuum up the scurrying invertebrates along with their eggs. With their long lips protruded into the loose soil they then alternately blow away dirt and suck up termites or ants, creating a cloud of dust in the process. When a sloth bear has been feeding like this in an area it leaves a telltale trail of dug-up termite mounds. The huffing sound that they make while feeding can often be heard through the forest even though the bear itself cannot be seen. A staccato-like burst of noise, it is composed of alternate blowing and sucking sounds.

Sloth bears do not specialize in digging plant roots and tubers to the same extent as the northern bears do. They may have been

Sloth bears live primarily in tropical forests and grasslands in southeast Asia and India.

unable to compete for this food source successfully with the wild pigs that were widespread in the tropics. They may occasionally utilize this food source, but their primary plant food consists of fruits. However, they remain generalists, and feed on seeds, honey, and flowers when fruits and insects are not available. They live primarily in tropical forests and grasslands. During the heavy rains of

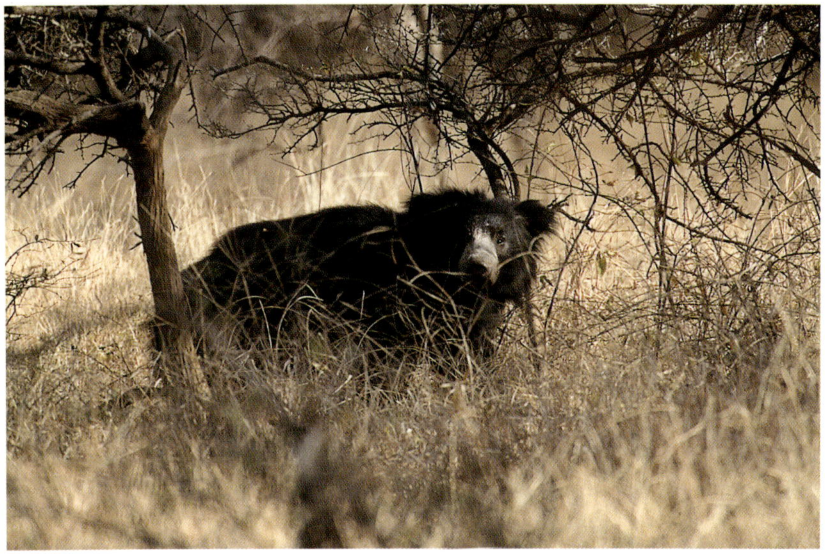

Sloth bears leave the grasslands and floodplains during the monsoons.

the monsoon period which begins sometime between April and June, they move upward in elevation to the drier forest areas. After the monsoon, as the ground dries out, they move back down to the riparian floodplain and grasslands. These areas have an abundance of termites, but they may be unavailable when the soil is very wet.

After mating, there is a period of about six to seven months before the young are born. Such a long period implies that there is delayed implantation before the embryo begins to develop. They generally breed in June and July in northern India and Nepal and cubs are born from November to January. Further south in Sri Lanka where there is less seasonality, there appears to be less breeding convergence and cubs may be born at any time of year.

Females give birth in dens which are dug into the earth, or in natural cavities, and may remain there for two to three months. After leaving the den, young cubs often cling to the long hair on their mother's back as she travels. This may be an adaptation so that the cub can accompany the mother over longer distances as she forages, rather than having her movements restricted to a pace that the cub can follow. The mother has an additional option to protect the infant if danger threatens; the cub can cling to her as she runs away from enemies. She may carry them this way for several months. Two cubs is the average litter size and three is rare.

Sloth bears have dark, fairly black coats with a mixture of brown and gray hairs in many individuals. They have long shaggy hair, and have lost the layer of warm underfur that northern bears retain. They also have a whitish-colored chest patch that is often in the shape of a U or a Y. This contrasting color pattern may serve as a means of communication; perhaps for attraction, threat, or identity. Bears that live in forest habitats such as sloth bears, sun bears, Asiatic black bears, spectacled bears, giant pandas and some American black bears all have these contrasting color patterns, while the two species of more open habitats, brown bears and polar bears, do not.

This may lend support to the theory that contrasting color patches help bears to communicate in forest habitats where vision is restricted. If so, it doesn't completely explain why brown bears that live in forested habitats in the Russian Far East, Europe, and the Pacific Northwest do not also have light color patches; although it is likely that they have occupied those habitats relatively recently in evolutionary terms. The lineage leading to brown and polar bears may have lost this characteristic as they adapted to the tundra, and it has not reappeared in bears that subsequently moved into forested areas.

When sloth bears, and other bears, stand up on their hind legs, the bright color patch becomes very visible. Bears in general stand up to get a better view of something, or to catch a scent higher up

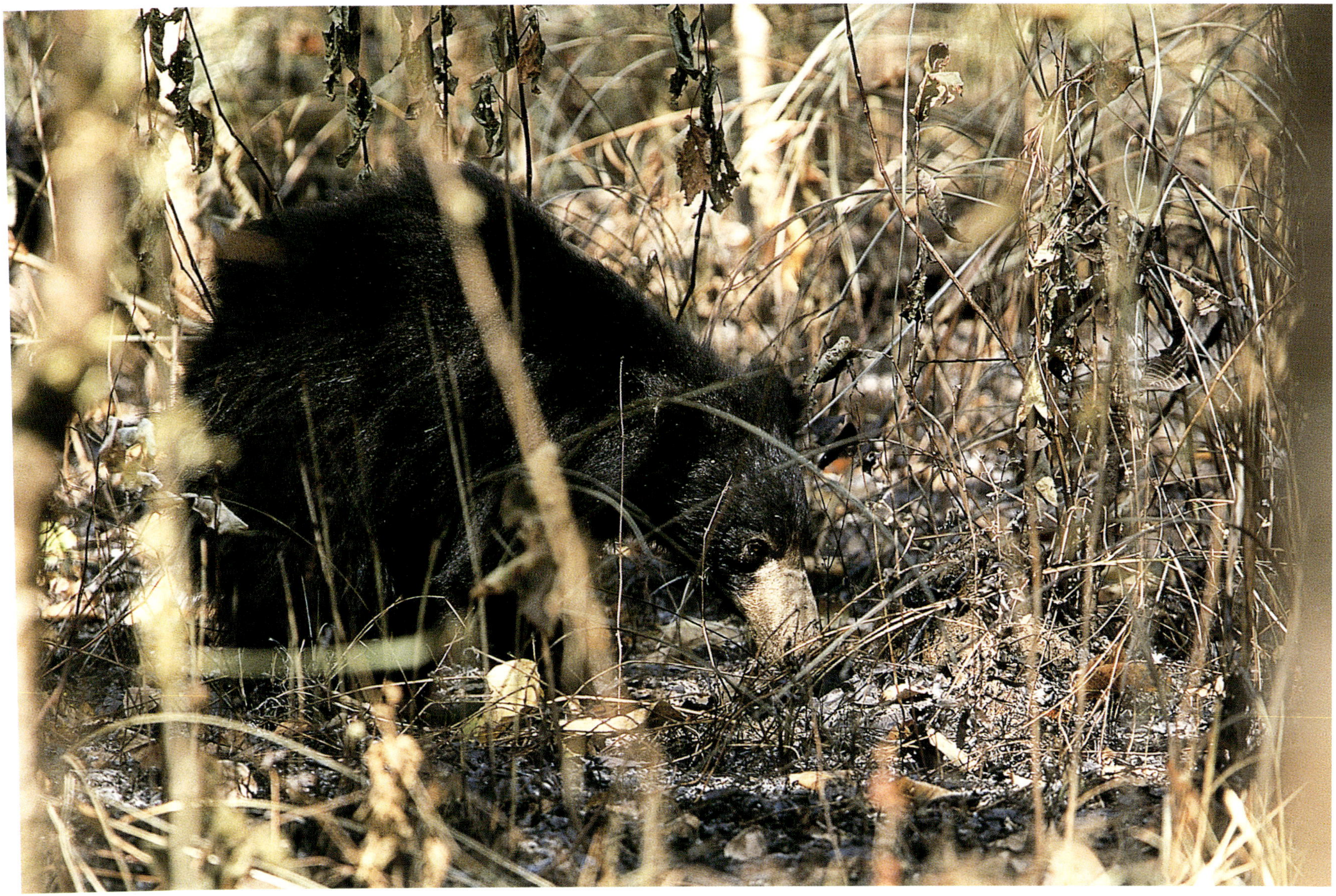

Sloth bears are primarily insectivores. They have large, mobile lips and long tongues which enable them to feed on ants and termites. They dig up the soil and blow away the dirt to expose insects.

in the air, probably when something approaches that they haven't identified. The contrasting color patch may identify them to the approaching animal, and may serve as a threat display in some cases, or identify them as a fellow sloth bear during the mating season.

Sloth bears are found on the island of Sri Lanka and on the Indian subcontinent, including India, Bangladesh, Bhutan, and Nepal. With the exception of Bhutan and Nepal, these are the most densely populated areas in the world for human beings. It comes as no surprise that sloth bears have few places left in which they can survive. They are considered to be declining throughout their range; officially they are classified as vulnerable by the International Union for the Conservation of Nature (IUCN). There are few data on numbers and distribution, but it is estimated that the total world population of the species is only 10,000 to 25,000.

The litany of threats has become familiar; deforestation, the spread of agriculture, poaching, etc. They are protected under the Indian Wildlife Protection Act which prohibits hunting, although they can be killed in defense of life or property. The capture of sloth bears used for street entertainment by traveling entertainers has a long tradition in India and is still a concern in some states. In addition, some bears are exported to Pakistan for staged fights with dogs. Perhaps more than any other species except possibly the giant panda, sloth bears are being squeezed out of existence by the sheer numbers and presence of human beings. Except in the most mountainous regions or in protected parks, humans are everywhere. Bhutan may be the bears best stronghold; they are protected by government and much forest habitat remains intact.

In India, sloth bears are concentrated in and around protected areas, but many are found outside these areas as well. It has been estimated that there is an average of about 12 sloth bears per 38 sq miles (100 sq km) in protected habitat, or about 5000 total bears. If the density is half as high in sloth bear habitat outside protected areas, there may be as many as 20,000 bears in all of India. The loss of forested habitat and its fragmentation into small isolated patches is probably the greatest threat. Many large forested areas were maintained during the rule of maharajahs, primarily as hunting preserves. With British occupancy during the 1800s a period of forest removal began which then accelerated after Indian independence in 1947. Most, if not all, of the protected areas that remain are remnants of the original royal hunting preserves. Sloth bears were once hunted with spears from horseback, and were later hunted with rifles until they became protected in 1972. Sloth bears are not currently protected in Nepal, although Asiatic black bears are.

Sloth bears are primarily found in lowland areas ranging into the Himalayan foothills where they overlap with the range of the Asiatic black bear in India. There appears to be little overlap between the two species in Nepal. Higher in elevation still are found the Himalayan brown bears, well above the range of the sloth bear. In eastern India, and perhaps Myanmar, they may overlap with sun bears in the hill country south of the Brahmaputra River. In this region all three tropical bear species probably coexist, although there are no recent confirmed records of sun bears.

Sloth bears are attracted to human developments in search of food such as honey or fruit, but their reliance on insects helps to keep them in more remote areas. In two years of following bears with radio collars in Chitwan National Park in Nepal, none traveled outside the park. If the population grows, however, subadults may be forced to disperse into human-occupied areas. In other parts of their range, as habitat is reduced, sloth bears are forced into marginal areas also. They can be aggressive and dangerous, and bear parts are valuable commodities in the trade for Asian medicines. Incentives for killing bears are therefore high.

Protection of all remaining sloth bear habitat is a critical priority for conservation, and public education combined with strict enforcement of anti-poaching laws is also necessary. To preserve the species in the long term, larger protected areas than those that currently exist will be needed, and it may be possible to reconnect some of the fragmented habitat.

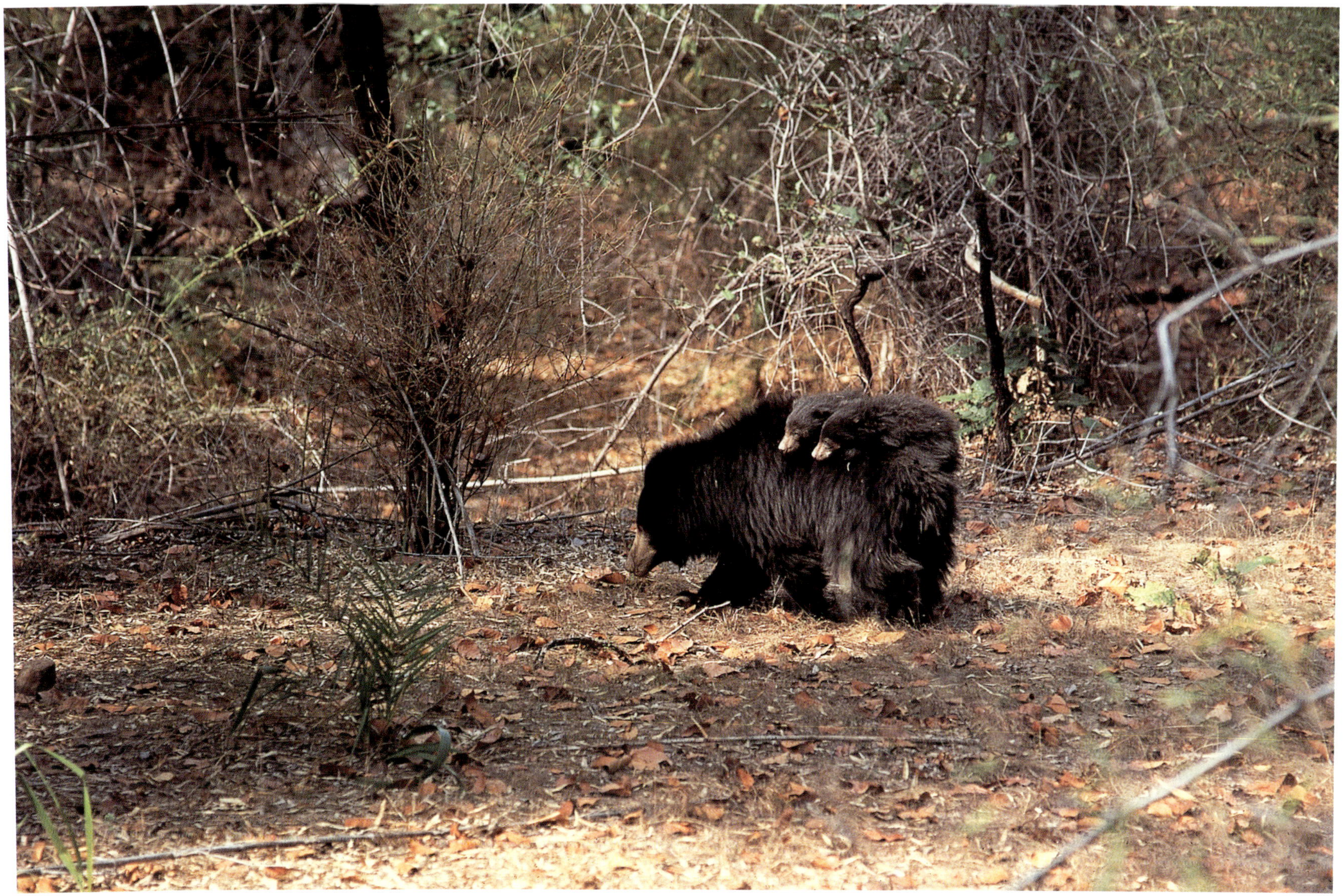

Sloth bear cubs often cling to the long hair on their mother's back. They accompany her in this way for several months until they are large enough to keep up with her on their own.

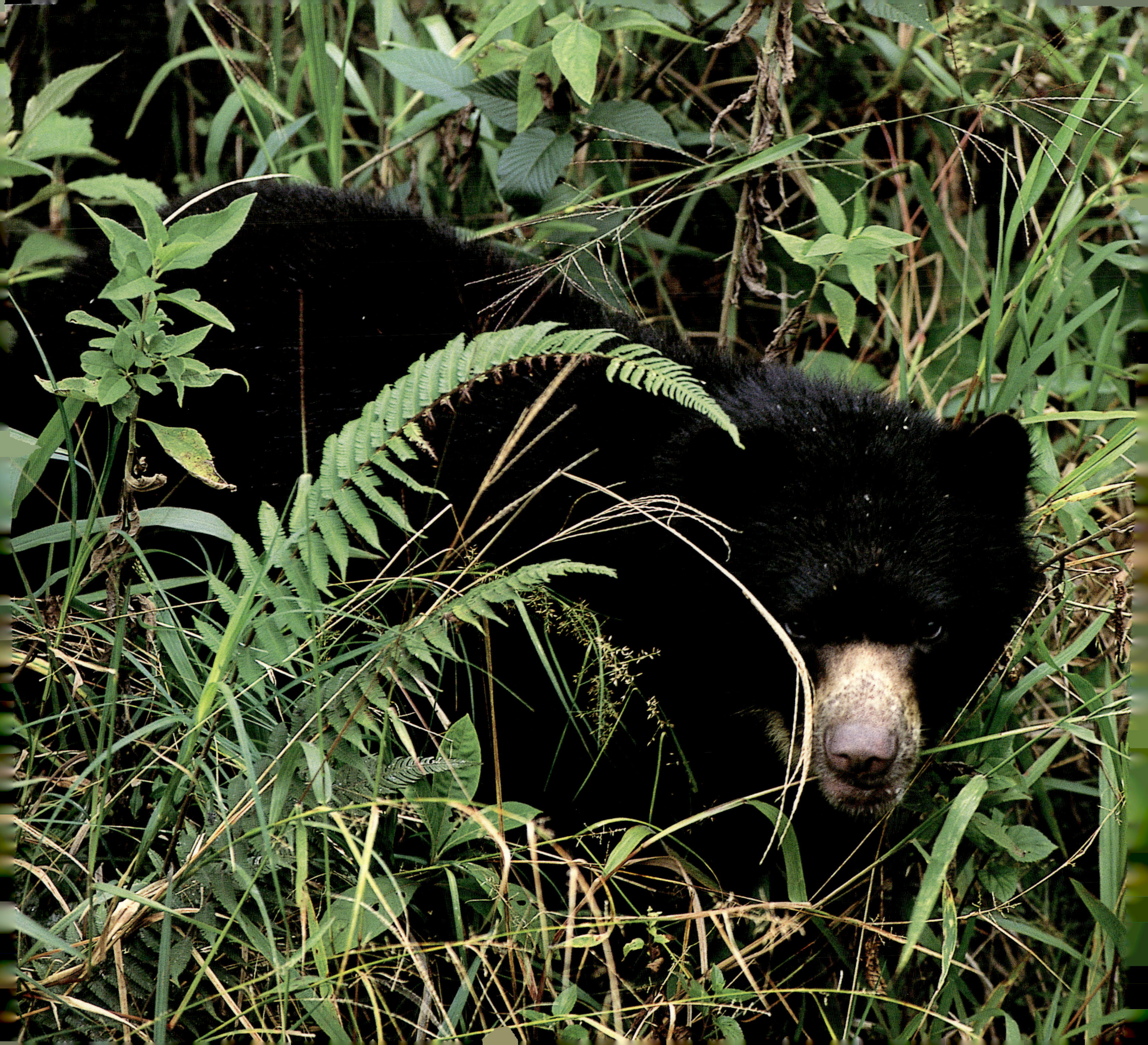

The Spectacled Bear

The spectacled bear evolved as the sole bear species isolated in South America after the end of the last ice age. Spectacled bears are medium-sized by bear standards, but they are the second-largest land mammals in South America. Only the tapir is larger. Its name refers to the light-colored markings surrounding the eyes. One of its common names in Spanish means bear with eyeglasses; another means the bromeliad-eating bear.

The evolutionary paths that this intriguing bear has followed to reach this niche are paralleled in complexity and variety by the actual trails across landscapes that its ancestors trod to reach their last stronghold in the Andes Mountains. From early Tremarctine (short-faced) bears in eastern Asia about 15 million years ago, this trail led across the Bering Land Bridge to what is now Alaska. These were the first bears to make this journey, and we must assume that conditions at that time were not greatly different than during the most recent ice ages of the Pleistocene (see the chapter on brown bears). Massive ice sheets covered what is now Canada and blocked any travel routes south for several thousand years. The vegetation was sparse and much of it was growing over permafrost. Winters were very cold.

We assume that these early short-faced bears were adapted to the cold and were omnivorous like the bear-dogs from which they evolved. They survived in the harsh northern climate and eventually made their way south to a land covered in grasslands and deciduous forests and populated with large mammal forms which have since disappeared. For well over 10 million years the short-faced bears radiated throughout North America. No new bears migrated from the Old World during this time, but the short-faced bears evolved into several new species as they were able to exploit unique opportunities presented by changing conditions in the New World. Just as the Ursid bears were able to adapt to warmer climates in tropical Asia where sloth bears and sun bears evolved, the Tremarctine bears were eventually able to adapt to tropical central America and exploit a more herbivorous niche.

The early spectacled bears radiated into South America slowly. Like other bears, their populations expanded incrementally, one female home range at a time, as they colonized Central America and then South America. It is likely that this expansion began during a cold period, perhaps during the next-to-last ice age, the Illinoian, which was the coldest of the Pleistocene glaciations. Conditions in the tropics would have been more temperate then, and the early spectacled bears would have had time to evolve to survive in warmer conditions. At one time they must have occupied a very large area; they still survive over a wide elevational range from lowland jungle to upper elevation cloud forests. On the western slopes of the Andes they are found from the edge of the coastal deserts at 820 ft (250 m) up to the snowline in Peru at 15,580 ft (4750 m) above sea level.

By the time that humans first spread across North America and further south, about 10,000 years ago, spectacled bears may have been present throughout Central America and down the western portion of South America. They were able to exploit a rich variety of food sources, and probably occupied the wetter regions, on the eastern slopes of the Andes, first. These areas of cloud forest contain the greatest number of plant food species utilized by spectacled bears, and are the population centers for the bears that exist today. We can imagine that bears slowly expanded south through the cloud forest (or similar humid habitats) until the best habitats were occupied. Then they might have dispersed into less optimal habitat as their populations grew. They were probably living as one large and fairly contiguous metapopulation stretching north to south along the Andes, when humans began occupying the land. As humans expanded

This spectacled bear is in a wildlife reserve in Colombia.

and their complex, agriculture-based MesoAmerican civilizations developed, bear habitat was greatly altered and bears were displaced. The spectacled bears probably disappeared from Central America before the Spaniards invaded. They fared better in the Andes, but it is likely that fragmentation of habitat there became significant as long as 500 years ago. At that time it is estimated that spectacled bears on the border of Peru and Ecuador inhabited a range of habitat types as wide as those currently occupied by brown bears worldwide; from extremely dry to extremely wet conditions and from near sea level to the upper limits of vegetation. They can occupy a wide variety of habitats, but are most common presently in heavy forest, perhaps because of displacement and persecution by humans. They are now confined to a narrow strip of habitat along the spine of the Andes; in fact only ten per cent of occupied bear habitat in Venezuela is found outside the protection of National Parks. They are difficult to observe, being largely nocturnal and arboreal in thick forest canopy, and therefore their status and distribution is uncertain in many areas.

Spectacled bears are omnivorous and feed on plants, small mammals, and even birds. However, they are primarily herbivorous, their preferred foods are fruits and bromeliads. They spend much of their time in the treetops where they will often build nest platforms for feeding and sleeping. Because their food grows on many branches that can not support their weight, they will sit and bend the branches inward to reach fruit and bromeliads. The bent branches are wedged into place to build a rough nest. Once a nest becomes large enough for sleeping, the bear will add layers of leaves, and may spend several days in the same nest.

They have large molars and premolars and advanced jaw musculature adapted for grinding vegetation, and are generally solitary animals, but often feed in groups. They are found along the spine of the Andes Mountains in all three ranges through Venezuela, Colombia, Ecuador, and Peru into Bolivia. They occupy dry thorn forests, rainforests of varying wetness, and grasslands, but their optimal habitat seems to be humid to very humid montane forest which is called cloud forest.

Birth rates and litter sizes are similar to other bear species, and successful reproduction depends upon the nutritional state of the female. The length of time between mating and birth varies greatly which indicates they are capable of delayed implantation, so that cubs are born at a time of local high food availability. Unlike the northern bears which are timed to give birth at the same time each year – in spring – spectacled bears, and other tropical bears, have highly variable food resources and less climatic consistency. Spectacled bear births are normally timed to occur so that the cubs are several months old by the time that fruits are ripe in the fall rainy season and they can eat them. When El Niño disrupts the normal climate and changes the development of fruit, there is some evidence that bears adjust to this by implanting the embryo at an appropriate time. This implies that there is some signal in the environment, climatic or nutritional, that turns on the proper hormonal response in bears. It is an intriguing possibility that should be elucidated by further research.

Their predators include mountain lions and jaguars. Today, spectacled bears are still faced with threats of human habitat alteration and fragmentation like the other bear species, as well as hunting and poaching for bear parts. One of the biggest agricultural practices to impact spectacled bears may be the increase in cultivation of coca for cocaine.

Protected areas have been recently established; 56 within the last 30 years. Eight of these areas are over 730 sq miles (1900 sq km) in area, which is considered by the Spectacled Bear Specialist Group to be the minimum size necessary to maintain viable populations. In protecting spectacled bear populations and habitat, conservationists are also efficiently working to maintain biodiversity. Bears tend to occupy the richest and most varied habitats and the core of surviving populations are found in those areas; in Bolivia for example bear habitat includes habitat for 63 per cent of all of South America's endemic mammals. As are bears in other parts of the world, spectacled bears are key indicators of ecosystem health. Preserving bear populations helps preserve the balance and the function of natural systems.

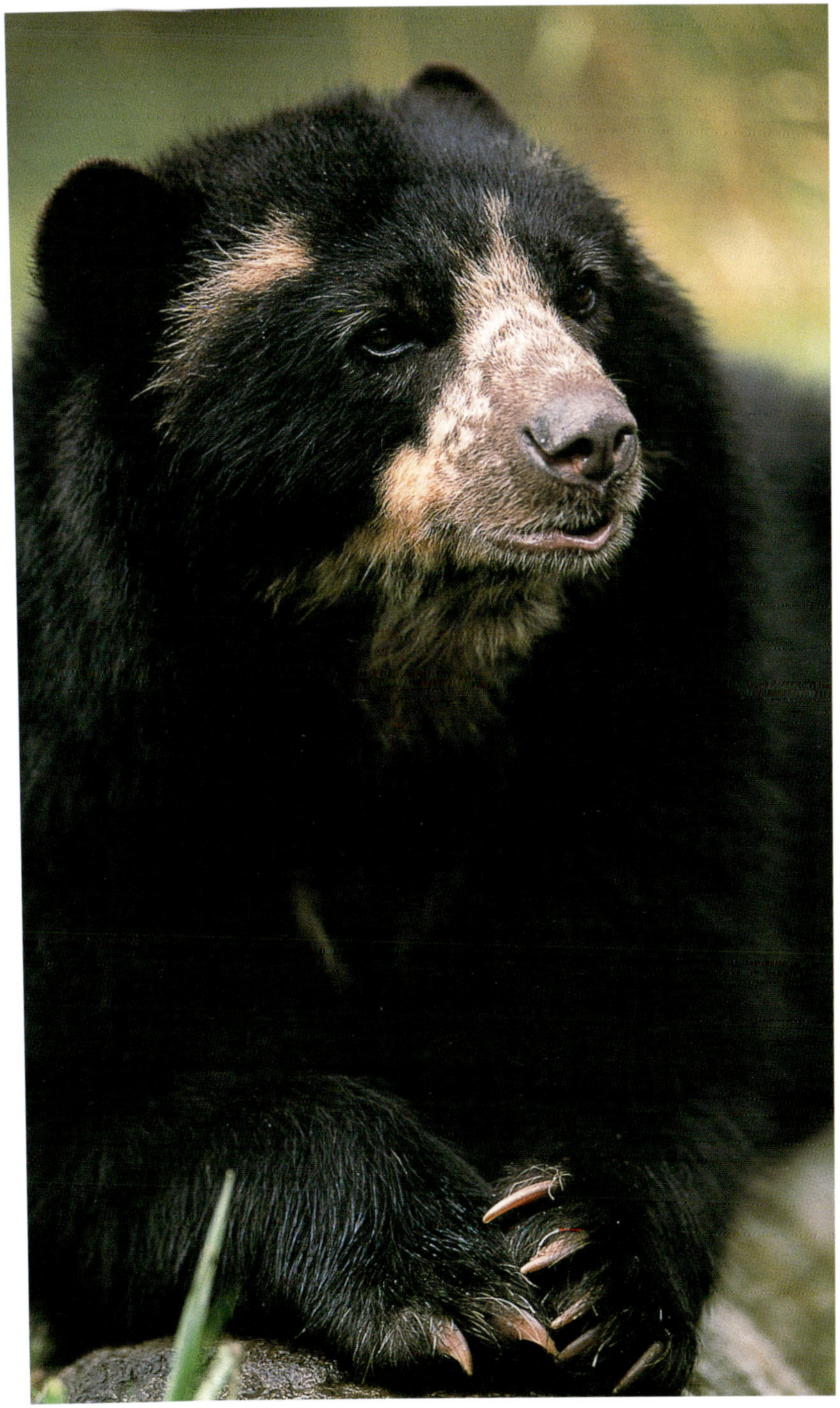

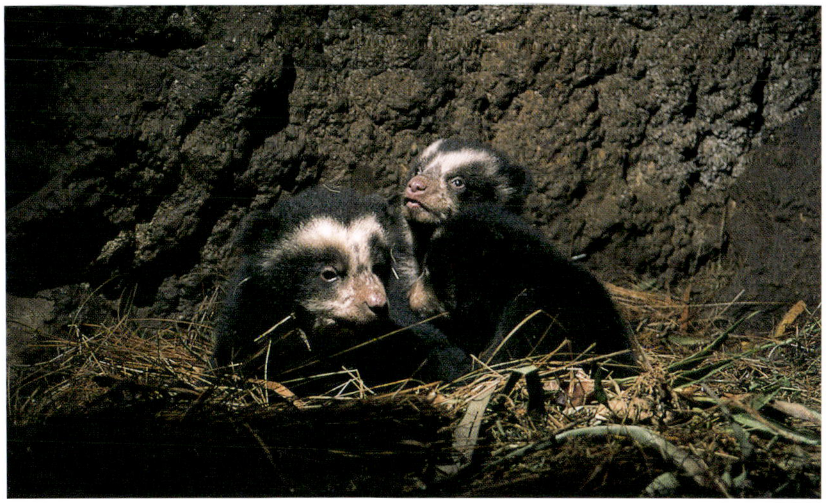

Spectacled bears can occupy a wide variety of habitats, but are most common presently in heavy forest, perhaps because of displacement and persecution by humans. Over the range of habitat they occupy, female spectacled bears with cubs tend to select inaccessible areas with security cover such as trees or cliffs. In the cloud forest they climb trees and utilize the forest canopy. In the grasslands they may find small forest patches on steep slopes. Along the margins of the Peruvian desert they often live by water holes with steep cliffs nearby.

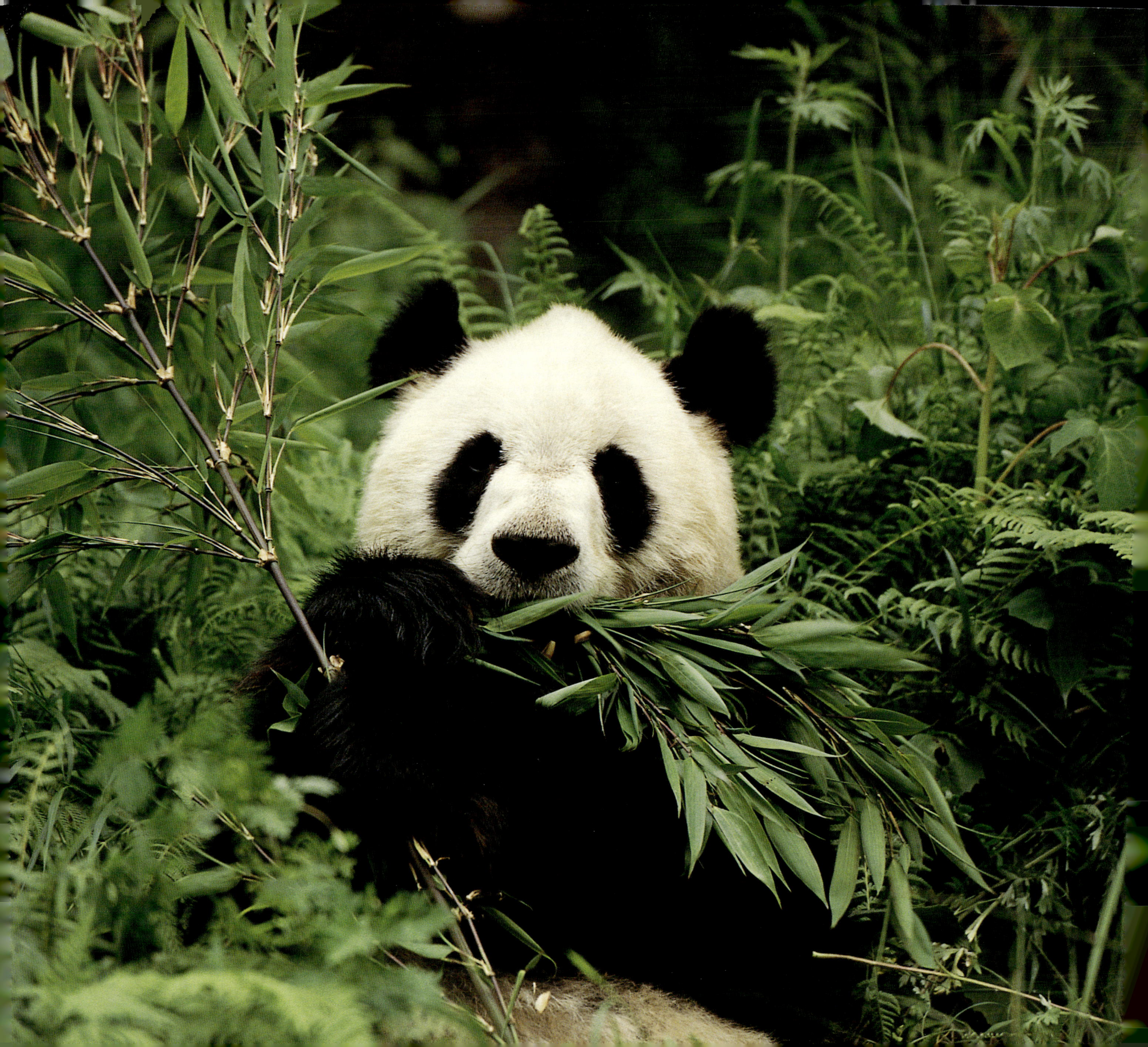

The Giant Panda

Pandas belong to the Ailuropodinae, the oldest family of the most primitive lineage of bears. Fossils of the oldest ancestral panda, *Ailuropoda lufengensesis*, which are found in southern China, are about 8 million years old. The earliest pandas were small, forest-dwelling creatures for millions of years until about the time of the late Pliocene 3 million years ago, when larger pandas developed. Pandas about half the size of modern giant pandas, *Ailuropoda microta*, were widespread throughout southern China about 600,000 years ago and were replaced by a larger species, *Ailuropoda melanoleuca baconi*, that was even larger than the modern giant panda, which evolved during the late Pleistocene. The fossil evidence suggests that in the late Pliocene and early Pleistocene, some 2-3 million years ago, the ancestral pandas were widely distributed over much of eastern and southern China as far north as Beijing. They ranged into what is now Taiwan, northern Myanmar (Burma) and northern Vietnam.

During their long evolution, pandas adapted to exploit the widespread and reliable plant resources of southern Asia. As they did so they lost many of the carnivorous and omnivorous traits of their ancestors and developed specialized adaptations for feeding on plants. One of the most stable food plants, for hundreds of thousands of years, has been bamboo. Recent ancestors, and the giant panda in particular, became increasingly dependent upon bamboo as a sole food source. Although bamboo can only be partially digested, and there are other more nutritious foods available, bamboo was apparently a constant and reliable source of food through changes in climate and changes in season. Evolution favored reliability at the cost of variety; but even bamboo in its many species provided ample variety. The major drawback for thousands of years was that most of a panda's time awake had to be spent feeding. A more serious drawback arose as human populations expanded. Specialization reduces options, and as the bamboo forests disappear the pandas are unable to adjust to other food sources. Omnivorous food habits have been the successful strategy of almost all the other bears, but the pandas lost that strategy and can never get it back.

Pandas are instantly recognized by their black and white coats. Most of the body is white with contrasting black fur on the ears, around and below the eyes, and on the legs where a black band connects each pair of legs across the back and shoulders. They have long, coarse, and oily guard hairs and a layer of underfur that is thicker than that of the tropical bears, but lighter than that of the northern bears. Their forelegs are larger and heavier than their hindlegs, which is an adaptation for climbing trees and for feeding and manipulating bamboo.

Like the other tropical bears, the early pandas were evolving in competition with other efficient predators, primarily the large cats. Unable to compete for prey species, and being preyed upon themselves, the early pandas evolved specializations in the direction of tree-climbing and the utilization of plant foods. We don't know what their diets consisted of, but the ancestral pandas were likely not as specialized in diet as the giant panda. Giant pandas forage almost exclusively on bamboo. There are a few records of pandas eating other plants or occasionally utilizing carrion such as deer, but about 99 per cent of the diet consists of the stems and leaves of bamboo.

In contrast to the prevalence of bamboo in the diet, the giant panda has not evolved efficient means of digesting the cellulose and other molecules in the plant. Giant pandas can only digest about 17 to 21 per cent of the dry biomass that they ingest. This inefficiency may indicate that the dietary shift to bamboo has occurred relatively recently in evolution. On the other hand, it is more likely that its digestive system, which originated in more carnivorous animals, has been unable to evolve toward a herbivorous diet as rapidly as the panda's

Giant pandas feed exclusively upon bamboo although they can only utilize about 20 per cent of its biomass.

morphology and behavior have done. As a consequence, pandas need to eat large amounts of bamboo daily; 20 to 40 lb (10 to 18 kg) is common. They select habitat where bamboo is plentiful and travel between food patches is reduced. They feed during both day and night; and are most active in the early morning and early evening around dawn and dusk.

During their long evolution pandas have developed many unique morphological and behavioral adaptations. It is possible that these adaptations originally enabled them to exploit a variety of different plant foods, many of which have more nutrients and are more digestible than bamboo. The panda's 'thumb' is unique in the entire animal kingdom; a wrist bone, the radial sesamoid, has become so enlarged that it now functions like a human thumb and enables the panda to grasp the stems of bamboo. The muscles of the 'thumb' allow it to oppose the five regular digits (which are similar to the paws of other bears) and grasp bamboo stems to hold them while eating. Giant pandas generally sit on their rumps while feeding to leave their forelimbs free for manipulating bamboo. They have a short muzzle with powerful jaw muscles and large teeth for grinding and crushing, all of which enable pandas to chew and swallow bamboo fibers. All of the molars and premolars are wide and flat topped.

If giant pandas had fed primarily on bamboo for much of their evolution, it is possible that other metabolic adaptations would have occurred along with their morphological changes. Herbivores in general have developed very long intestines which support symbiotic bacteria and protozoans that aid in the digestion of plant materials. Pandas, however, have a short digestive tract like a carnivore. This suggests that they were generalist omnivores like many other bear species until relatively recently in evolution.

However, natural selection can only occur when random mutations provide differences that affect survival and reproduction. Even the slightest advantage, over long periods of time, can direct the course of evolution. Because mutation is a random process, it is possible that pandas have relied on bamboo for millions of years but the genetic opportunity to adapt through changes in digestion and metabolism never occurred. Adaptations in morphology and behavior have clearly been possible. Metabolic changes are more fundamental, however, and depend upon the interaction of many complex chemical processes; the panda's metabolism may have progressed to a point from which a change to a more efficient form of herbivory was extremely improbable if not impossible. Once the earliest ancestors (ancestral even to the bear-dogs) started down the evolutionary path of carnivory, there may have been no turning back in terms of metabolism.

At any rate, pandas today are completely dependent upon bamboo. At present they have about 30 species to choose from. In the not-too-distant past, bamboo was the dominant plant in all of southern China. As a consequence, pandas once occupied all of southeastern China and even part of what is now Myanmar. To the early pandas, the dense bamboo forest probably offered security from large predators and a constant, reliable food source to depend upon. After a bamboo plant develops flowers and is fertilized, the plant dies. Often a single species covering large areas will flower at the same time and that food source will be lost until new plants grow. The diversity of bamboo species in the past ensured that throughout the pandas' original range there were several types to choose from in the event one or more species became unavailable. Despite bamboo's poor digestibility, the security and reliability of the bamboo forests enabled the giant panda to specialize on bamboo as its sole source of food. When food became scarce in one area, pandas could move to another area where it was plentiful. There was a severe bamboo die-off in the late 1970s and early 1980s during which many pandas had to be rescued from the wild as they neared starvation. In the Min Mountains 138 pandas were found dead during this period by one rescue team. The rescued pandas and their offspring survive in zoos.

Giant pandas have evolved from the oldest lineage of bears. They are very specialized in relation to other bear species.

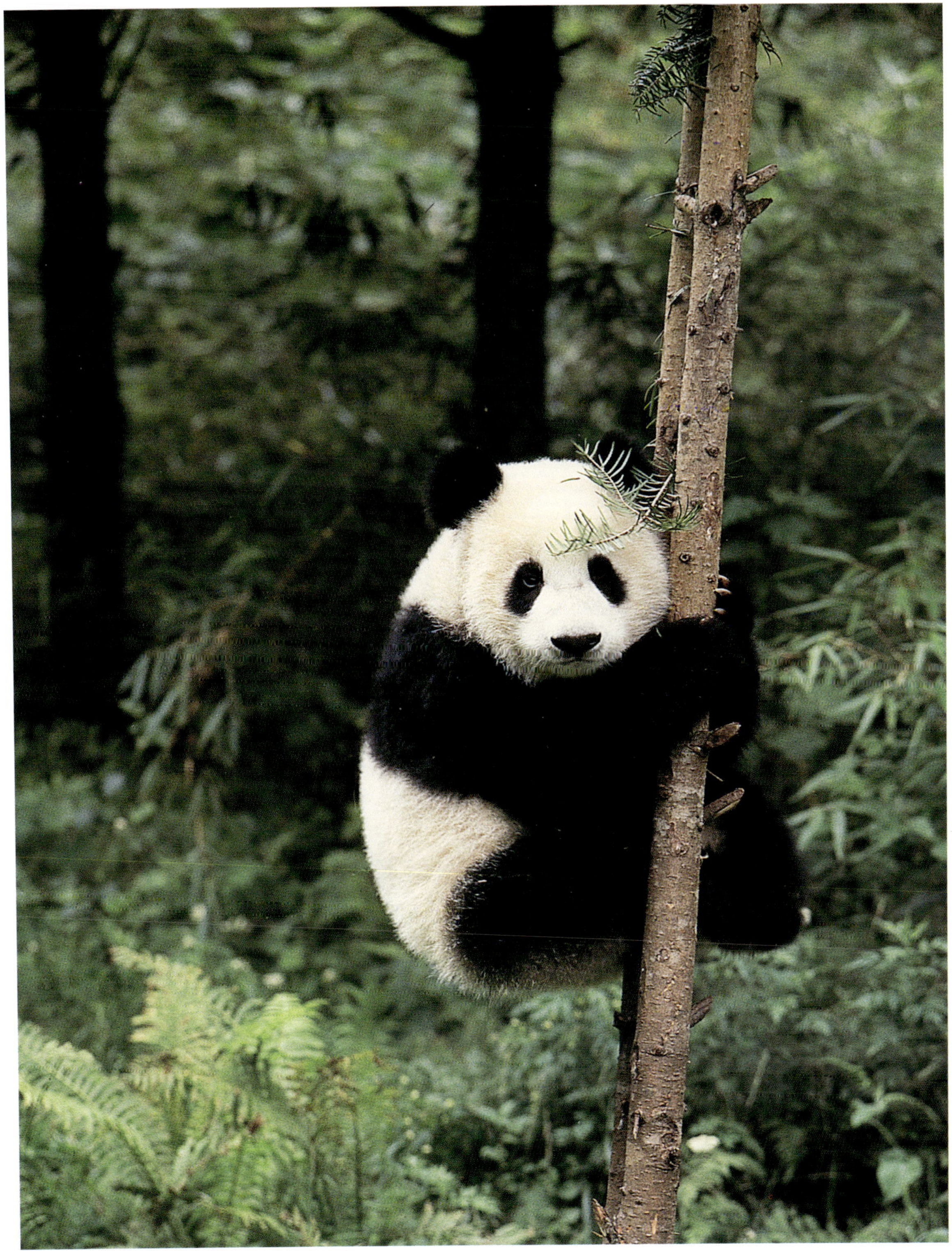

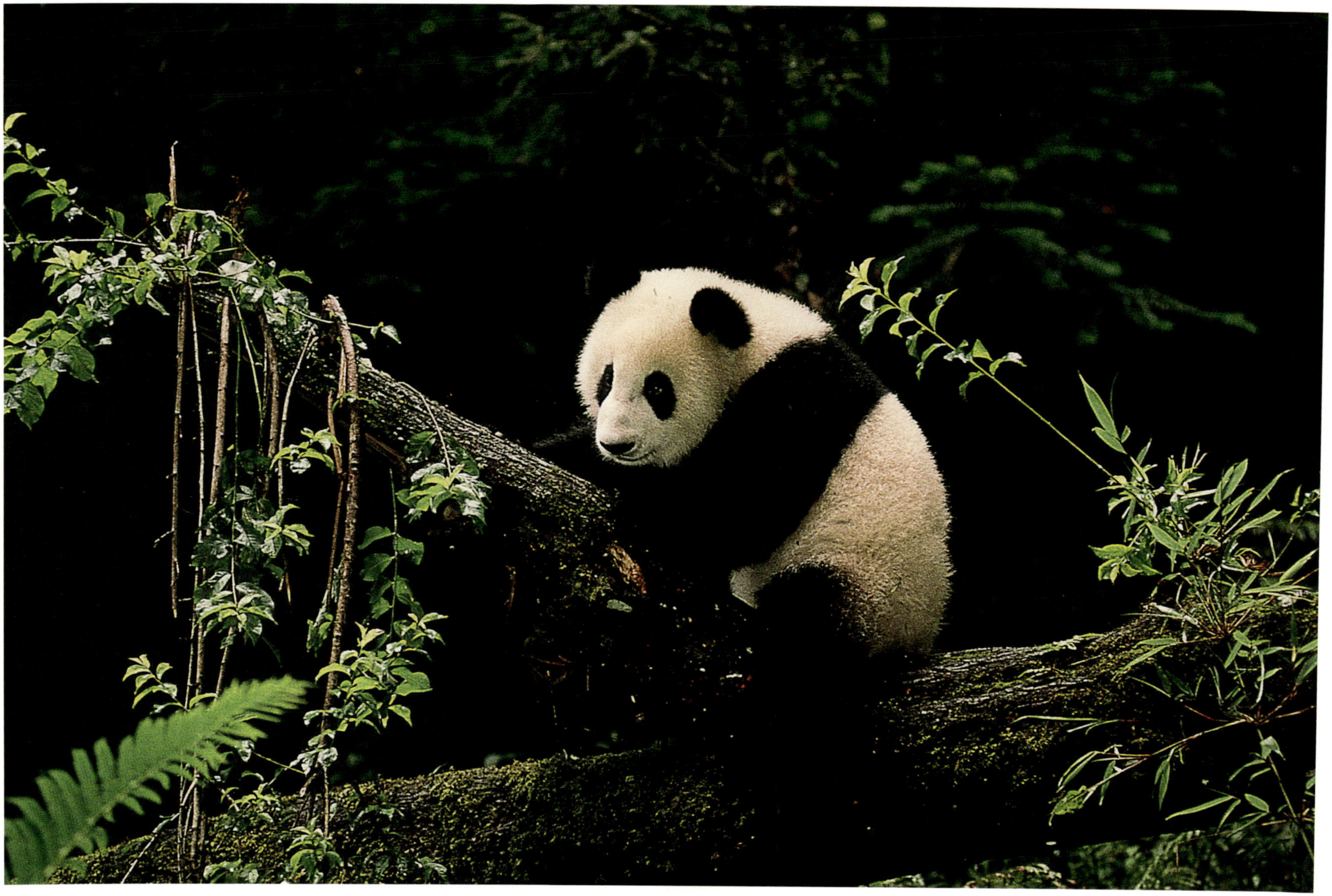

Panda cubs remain with their mothers for 18 months or more. This one-year-old cub is still dependent and is learning what types of bamboo are most palatable at different times of the year and where to find them.

Bamboo would still be a stable food source except for the rapid expansion of humans in southern Asia and the development of agriculture. As humans increasingly dominated the landscape the giant panda was forced to retreat. Today only about 1000 giant pandas remain. They live in six remote and isolated mountain regions and spend the summer in higher elevations above 7000 ft (2200 m). In these regions they live in temperate montane broad-leaf forests and broad-leaf/conifer mixed forests up into the subalpine conifer forests. Bamboo species are common in these forests and are often the dominant form of vegetation. There may be as many as 33 species. However, they are primarily small or dwarf species less than 16 ft (5 m) in height, and only about 15 species are widely available and preferred. Even the best of this habitat is marginal in relation to what pandas need and what was once available to them.

Pandas move up and down in elevation during different seasons in order to select certain bamboo species. The growing shoots are most nutritious. Once the shoots are fully grown they become tough and fibrous and pandas move upward to where emerging shoots of other species are available. They continue to eat new shoots as long as they are available and then concentrate on leaves during summer when they are most numerous. In winter they rely more on stems and whatever leaves are not dead. In the winter they generally depend on lower areas, between 3900 to 6500 ft (1200 to 2000 m), where they also mate and give birth. This lower habitat is particularly threatened by the continued expansion of the human population in China.

Giant pandas live a solitary existence for most of the year, keeping track of their neighbors and maintaining distance among them both spatially and temporally by the use of scent. In the Quinling Mountains they have been observed traveling in groups of two or more. They have highly developed scent glands in the anal area that are used for scent marking. Pandas rub their anal gland area against trees and other objects and spray urine at scent-marking stations. They also claw the bark of scent-marking trees. Communicating through scent marking allows individuals to avoid each other; or to find each other if they wish. As the mating season approaches they communicate more frequently through scent marking and with vocalizations. Females have a repertoire of moans, bleats and barks, while males tend to bark and roar. The scent of females serves to attract males, which may mate with several females. Males will fight each other over females in estrous; the source of their competition will often climb a tree while her suitors decide who gets to breed.

It is likely that a female will also breed with more than one male during her two- to seven-day estrous period, as brown bears do. Dominant males do most of the copulating but may not remain and guard the female throughout her estrous period, thus giving subordinate males a chance to copulate. The mating season lasts from mid March to mid May, but females that are not impregnated may come into estrous again in September and October and even occasionally in January and February. Successful mating appears to depend upon a high degree of compatibility between the male and the female; this is particularly true in captive breeding animals. Early attempts to breed pandas in zoos often failed because the pandas did not like each other; introduction of another, compatible, mate from a nearby cage has been successful on at least one occasion.

Pandas have been able to reproduce in zoos, but only in a few cases. One or two cubs are usually born, but only one generally survives to be raised. The length of time from mating until birth has been observed to vary greatly, as also in sun bears, which implies that there is a period of delayed implantation that can vary from one to four months. Giant pandas have been observed raising cubs in the wild by Chinese researchers. The cubs are born nearly hairless with eyes closed. The mother stays in the den for about ten days after the birth, feeding and caring for the cubs. She may be in a type of dormant state during this period, although pandas do not hibernate. Biologists have been able to approach very cautiously and even handle the cubs at this stage. The female panda was very habituated to their presence by this time after months of close observation, but her acquiescence may have been facilitated by a drowsy or dormant condition as well.

Dens are usually situated in rock caves or in trees with hollow bases. Conifer trees of a size large enough to furnish a den site are well over a hundred years old and may be very difficult to find as the forests are harvested. After the early stage, the mother leaves the cubs sleeping in a den while she goes outside to feed and drink for short periods. This stage lasts about four to six weeks. Although there are many dangerous predators in the bamboo forest – Asiatic black bears, leopards, golden cats, and yellow-throated martens – the mother is able to defend her cubs. She also moves them to other dens on occasion; probably to help avoid predation.

When the cubs are able to travel, the mother leaves the den. The mother must carry the cub which is uncoordinated until about five or six months old when it can move on its own. Cubs then travel with their mothers until they are about 18 months old; nursing and learning how to find and eat bamboo on their own. After the cub strikes out on its own, the mother will not generally mate again the next year or two; thus the reproductive interval is at least two years. The offspring will not reach sexual maturity until at least 4½ years of age, and maybe not until they are 7½. Females are reproductive for 11 years or more. In the wild, pandas may live as long as 22 years once they reach adulthood. The oldest panda in captivity lived to be 30 years old.

Outside of the mating season, pandas do not often meet. They know of each other's presence from the scent-marking trees which are generally located along travel routes. Males appear to leave their scent more often than females. They rarely vocalize, except during the few times when they meet other pandas. At such times they may use noises that have been described as moans, honks, yips and barks. Males utilize larger home ranges than females, and the home ranges overlap. Males generally include several female home ranges within their own.

The pupils of the panda's eyes are vertical slits as in members of the cat family. This may be an adaptation for night vision. Because they are quite different in color, morphology, and behavior from the other bear species, pandas were the subject of a long-running controversy: were they bears or not? This debate was argued back and forth for nearly 130 years until finally being settled in the 1990s when genetic evidence weighed in to greatly support their inclusion with the other bears. Since 1869 many scientists have argued that they should be placed in the raccoon family. Others thought that they constituted their own separate family. Even within the past three decades prominent scientists have argued for either bears, raccoons, or separate status. There is now no doubt, based upon concordance of DNA and protein studies, that pandas are more closely related to bears than to any other group of species, and are close enough to be included in the family Ursidae. Another species, which was commonly called the red panda, is only superficially similar to the giant panda, and both morphological and genetic evidence has grouped it with the raccoons, which are the closest relatives of bears. The bear and raccoon lineages diverged about 35 million years ago. Pandas then diverged from the ursid lineage about 20 million years ago.

Giant pandas are shy and secretive and will generally remain silent and still when humans pass nearby. They will move away if possible, but will sometimes charge. Like other bears, females with young are usually the most aggressive. When they become weak or ill pandas have been known to enter human settlements or farms and even to eat human foods. Because of their dependence on bamboo, they do not depredate crops or attack livestock. They can easily be habituated to humans and trained.

There are now only about 25 'islands' of panda habitat left; two-thirds of these support fewer than 50 pandas. This means that about 16 of these isolated populations will soon go extinct unless more habitat is restored. It is possible that pandas can be maintained for a while in zoos; but there are only about 116 in captivity worldwide, and reproduction in zoos has met with limited success. Only about 17 giant pandas are found in zoos outside China, and the current Chinese government policy is only to 'loan' pandas for substantial sums of money to other nations. Although many Chinese are concerned about preserving pandas, the intense pressure for more land from an

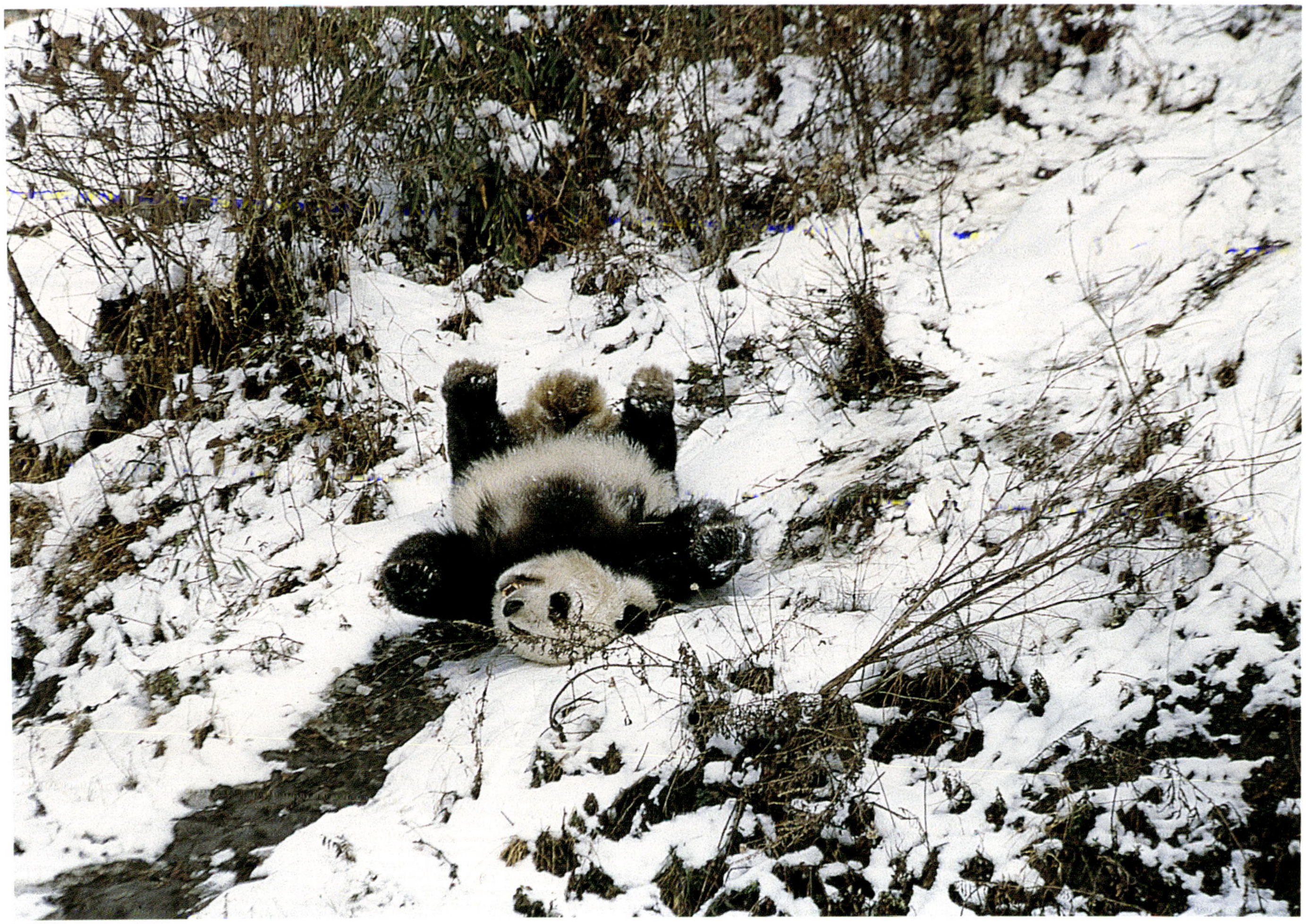

What is black and white and black and white and black and white?
Pandas symbolize the diversity and tenacity of life. This panda rolling in the snow does not realize that it is on the brink of extinction; just as humans are the cause of its decline, only humans can now prevent it from ceasing to exist altogether.

increasing human population makes the preservation of current habitat very difficult. Restoring other lands that are now used for agriculture is an even greater challenge. In order to survive in the wild, giant pandas need more space to live.

Although giant pandas once ranged across most of southern and eastern China, by 1800 their range had shrunk so much that they occupied only two mountainous regions. By 1900 they were found only in the larger region which includes the Quinling Mountains and the edge of the Tibetan plateau. Within a few years, the expansion of agriculture in the river valleys had fragmented this once-connected population into six mountain ranges that are isolated from one another by human settlements and farmland. Each of these six mountain ranges still has resident pandas but even within them the panda habitat is fragmented. About 80 per cent of the remaining pandas are found in Sichuan Province, divided among four mountain ranges. Pandas rarely move between these mountains. About 35 per cent of all pandas live within protected reserves. As discussed in the final chapter, such small population sizes, in isolated patches of habitat, increase the risk of local extinction in each patch. Birth and death events, and reduced genetic variability, can combine to reduce populations. Environmental factors such as fires in bamboo groves and widespread dieback of bamboo after the flowering phase can quickly destroy entire populations when there is little chance of animals moving to unaffected areas. The predicament of the panda is a case study in the processes that lead to extinction.

Pandas have become symbols for the conservation of endangered species. They are critically endangered, and they are extremely appealing to people. Although they have been killed, and continue to be killed, by poachers for economic gain, their demise has been largely an indirect by-product of human population growth. Perhaps more than any other species, giant pandas epitomize the quandary of conservation. Although most people do not want to kill pandas, or other bears, the survival of individual people often precludes the survival of pandas. The choice of clearing bamboo forest in order to plant crops, or cutting trees for firewood can be almost a matter of life or death for villagers or their children. By destroying this habitat, they are indirectly killing pandas, and pushing them closer to the brink of extinction. They don't see the pandas actually die in most cases, but they will be unable to produce cubs and raise them successfully. People are generally unaware of the effects of reduced reproduction; and they are only doing what they feel they need to do in order to survive themselves. Conservation of giant pandas, and of other bear species, requires a concerted effort by people, and involves elements of biology, sociology, economics, politics, education, law enforcement, and other disciplines. Further discussion on conservation approaches continues in the final chapter.

Pandas are fully protected in China. Hunting has been illegal since the 1960s. As many as seven poachers were arrested in 1987 and the maximum penalty for killing pandas was increased from two years in prison to life imprisonment or death. Despite the severity of punishment, poaching still remains a threat. The value of a panda hide can be the equivalent of two or more years, income for a rural villager, and several hundred thousand dollars to the final seller, due to a demand for panda pelts in the richer Asian nations. At least three poachers have been sentenced to death. Pandas are sometimes killed accidentally by snares set for other animals which it is also illegal to kill. Any protection of giant pandas will need to provide economic benefits for rural villagers and alternate sources of wood for shelter and energy so that protection will be in their best interests as well as the pandas'. The story of the decline of the giant panda is currently being repeated with all seven other species of bear, but they each have more time left than the panda, which is on the brink of extinction, and if incredible efforts are not made to protect and restore habitat they may go extinct in the wild within our lifetimes.

Giant pandas exist today only in small, isolated patches of wild bamboo forest.

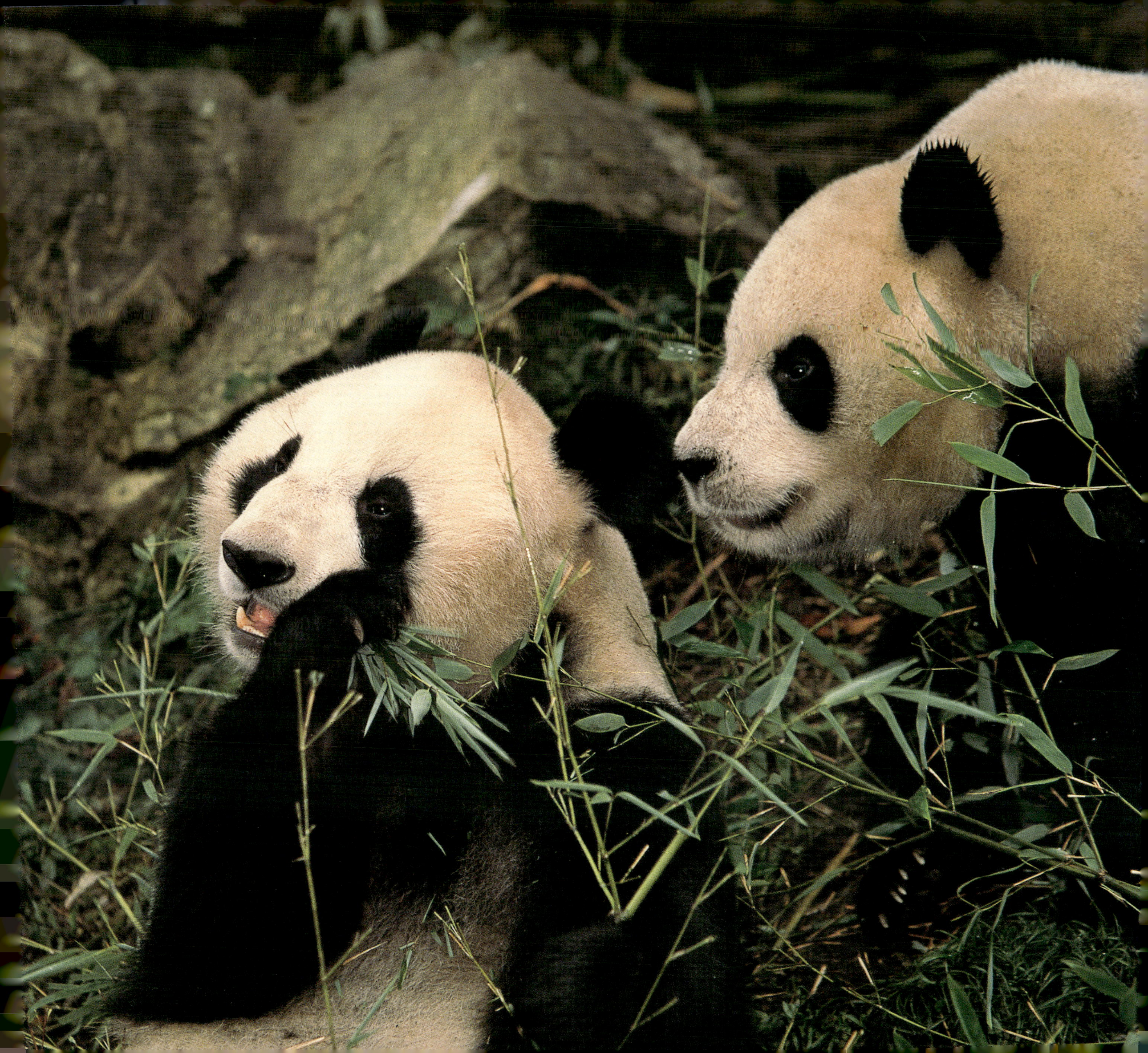

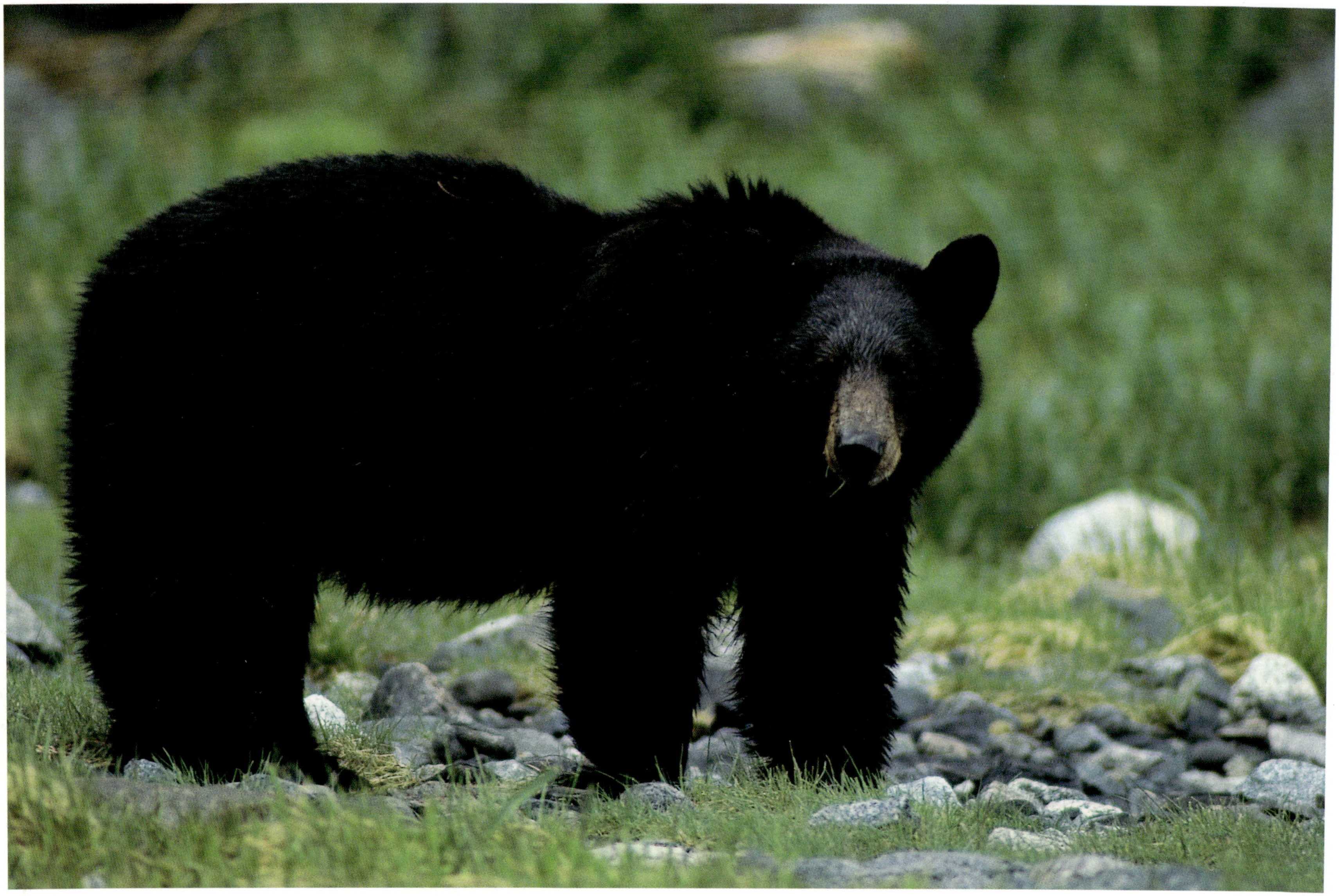

Bears and Humans

Evolution is a slow dance with death. It is a complex dance, playing out over millions of years, with a myriad of partners on a constantly shifting dance floor. The steps you take are determined by the positions of the other dancers and the condition of the pavilion. No two dances are the same. Any missteps are culled by death; the only dancers that survive are those that dance in nearly perfect rhythm.

Humans and bears have been partners in this dance for less than a million years: since long after Lucy, perhaps the first modern human primate, walked the land. Both bears and humans converged from markedly different ancestors to occupy similar niches by the time of the Stone Age. Bears descended from terrestrial carnivores living somewhere in central Asia. Humans descended from partly arboreal herbivores living somewhere in Africa. As bears developed adaptations to omnivory, they retained many of their carnivore features. Humans retained many of their herbivore features, but as they evolved they developed adaptations and behavior enabling them to function as carnivores.

Bears and humans evolved in concert with other species in their environment; competitors, predators, prey, and plant foods. For less than a million years bears and humans have influenced each other's evolution, but they have been important influences because they competed closely for most of the same resources. Before humans became a factor, the other large predators were major forces in natural selection for bears. Because of the precedence of the large cats, bears that evolved in southern Asia became less carnivorous and adapted to roles as frugivores, insectivores, and herbivores. They became somewhat secretive and nocturnal.

The bears that evolved in the north, however, had fewer big cats to deal with. Instead, their major competitors were wolf-like. In an evolutionary response, bears were more successful at becoming larger and stronger. This enabled them to take kills away from wolves and other smaller predators. At the same time, strength and claws enable them to dig for rich tubers and other consistent, unexploited plant foods. Wolves in turn developed a social organization that improved their hunting efficiency and enabled them to defend their prey from bears. This balance of power is still a delicate one today. The brown bears that evolved to compete with wolves, and then later in time encountered big cats, are some of the largest, most aggressive bears of all. In order to displace cats from their kills, these bears succeeded by becoming bigger and fiercer.

Bears and humans first encountered each other in Europe and Asia. For many thousands of years their competition was a stand-off, like bears and wolves. A single human or two was no match for a brown bear and humans were killed, displaced from food sources, or tolerated depending upon the needs of the bear. However, a large group of humans, if they were desperate enough and well armed, could drive a brown bear (or a pack of wolves) from a kill. They could even kill them if necessary. Earlier humans had probably developed such hunting strategies in Africa where large groups armed with stone implements had the opportunity to acquire kills that had been taken by leopards, cheetahs, hyenas, and occasionally lions, if they were aggressive enough. The abundance of this source of protein may have even served to start humans down the evolutionary path towards meat eating.

As humans moved northward out of Africa, however, they became major competitors with bears wherever they found them. Our ancestors migrated out of Africa about a million years ago. These people are classified as *Homo erectus* and they first spread north and eastward into southeast Asia. In southeast Asia, the bears were not the top carnivores and had already adapted to avoiding other predators.

American black bears are true generalists; they coexist with grizzlies primarily by avoiding them.

They were probably not bothered too much by humans. Early humans had other, more dangerous predators to deal with too, and were probably not bothered too much by bears. Humans and bears adapted to each other and shared habitat and foods in central and southeast Asia for over 900,000 years.

During one of the warmer, interglacial periods about 850,000 years ago, several new species invaded Europe; one of these was the brown bear, *Ursus arctos*. Brown bears had existed as a distinct species for at least 250,000 years by then but had been confined to central Europe. They probably remained south of the permafrost for most of that time, but some populations were gradually adapting to life on the tundra.

Early humans moved into Europe about 500,000 years ago. These ancestral people, in the transition from *Homo erectus* to *Homo sapiens*, may have come from southcentral Asia and may have had some contact with ancestral brown bears there. When they occupied Europe there was another species of bear present, the cave bear *Ursus spelaeus*. Although cave bears were as large as the biggest Kodiak bears today, they were primarily plant-eaters. Their large molar teeth were adapted to chewing and grinding. They must have also fed on carrion as indicated by the large size and heavy musculature they attained. In some respects, they resembled the short-faced bears which evolved separately in North America.

Early humans and cave bears probably avoided each other as much as possible. Solitary humans could have easily been prey, and even a large group of humans would not attempt to kill a cave bear. However, it is likely that both species ate many of the same plant foods and might have tried to bluff each other away from carrion. Cave bears denned during the winter and females gave birth in caves that were in continuous use for hundreds of thousands of years. In many caves there are the remains of the bears that died during winter sleep, and there are literally thousands of fossils. During the winters, early humans must have also sought shelter in caves whenever possible. They may have killed occasional cave bears at these times, but there is no evidence of humans doing so. Early humans developed a great respect for cave bears.

When brown bears appeared in Europe they were smaller than cave bears, but much more carnivorous. They must have been very dangerous for early humans. There is some fossil evidence that humans hunted and killed brown bears, and bears most certainly killed humans. In the presence of this smaller, meaner, and probably quicker cousin, the cave bear must have seemed like a benign older gentleman to the humans that feared and respected them both.

During the Pleistocene in Europe, continental glaciers periodically descended from the north. During most of these ice ages, Scandinavia was completely glaciated and the major European mountain ranges (the Alps, Pyrenees, Cantabrians, Transylvanians, and Caucasus) all had extensive ice caps. Permafrost and tundra extended south as far as southern France.

During these times, European plants and animals were forced to move south below the permafrost and populations were isolated in refugia on the Mediterranean peninsulas of Iberia (Spain), Italy, Greece (and the Balkans), and Turkey. During cold periods, early humans coexisted in these pockets with cave bears, mammoths, mastodons, and other animals. Competition for food and other resources intensified. During warm periods, the flora and fauna would disperse northwards again as conditions became favorable. Invariably, some species went extinct in the isolated refugia, but as Europe warmed again other individuals of those species recolonized from farther south.

About 130,000 years ago the Neanderthal race of humans evolved in Europe and occupied it until about 40,000 years ago when they were replaced by Cro-Magnons. Neanderthals lived in tolerance with both the cave bears and the brown bears, moving slowly generation after generation south and then north in response to the ice ages

Bears and humans are omnivorous and share many of the same foods. In many cultures bears are referred to as kin.

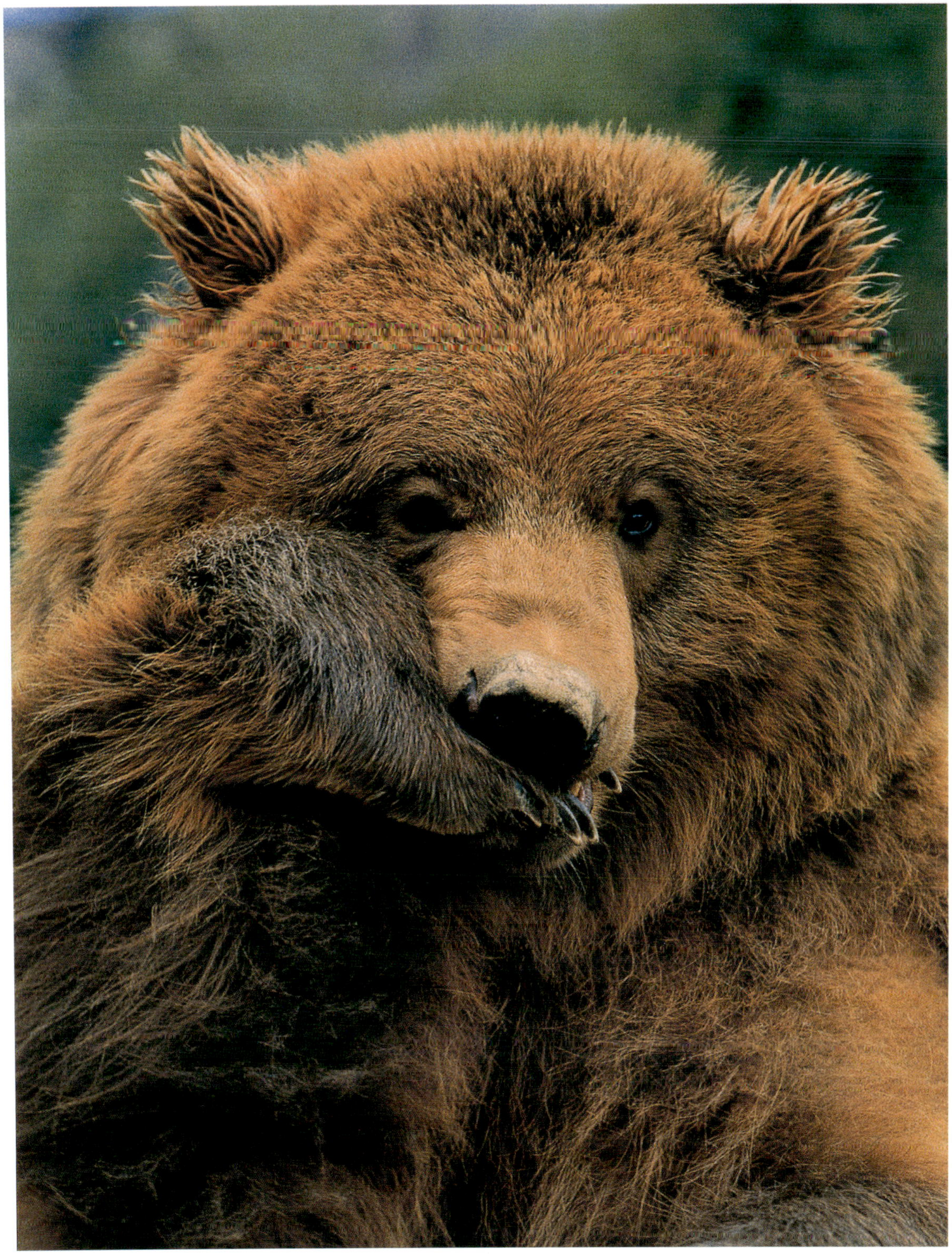

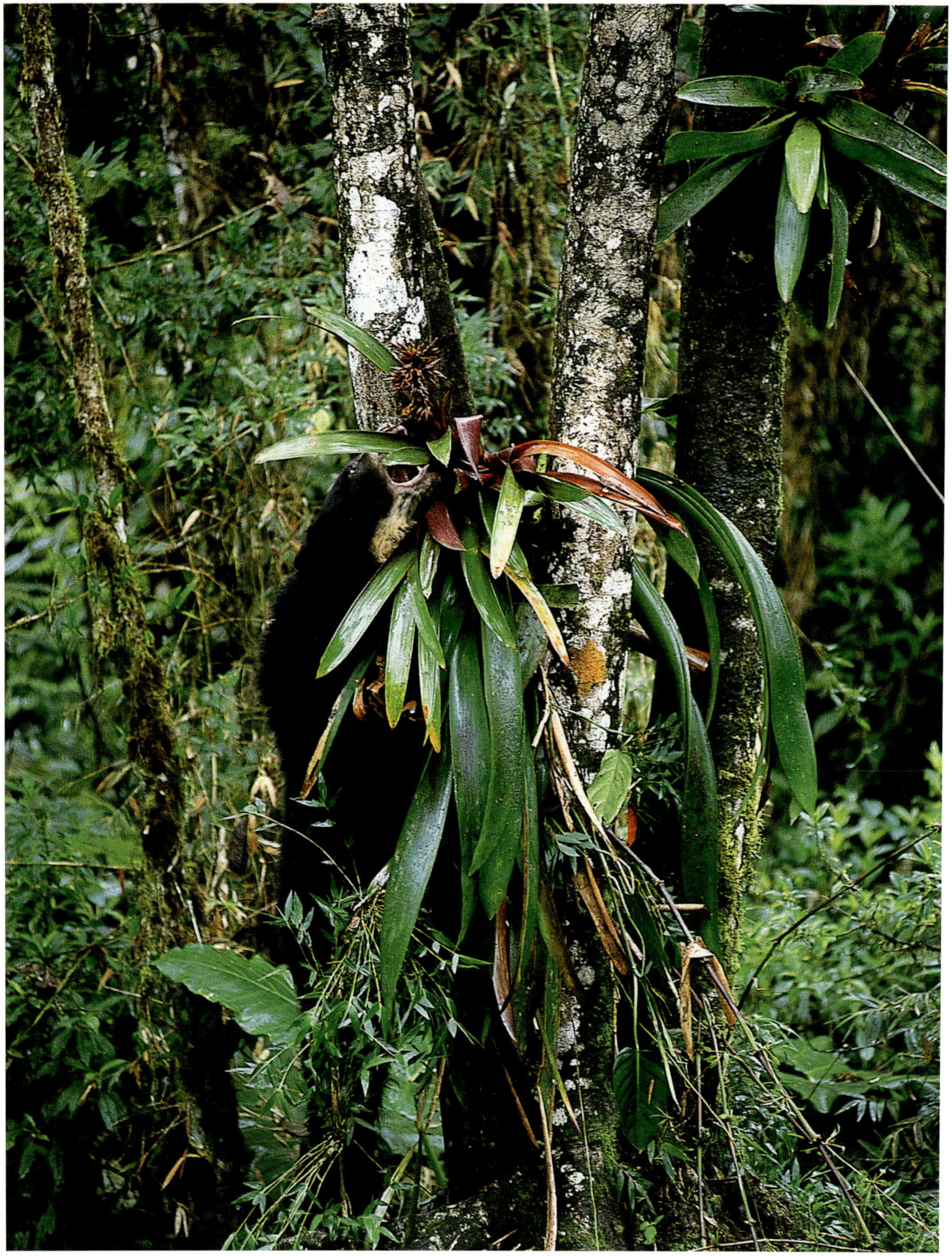

Both bear and human populations were greatly reduced in numbers when they were forced into the isolated pockets of habitat on the peninsulas. In these refugia, populations were small, and natural selection was pronounced. Both bears and humans may have evolved rapidly. At some point, humans developed into modern forms; the first of these were discovered in Cro-Magnon cave in France, and were given that name, but similar people with similar cultural artifacts were also inhabiting parts of Africa and southwestern Asia at the same time. We may never know exactly where modern humans first developed their tools and weapons, but they quickly spread throughout the inhabited world.

During the same time period that humans were developing social organization, the brown bear may have gained some advantage by adapting to colder areas on the permafrost tundra north of the refugia. Mammoths and caribou were probably widespread and would have been available as prey. During cold periods there would have been increased survival value to brown bears that adapted to the tundra. They certainly thrive in such areas today. They would have weathered the ice ages with larger populations than the cave bear. On the tundra they would have been the top carnivores and had the whole array of Pleistocene mammals to choose from for prey. Mammoths, mastodons, ground sloths and the other large megafauna were probably too big to kill directly, but brown bears had little competition for weakened animals or carrion.

A similar scenario must have existed all across northern Asia during the Pleistocene. In central Asia, however, populations were not crowded into such small, isolated refugia during cold periods; there was more contiguous habitat available. Bears and humans probably just moved north and south with the climate. Bears could adapt to the tundra along a broad front. In the south there were tigers, lions, leopards, wild dogs and other serious predators, but they moved even further south as the climate cooled. The brown bears could not outcompete them for prey at the northern edges of their range where they came in contact.

As a consequence, perhaps over hundreds of thousands of years, brown bears evolved as selection favored individuals that were more successful in exploiting the northern margins of their habitat. Other species were also doing this including the mammoths, wolverines, and several ungulates such as caribou. The permanent tundra that moved north and south following the glaciers was a fruitful niche for a predator to exploit, and the brown bears gradually adapted to it. They also adapted to seasonally abundant plant foods, particularly roots and tubers that had to be dug.

Humans colonized the colder climates later than bears, but they did it with technology rather than evolutionary changes. The common ancestor of brown bears and black bears was probably somewhat adapted to the cold steppe by at least 3.5 million years ago when black bears migrated to North America. Brown bears became even more adapted by 300,000 years ago when the first wave of brown bears migrated across the Bering Land Bridge to Alaska and the New World. There are no fossils from this period, but the date has been inferred from mitochondrial DNA sequence data. The first record of humans inhabiting what is now Siberia comes from fossils dating back only 20,000 years. It was at this time that humans had developed enough technology, in the form of clothing, fire, and weapons, to be able to survive in the harsh climate. Once they were able to colonize, they spread rapidly. By at least 15,000 years ago, humans followed the bears across the Bering Land Bridge.

During this, the last (Wisconsinan) glaciation of the ice age, the last wave of brown bears also migrated across. Horses and camels from North America crossed in the opposite direction. As the climate warmed, and the sea levels rose, humans and bears on both sides of the Pacific continued their evolutionary dance. Humans were on the verge of new technology and were beginning to develop tools and

Spectacled bears feed on a variety of plants in the tropical forest canopy; particularly bromeliads.

weapons with multiple parts such as spear-throwers, bows, and arrows. They were also developing sharp stone blades and spear points. They had co-existed with bears for hundreds of thousands of years with bears being clearly dominant, but humans were evening the balance. With the development of better weapons, and the domestication of dogs, both humans and bears became about evenly matched. Dogs were domesticated independently by at least three different groups of humans about 12,000 years ago; in North America, in China, and in southwestern Asia. Both dogs and stone points were still no match for bears, but in many cases groups of armed humans with dogs may have been able to drive a well-fed bear from a carcass.

In the New World the evolutionary dance had more the elements of a race. As the continental glaciers receded and opened up a route to the south about 11,000 years ago, two vast continents became accessible for both humans and brown bears to colonize. At that time in Eastern Beringia (interior Alaska), humans, brown bears, mammoths, wolverines, and other species had been living together for thousands of years. As the Mackenzie Corridor opened up between the Laurentian and Cordilleran ice sheets, these species were poised to expand into the warmer lands to the south. The humans had the technology of chiseled stone points that we call the Clovis culture, from Clovis, New Mexico, where it was first discovered. The oldest Clovis site was occupied about 11,400 years ago. These early Americans resemble the modern Northern Asian mongoloid races from which they dispersed.

The conventional view until recently was that both Clovis humans and bears migrated south along the Mackenzie corridor as the ice receded. New data, from fossils and from frozen specimens, suggests that a coastal route to the south may have been the first route. The DNA evidence for brown bear migration is discussed in more detail in the chapter on origins. During interglacials, brown bears were able to migrate into North America. There were four such warm periods during the Pleistocene and it is likely that brown bears came across the Bering Land Bridge during three of them. About 50,000 years ago, all the known lineages of North American brown bears were intermixed in Eastern Beringia. There is some evidence that humans were also present at that time. Although there was no ice blocking their movement south, bears did not migrate until after the end of the last ice age which reached its peak about 18,000 years ago. Humans came over around 15,000 years ago and probably lived on the tundra and the coastal islands for several thousand years until they were able to move south. At that time, it is likely that both bears and humans went south first along the coast, and then later along an interior route between the two continental ice sheets.

The evidence for a human coastal route comes in part from fossil remains on coastal islands, and from earlier remains to the south of the ice sheets that are unlike the majority of early Americans. Some of these early human remains date back over 11,000 years in South America. Skulls of Kennewick Man from the Pacific Northwest and Spirit Cave man from Nevada, as well as others, may be most similar to more ancient Asians; like the Ainu of Japan. It appears possible that there may have even been humans living south of the ice when the Clovis people, and the brown bears, began to migrate south. This is a possibility that can never be disproved, and which may be further illuminated by discoveries in the future. It is an intriguing mystery that will be slowly solved, if ever, as more fossils are found.

Imagine what it must have been like as the last ice age came to an end. The land connection between Asia and North America was broken around 13,000 years ago as the melting glaciers raised the sea level. What had been one vast, open expanse from Canada to Europe was severed. One group of humans and bears became isolated in Eastern Beringia in what is now Alaska and Northwest Canada. Although the climate was warming, it was still very cold and it remained cold for several thousand years. Like today, the daylight lasted 24 hours above the Arctic Circle in mid summer. Conversely, the darkness lasted 24 hours in mid winter, and ice covered the Bering Strait. It is also possible that humans could have continued to travel between Asia and North America during the winters.

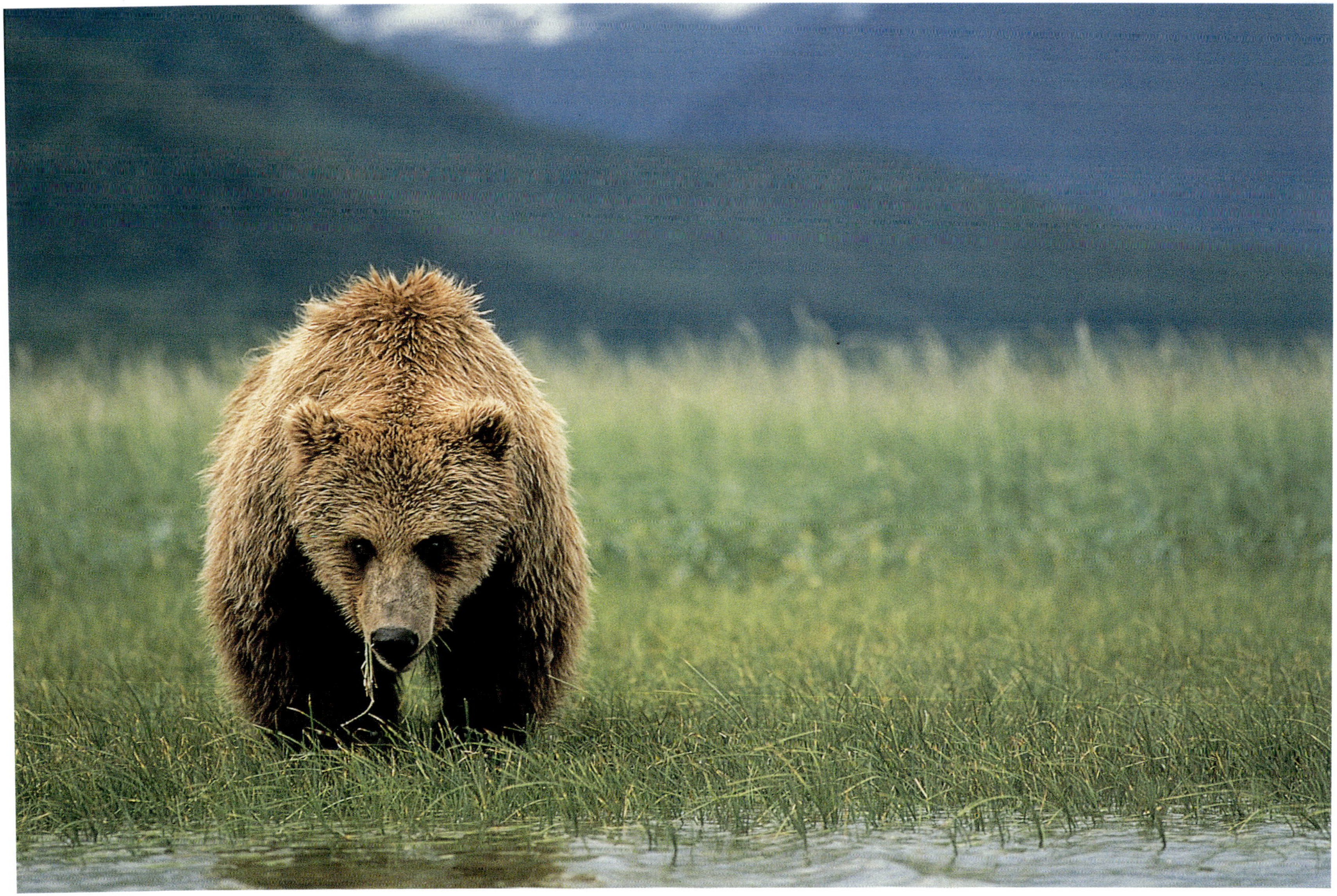

Coastal estuaries are important habitat for brown bears in the spring. At this time they graze on sedges and grasses until other more nutritious foods become available; they are also very vulnerable to hunters and poachers.

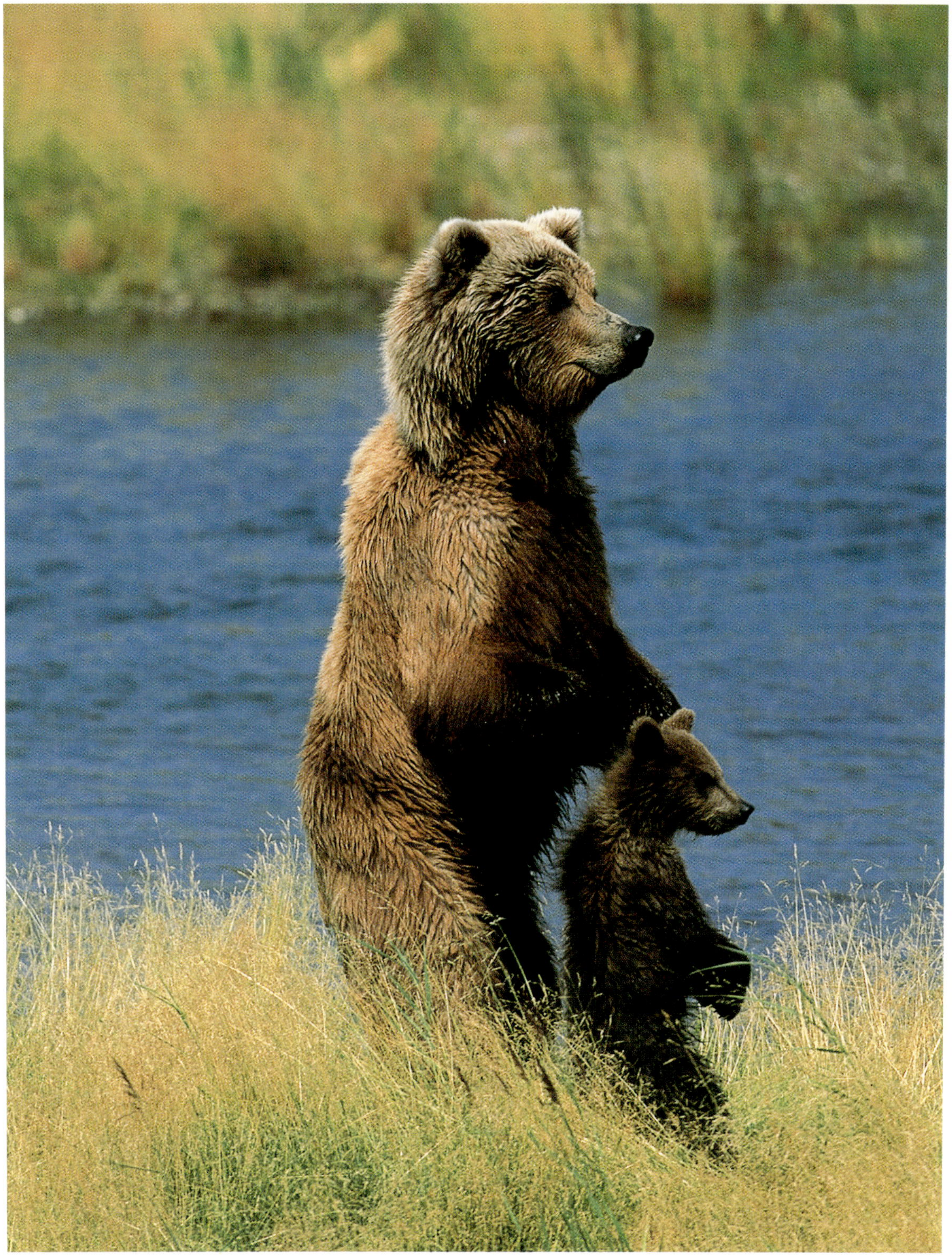

It is more likely that people stayed put. It is also likely that there were more people along the western coast than there were inland. Much of the Southern coast of Alaska, out through the Aleutian Island chain, remained covered by the Cordilleran Ice Sheet for a long time. This ice sheet reached its peak about 15,000 years ago, and then began to recede, but it still covered most of the Southern coast 13,000 years ago. There were a few ice-free areas where humans could reach the coast, and there were Islands that remained ice-free throughout the last ice age. Kodiak Island, however, was probably ice-covered until 11,000 ago, at which time the ancestors of the Kodiak subspecies of brown bears colonized it.

Most of the land above the ice sheets was permafrost covered with cold-tolerant plants somewhat similar to the tundra we have today. The soil below a certain depth remained frozen all year. It was mostly treeless. There were a few mild spots, however, that held trees. The vegetation may have been primarily a grassland, but sagebrush was also widespread. This has been called tundra-steppe. Mammoths, horses, and bison, all of which are grass-eaters, were the most abundant according to the fossil record. However, plant pollen samples indicate that grass was not very widespread. Whatever the habitat looked like, humans probably roamed the open plains throughout the summer in groups foraging for both plant and animal foods. As winter approached they built shelters and stockpiled food and fuel to see them through the cold and dark. Similar scenarios must have taken place in the peninsular refugia of Europe in what is now Spain, Italy, and Greece. Humans and bears may also have been isolated together in Northern Japan and the Russian Far East.

Bears slept all winter, secure from most disturbances. The giant short-faced bear (in North America), the cave bear (in Europe) and the brown bear survived on their fat reserves, gave birth to their young, and emerged in the spring. In a similar fashion, humans spent most of the winter in earth-covered shelters, and emerged in spring. As the ice-sheets receded for the last time, humans and bears in North America were ready to move south.

The race for population expansion between brown bears and bands of Clovis hunters was no contest. Humans were much more mobile. Both humans and brown bears probably reproduced at about the same rate initially; nomadic early humans could successfully raise only one child per female every couple of years or so. Once a child was old enough to walk and to keep up with the tribe, a female could carry a new infant. Older children could help care for the toddlers. Brown bears probably had a reproductive rate that was similar to modern times; about two cubs every 2 to 4 years depending upon the environment. However, bears colonized new areas much more slowly than humans because female bears did not travel as far. In those times, as now, brown bear cubs were weaned at about 1 to 4 years; in colder and less productive climates they develop more slowly and spend more of the year in winter sleep. When they are weaned, the mothers drive away the male offspring for reasons that are discussed in the chapter on brown bears. Avoidance of inbreeding may be a major factor. The female offspring, however, remain near their mothers as they reach adulthood. In a few instances, female offspring may move away from their mothers but they never move very far. They may move dozens of miles compared with the hundreds of miles that their male siblings typically move.

The male segment of the population travels extensively; distances up to 500 miles (800 km) have been recorded for dispersing subadult males. The population as a whole, however, can only expand at the rate of female dispersers. The occupied range of a brown bear population expands one female home range at a time. Males may temporarily occupy a much wider area, but it does not increase the population since they find no females to mate with.

Thus, human populations expanded from Alaska to Patagonia in just a couple of thousand years. Brown bears got only as far as

A female brown bear and her cub stand up to get a better look at an approaching male.

Mexico, and it took them over 10,000 years to get there. By 1750 they had reached the greatest extent of their distribution in the New World and their populations began rapidly to decline. After the ice age in Europe, brown bears expanded north on two fronts; through Western Europe from the Iberian refugium and through Eastern Europe and Western Russia from the Balkan refugium. At one point they occupied all of Europe, Scandinavia, and even the British Isles. As human populations grew, settled the land, and removed the wildlife habitat, bears began to decline. By the time of the Industrial Revolution they declined rapidly.

The reason bears in North America began to decline was the introduction of firearms by human populations that had recently left Europe. Both the new human populations and some of the indigenous human populations used firearms to kill bears. The European colonists, however, seemed determined to exterminate brown bears wherever they encountered them.

The same scenario was beginning to play out everywhere in the world at this time as firearms became available. In many parts of the world, bear populations had already begun to decline before the advent of firearms. For hundreds of thousands of years, bears of all species had coexisted on somewhat equal terms with early humans. However, modern humans were different. Modern humans were more difficult to coexist with because they began to settle down, alter the landscape, and remove all the predators and competitors they could. The two greatest factors in the competition between humans and bears stem from 1) large-scale alteration of habitat as humans developed civilizations, and 2) the development of firearms which enabled bears to be killed wherever they were encountered. Firearms were not widespread until the 1500s, and agriculture began to develop only about 10,000 years ago. The development of agriculture began independently in several places including the Fertile Crescent (southwestern Asia), China, and South America. For hundreds of thousands of years before that, hunter-gatherer humans and bears had established an uneasy truce.

As early crops were domesticated, humans began to alter large areas of the most productive land for agriculture. This was also land that had been most productive for many of the plant foods that bears fed upon. The practice of agriculture had two long-term effects upon bear populations. It directly altered bear habitat and removed many important bear foods; these were replaced by other foods which bears could eat, but which humans carefully guarded. Agriculture, and a sedentary lifestyle, also allowed human populations to attain greater densities than ever before. More humans meant more competition with bears for resources and space.

Some of the earliest records of bears by humans come from cave engravings in France, which were made about 30,000 years ago. Before this, bear bones and patches of fur were placed in Neanderthal burial sites. All cultures that have coexisted with bears include them in their stories, myths, legends, and art. It is beyond the scope of this book to describe how humans have viewed bears throughout history except to point out the obvious; bears are very much like us in many ways, but in early times they were much more powerful.

Bear legends often take the form of bears as men, or half-bear/half-men, of women who had children with bears, or children who were raised as bears; all celebrating this similarity. Bears are often viewed as brothers, grandfathers, wise and knowledgeable, and as healers. Early humans lived closely with bears and watched them; they probably learned which plants were most nutritious at certain times and may even have learned of plants with medicinal properties. As humans formed societies and insulated themselves from the rhythms of nature we lost this kinship. We became more powerful than bears and we lost our understanding and respect. It is now time for many of us to learn it again.

Most barriers to travel are man-made. This black bear and her cubs are trying to cross a fence in Tennessee.

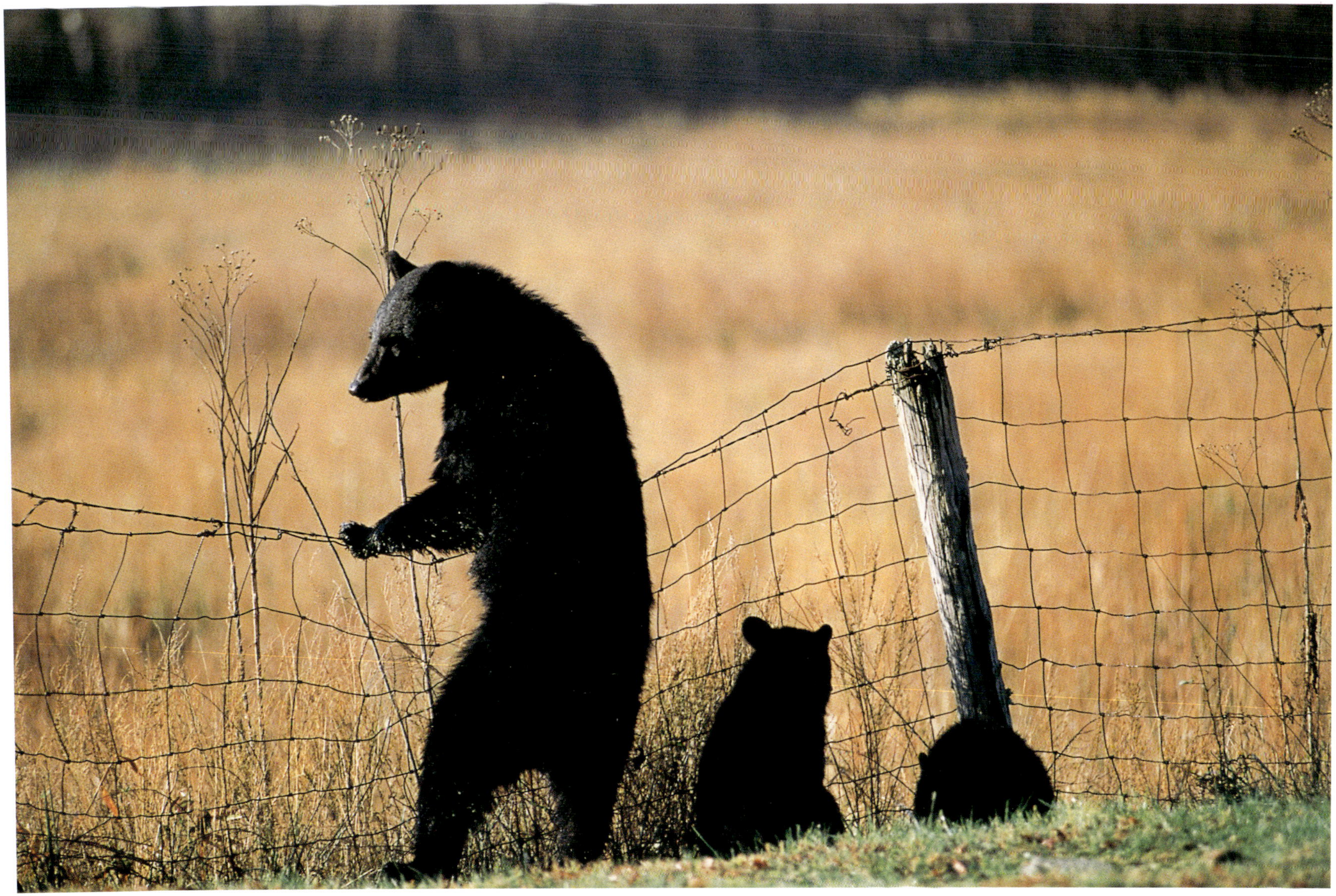

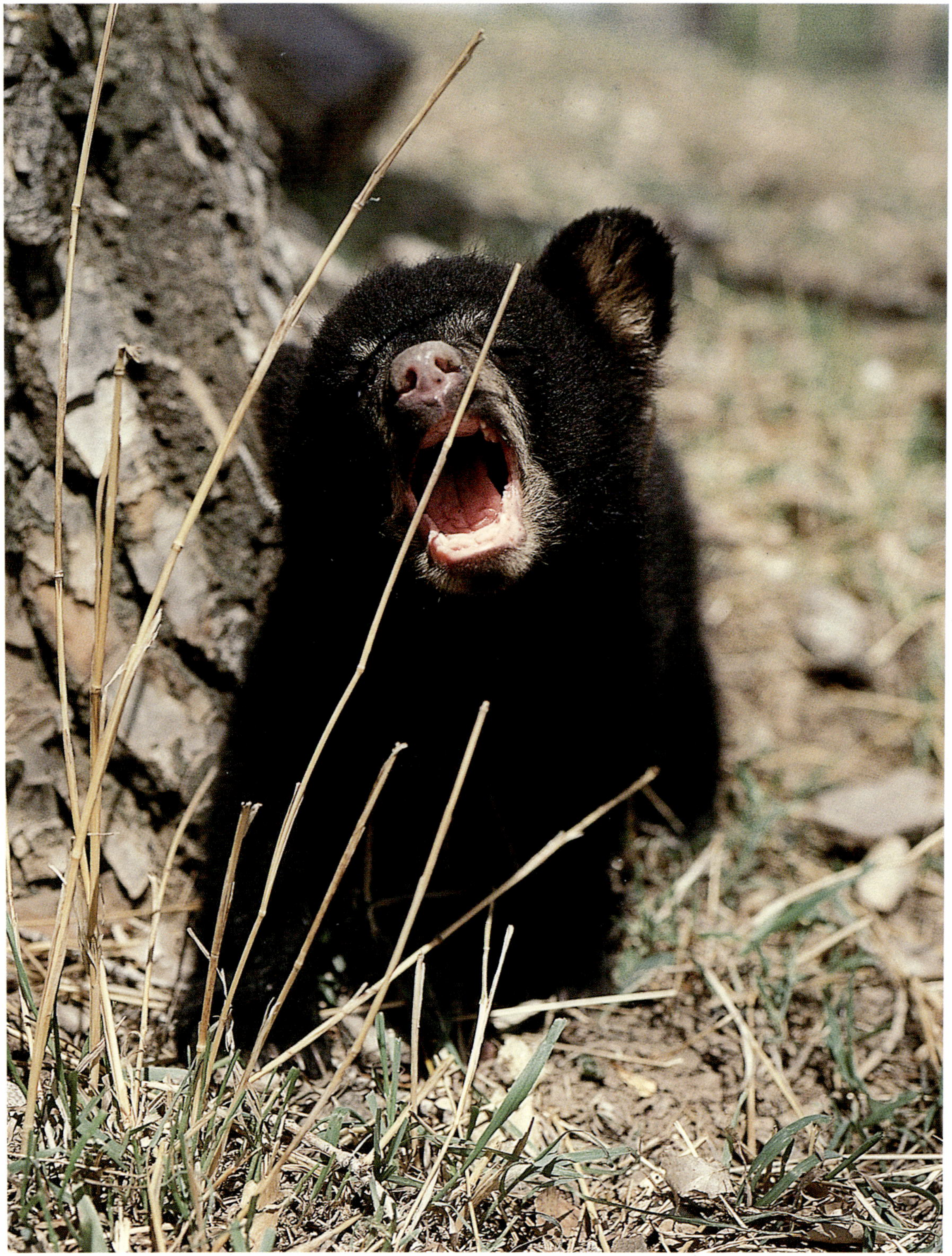

Conservation

Humans and bears coexisted until technologies arose to give humans an advantage. As human populations have grown, people have required more space. In the competition for space humans are now easily able to exclude bears and other species from the land. This has happened fast enough to drive species to extinction and to threaten them even in protected areas. Small populations tend to go extinct. If an entire species is reduced to one small population, the entire species will almost certainly wink out of existence, never to return. In the early 1970s scientists introduced a systems approach to the study of extinction, distinguishing between deterministic (caused) and stochastic (random) factors.

These ideas were further refined so that now we understand that the primary factors affecting the survival of small populations are: 1) deterministic extinction, which occurs when something essential is removed (such as space, shelter, or food) or when something that has negative effects (like a competing exotic species or a disease) is introduced, 2) environmental stochasticity, or random changes in the environment such as drought, global warming, or severe winters, 3) demographic stochasticity, or the chance variation in individual birth and death (demographic) events, which has very large effects once a population becomes very small, 4) genetic deterioration, which can reduce fitness through increased genetic drift, inbreeding, and the subsequent loss of heterozygosity and genetic variance, and 5) catastrophes, or rare but widespread events that can extinguish a population or species, such as a huge meteorite, an epic flood, or the eruption of a large volcano.

Loss of habitat and fragmentation are the immediate threats to bears today. Fragmentation of bear habitat and small bear population sizes are the result of centuries of competition with human beings. Once a population becomes small (fewer than 100 animals) the stochastic or random factors become much more important. Although populations tend to become extinct from the direct random processes of small populations such as few females of breeding age, inability to find a mate etc., those demographic effects are made worse by genetic effects.

Animal breeders have found through centuries of experience with domestic animals that negative genetic effects become very serious in herds of 50 animals or less. Isolated populations of wild animals such as bears and bighorn sheep smaller than 50 adult animals have historically gone extinct. Conservation biologists have termed this process an 'extinction vortex': in small populations, bad genes reduce the growth rate and the population gets smaller. In a smaller population there are less opportunities for successful mating, severe weather, poor nutrition, and mortality have much more of an impact, and the genetic problems are perpetuated. The population spirals down until it goes extinct. Below about 25 animals there is virtually no chance of recovery unless new animals are added to the population. Even this will not help if there is not enough habitat with food and cover to support them.

The best way to preserve bears is to give them enough space to survive over the long term. Large protected areas are often called Conservation Areas or Reserves. A Conservation Area can be considered a refuge from extinction. An adequate reserve will buffer a species from the five causes of extinction for a certain length of time. A key concept is the equilibrium theory of island biogeography: the number of species on an island is a function of the immigration rate, the extinction rate, the area of the island, and its distance from a source of immigrants. The smaller the island, the fewer species it can support. This theory is important for conservation because many of the remaining core areas of wildlife habitat can be seen as islands of habitat.

Bears have a wide repertoire of vocalizations. This American black bear cub is sending his mother a message.

None of the grizzly bear populations in the contiguous United States, even if isolated on the largest island of protected habitat currently existing in the Northern Rocky Mountain region, will ultimately be large enough to sustain sufficient levels of genetic diversity over hundreds or thousands of years, although they may 'hang on' without actually going extinct for this time period. Smaller bear populations in

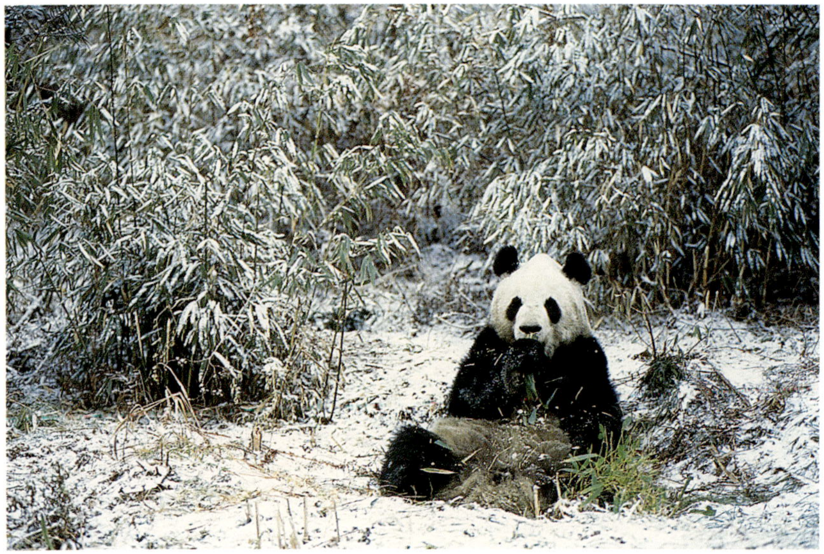

There are only about 1000 pandas left.

other areas such as Europe or Southeast Asia, are at much greater risk of extinction. To increase the size of habitat islands effectively, they must be linked by habitat across which animals can move. The greatest barriers to movement are generally man-made: highways, towns, subdivisions, and other developments. Many bear populations have reached the point where they cannot persist on their own without human help. The Pacific coast of North America is a case in point. It is one of the richest natural areas on earth. It is one of the few places where humans were able to maintain an essentially hunter-gatherer economy yet still have the time and resources to develop complex cultures. They shared the riches of the coast with bears.

In modern times, coastal land uses have changed drastically, primarily by industrial-scale timber extraction. Modern economies have accelerated competition between men and bears. Demands of growing human populations have fueled this need. As a result, humans and corporations are motivated to exploit renewable resources such as timber and fisheries at a much faster rate than they can be replaced. It is often a case of too much and too fast. To counteract the threats of logging, overhunting, and development, conservationists have been struggling for decades to provide protected areas for bears. Today there are a few safe places such as the Admiralty Island National Monument, the Misty Fiords National Monument, the Khutzymateen Valley Wilderness, the Kitlope Wilderness, and the Spirit Bear Wilderness. In isolation, these areas are not enough to ensure the persistence of bear populations. Conservation groups and government scientists are working to protect additional habitat and to design a system of connected habitat so that bears can move to areas that they need to survive.

To sum up what has been discussed throughout this book, let us consider how bears can help us in designing protected areas. This is applicable to any species of bear. Genetic studies of grizzly bears have shown that grizzly bear populations all across Alaska and Canada are connected genetically; genes flow slowly from one population to another. Dispersing male bears are the agents of this gene flow. If they can't reach an isolated place where other bears live, the connection is broken and no new information is transmitted. This reduces genetic variation and leaves the isolated population with fewer and fewer genetic options for coping with changes in the environment. The few genes they do have can also be lost over time by random events; they may not be passed on during reproduction.

Two hundred and fifty years ago, grizzly bears ranged from Alaska to Mexico in the western U.S. Genetic information was exchanged across a network of population centers by the movements of dispersing male bears. This network was begun only about 50,000 years ago when grizzly bears first migrated to North America from Asia across the Bering Land Bridge. About 11,000 years ago this genetic network began slowly to expand across the Western United States. By about 1750 grizzly bears reached the greatest extent of their distribution and began to decline. This decline was caused by the greater expansion of humans; a much more prolific species.

As human populations expanded they altered the habitat so that much of it would not support grizzly bears. After the development of firearms, humans were able to remove grizzly bears directly from areas that humans wanted to occupy. By the 1920s grizzly bears were reduced to tiny isolated populations in a few western states. All but the largest populations have since winked out of existence even though they were not killed off directly by humans. Due to a variety of interrelated factors, one of which is the loss of genetic variation, populations of fewer than 50 animals generally go extinct within a few generations. Not only grizzly bears, but bighorn sheep, wolverines, lynx, and other species we may not be aware of have since disappeared from isolated 'islands' of habitat. Many of these isolated 'islands' are our national parks.

Predators such as bears are just the tip of the iceberg; we are losing populations of plants and animals at alarming rates. In one sense this is a moral and spiritual failure on our part. On a more practical level what we are ultimately losing is information. We are losing information on how life operates. We are losing data and systems that capture energy from the sun and pass it along to support species and ecosystems; and one of those species is us. We need to keep the systems intact so that we can continue to lead healthy, interesting lives. We need to keep the information intact because it could be very important for us at sometime in the future. If we lose genetic and ecological information, from almost any plant or animal, we are reducing our own options.

Grizzly bears eat most of the same foods that we do. They are capable however, of putting on incredible amounts of fat every year as they prepare for hibernation; but their high-cholesterol diet does not cause arteriosclerosis or other heart-related illnesses that plague humans. They sleep for several months without urinating or defecating, and toxic substances such as urea are recycled back into amino acids rather than poisoning the body as they would in humans. Proteins are maintained rather than being lost as they are in fasting humans. Bones do not lose calcium as they do in bed-ridden humans. How do they do these things? The answers are in the genetic code. To eventually find them, we need to maintain viable populations of native species.

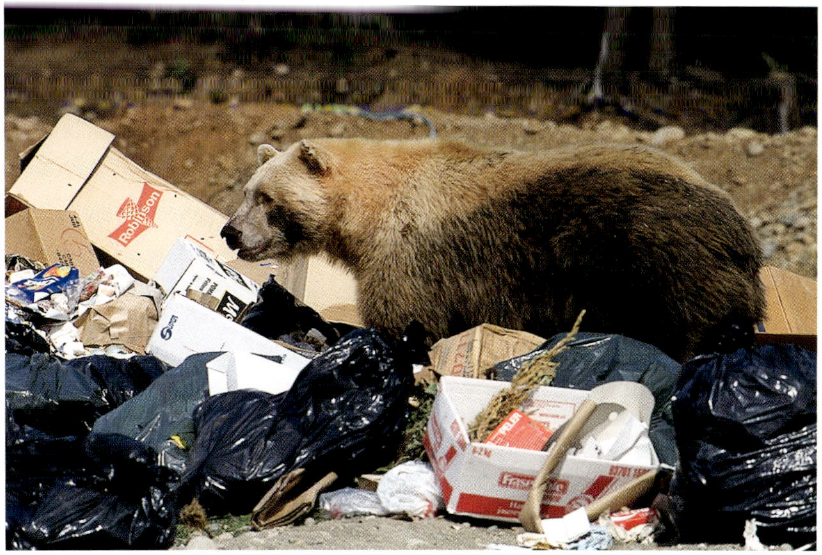

Bears that become habituated to humans eventually end up dead.

Due to their intolerance of human beings and utilization of diverse foods over large areas, grizzly bears require specific considerations when developing a conservation design for a region. These characteristics also make the grizzly bear a good choice as an 'umbrella species' – a species whose needs are coincident with many others species and thereby provides an 'umbrella' of protection. Although grizzly bears are intelligent, adaptable animals, their survival is dependent upon their ability to find high-quality food sources. Contact with human beings for any reason increases the probability that the bear will be killed. Basically, bears need areas where they can find good-quality food without being killed by humans.

The largest blocks of suitable habitat, which are found in roadless areas with little human disturbance, represent the 'core' areas of a conservation area design. At regional scales, connecting large core areas of wildlife habitat requires corridors – land managed for its function as routes for wildlife movement and dispersal. Conceptual models of core areas, movement corridors and buffer zones have been proposed by several prominent scientists as frameworks for long-term regional scale conservation of wildlife.

Movement corridors are important to bears and other wildlife for daily, seasonal, and for lifetime dispersal movements. Dispersal patterns of subadult bears as they reach sexual maturity are an important factor determining gene flow, population genetic structure, and ultimately genetic diversity in populations. Animals dispersing from 'source' populations can be recruited into declining or 'sink' populations to maintain demographic stability. If we want to preserve bears and other species for future generations, we need to set aside remote areas of habitat to serve as cores, and to link the core areas up with habitat through which animals can move.

Conservation Area Design, and the maintenance of conservation networks, requires a degree of sacrifice by humans. We must be willing to give up some areas for other species to survive. This is what saving the rainforest, or saving the desert tortoise, or saving the bears, is all about. It is not an unrewarded sacrifice however; it is essential to maintaining our current quality of life, and of improving the quality of life for others. If we reduced the natural world to monocultures of a few agricultural plants, and a few domesticated animals, we would have very few options in the face of environmental change. To feed human populations and to support our civilizations, however, we need these simplified agricultural systems, at least until we devise more complex ones. The critical balance that society needs to find now is how to maintain the function of natural systems at the same time and in the same areas, that we maintain our own domestic systems.

We need to maintain this balance; between the immediate needs of human beings, and the long-term needs of natural systems including humans. Designs to do this must cut across many artificial human boundaries and be based on the ecological and evolutionary networks we need to maintain. Borders and boundaries are irrelevant to gene flow, nutrient cycling, or seed propagation. Such plans have primarily been formulated by independent scientists and non-governmental organizations. However, as the science progresses, and as government agencies develop cooperative strategies, inter-agency approaches are also beginning to develop conservation area design strategies.

In the U.S., visions such as The Wildlands Project and the Yukon-to-Yellowstone Conservation Initiative have developed on a local basis by groups and individuals that work on areas where they live. These are projects designed to improve or maintain natural ecosystems, native species, and air and water quality by protecting core areas of wildlife habitat and habitat connections within the matrix of human-altered landscapes. They are projects designed to maintain human options as well as maintaining options for other species. Based upon core areas that are already protected as national parks and wilderness areas, scientists are working to determine what additional areas, if any, are needed in order to maintain viable populations of large carnivores such as bears.

If large carnivore populations are preserved, then most other native animals and plants will also be protected. This applies to other species than bears, and applies to all ecosystems on the planet. The best hope for preserving species is to provide habitat. The best way to provide more habitat where it is fragmented into isolated patches is to connect the patches somehow so that animals can move between them. The best thing that individuals can do to promote conservation is to tolerate wildlife nearby, avoid attracting them to areas where they will cause conflicts, understand their needs, and give them the space they need. I hope this book is a step in that direction.

Borders and boundaries are irrelevant to bear populations. Individual polar bears travel over hundreds of thousands of square miles.

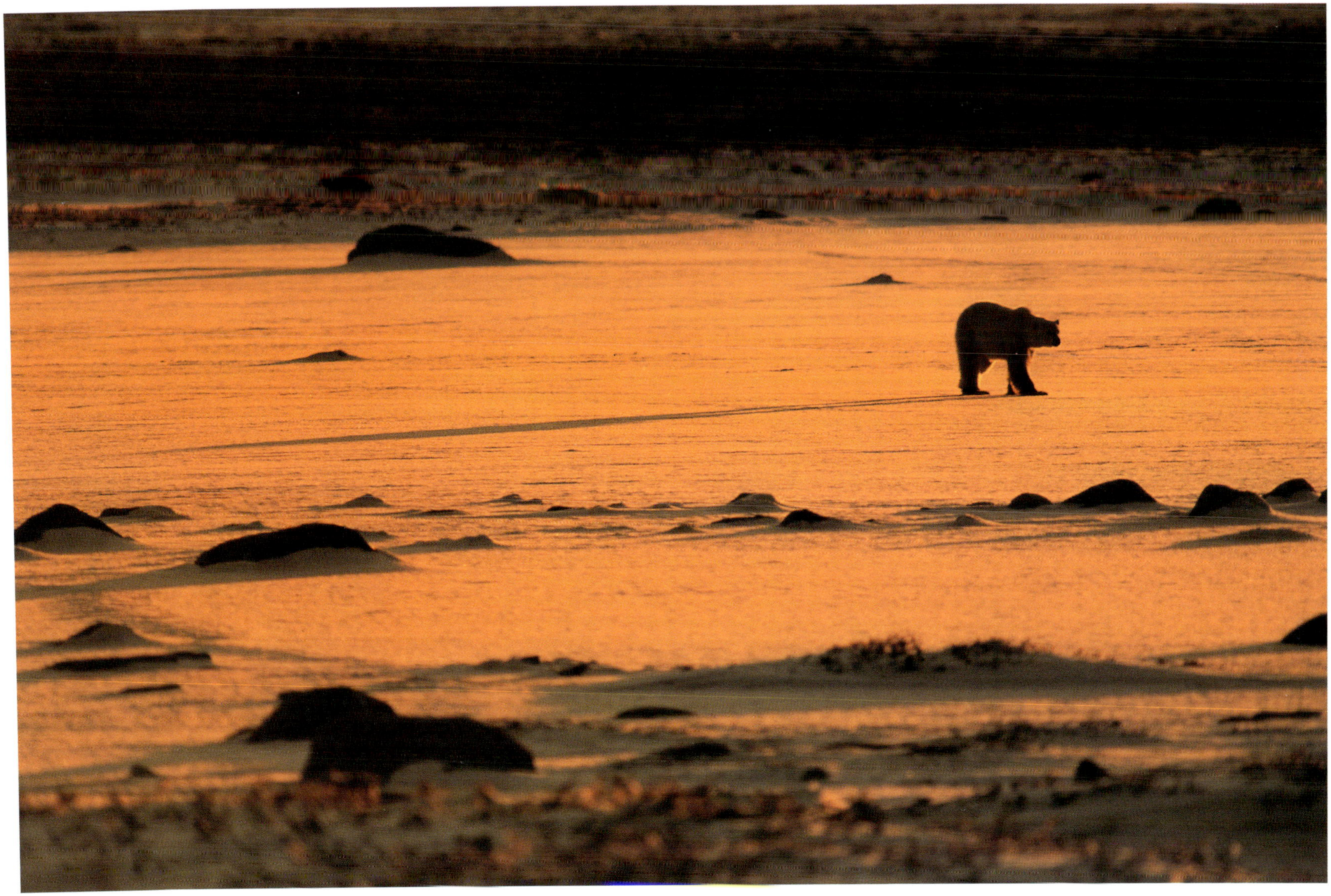

Brown Bear (*Ursus arctos*)

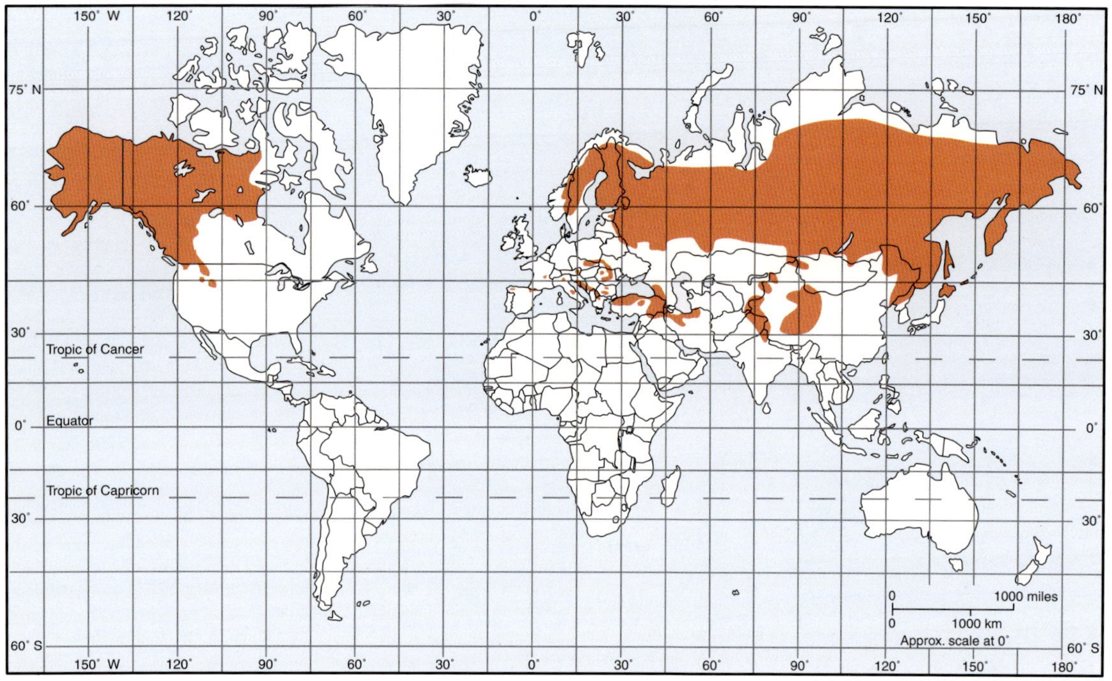

Common Name: Brown Bear / Grizzly Bear
Scientific Name: *Ursus arctos*
No of Young: Average 1 to 4 cubs, usually 2
Age at Maturity: Males: 8 to 10 years
Females: 4.5 to 7 years
Size: Varies considerably between populations.
Weight: Average weights:
Adult Males: 135 to 390 kg (300 to 860 lb)
Adult Females: 95 to 205 kg (210 to 450 lb)
The largest bears occur on the west coast of British Columbia and Alaska, where adult males may weigh over 300 kg (660 lb), females over 200 kg (440 lb).
Longevity: 20 to 25 years in the wild.
Diet: Vegetation – grasses, sedges, bulbs, roots, insects, fish, small mammals. In some areas moose, caribou and elk.
Habitat: A wide range from subalpine mountain areas, tundra and dense forests.
Distribution: Localized populations in Europe, northern Asia, Japan, western Canada, Alaska, Wyoming, Montana, Idaho and Washington.

Polar Bear (*Ursus maritimus*)

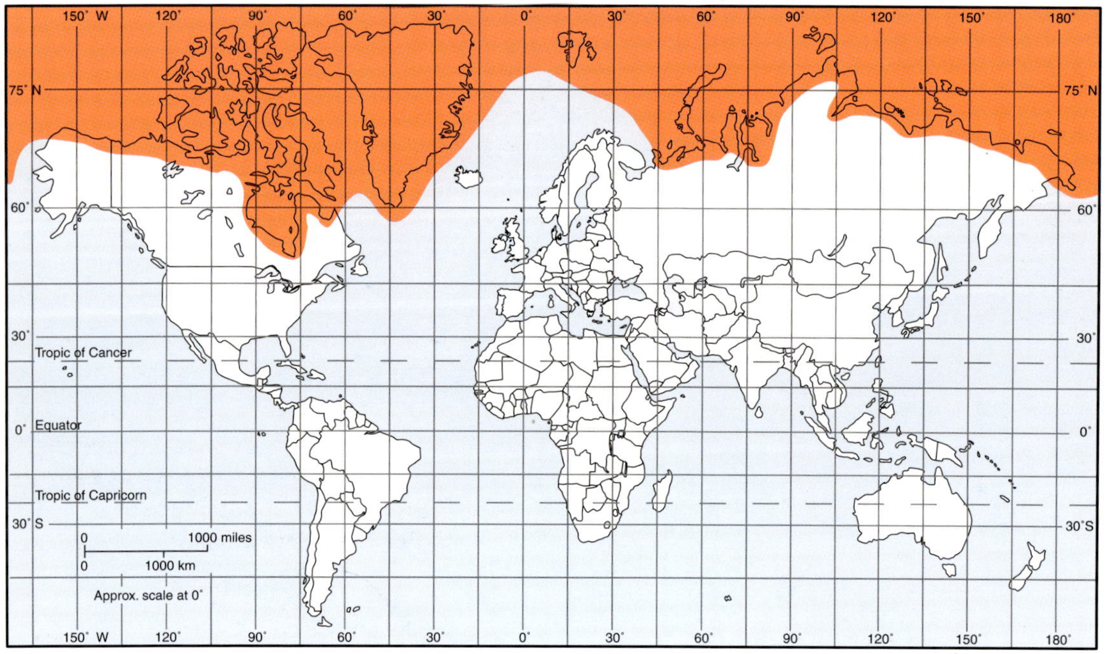

Common Name: Polar Bear
Scientific Name: *Ursus maritimus*
No of Young: Average 2
Age at Maturity: 3 to 5 years
Size: Adult Males: 240 to 260 cm (95 to 105 in)
Adult Females: 190 to 210 cm (75 to 85 in)
Weight: Adult Males: 400 to 600 kg (880 to 1320 lb)
Adult Females: 200 to 300 kg (440 to 660 lb)
Diet: Seals, walruses, narwhals, belugas, grass, kelp, berries.
Habitat: Annual ice adjacent to shorelines throughout the circumpolar Arctic.
Distribution: Throughout the circumpolar Arctic, as far south as Newfoundland.

American Black Bear (*Ursus americanus*)

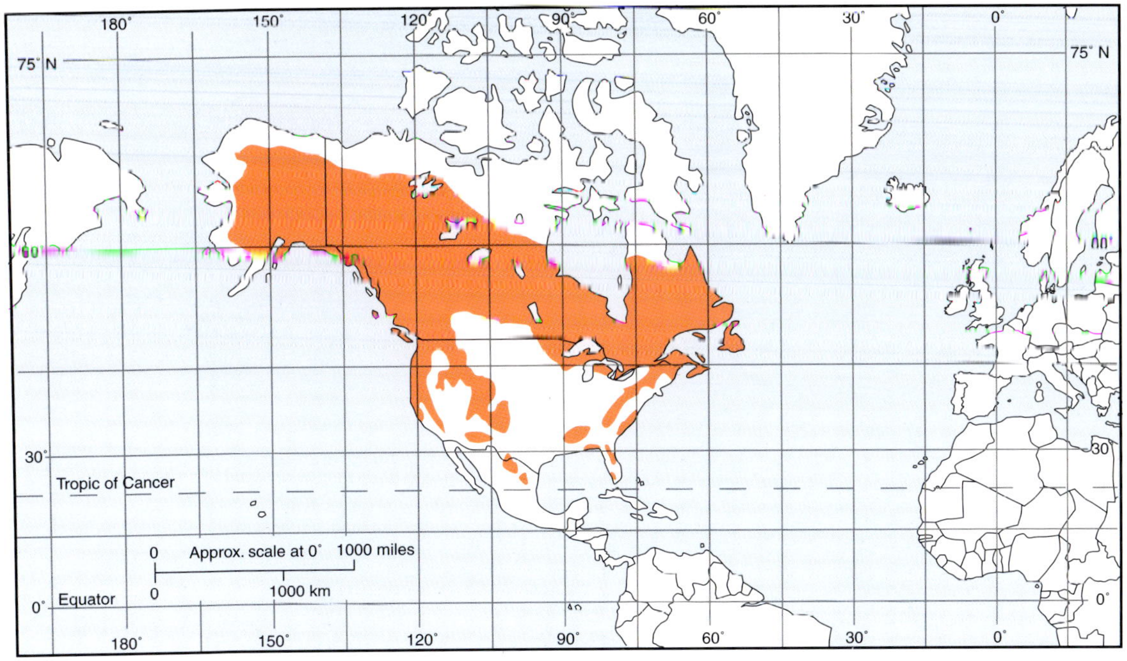

Common Name: American Black Bear

Scientific Name: *Ursus americanus*

Gestation: 6 months

No of Young: 1 to 5, average 2

Age at Maturity: Males: 4 to 5 years
Females: 3 to 4 years

Size: Adult Males: 130 to 190 cm (50 to 75 in)
Adult Females: 130 to 190 cm (50 to 75 in)

Weight: Adult males: 60 to 300 kg (130 to 660 lb)
Adult females: 40 to 80 kg (90 to 175 lb)

Longevity: 20 to 25 years in the wild.

Diet: Nuts, berries, insects, grasses, roots and other vegetation, young deer and moose calves, spawning salmon.

Habitat: Forests.

Distribution: Throughout North America and Canada, northern Mexico.

Asiatic Black Bear (*Ursus thibetanus*)

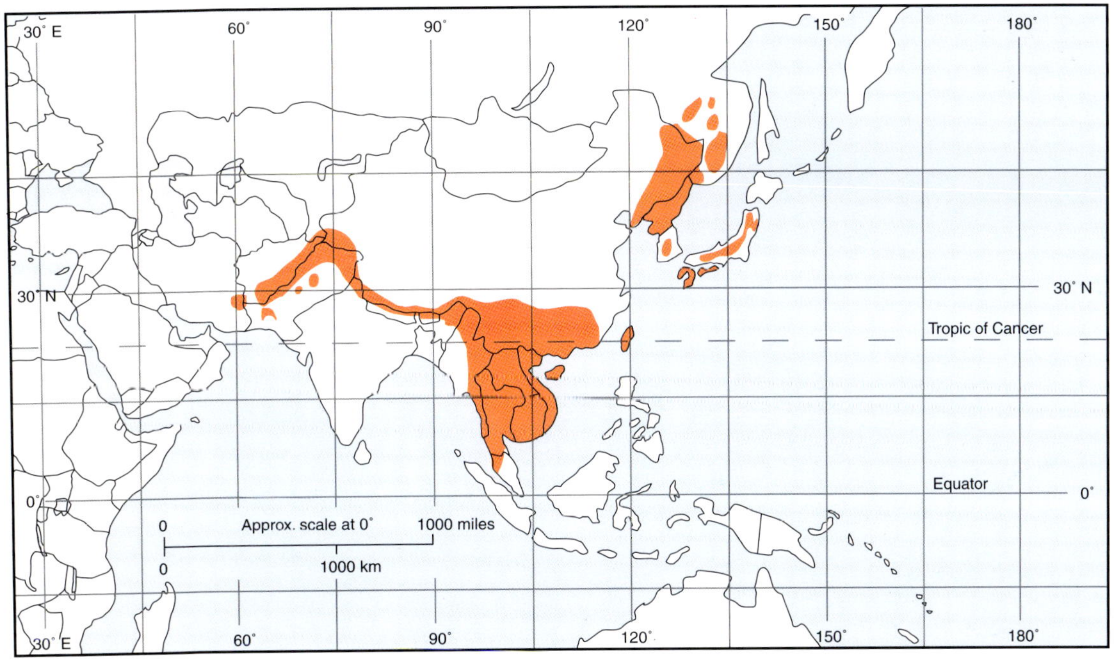

Common Name: Asiatic Black Bear

Scientific Name: *Ursus thibetanus*

Gestation: 4 to 6 months

Age at Maturity:
Females: 3 to 4 years

Size: Adult Average: 130 to 190 cm (50 to 75 in)

Weight: Adult males: 100 to 200 kg (220 to 440 lb)
Adult females: 50 to 125 kg (110 to 275 lb)

Diet: Fruit, bees' nests, insects, invertebrates, small vertebrates, carrion.

Habitat: Forested areas in hills and mountains.

Distribution: Southern Asia, from Afghanistan, Pakistan and North India, Nepal, Bhutan, Burma and Northeastern China, and Taiwan to Southeast Russia, and the Japanese islands of Honshu and Shikoku.

Sun Bear (*Ursus malayanus*)

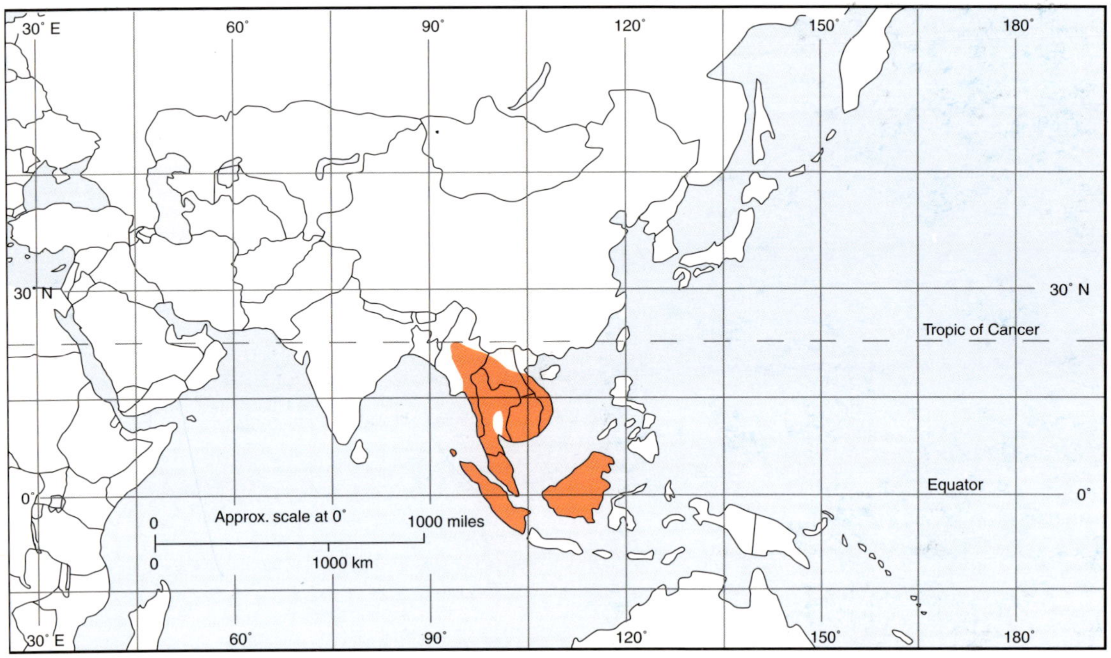

Common Name: Sun Bear

Scientific Names: *Ursus malayanus / Helarctos malayanus*

No of Young: 1 or 2 cubs

Size: Adult average: 120 to 150 cm (48 to 60 in)

Weight: Adult males: 27 to 65 kg (60 to 145 lb); males are 10 to 20 per cent larger than females.

Diet: Termites, small mammals, birds, palm trees, bees' nests.

Habitat: Lowland tropical rainforests.

Distribution: Southeast Asia: Burma, Bangladesh, Laos, Cambodia, Vietnam, Thailand, Malaysia, Sumatra and Borneo.

Sloth Bear (*Ursus ursinus*)

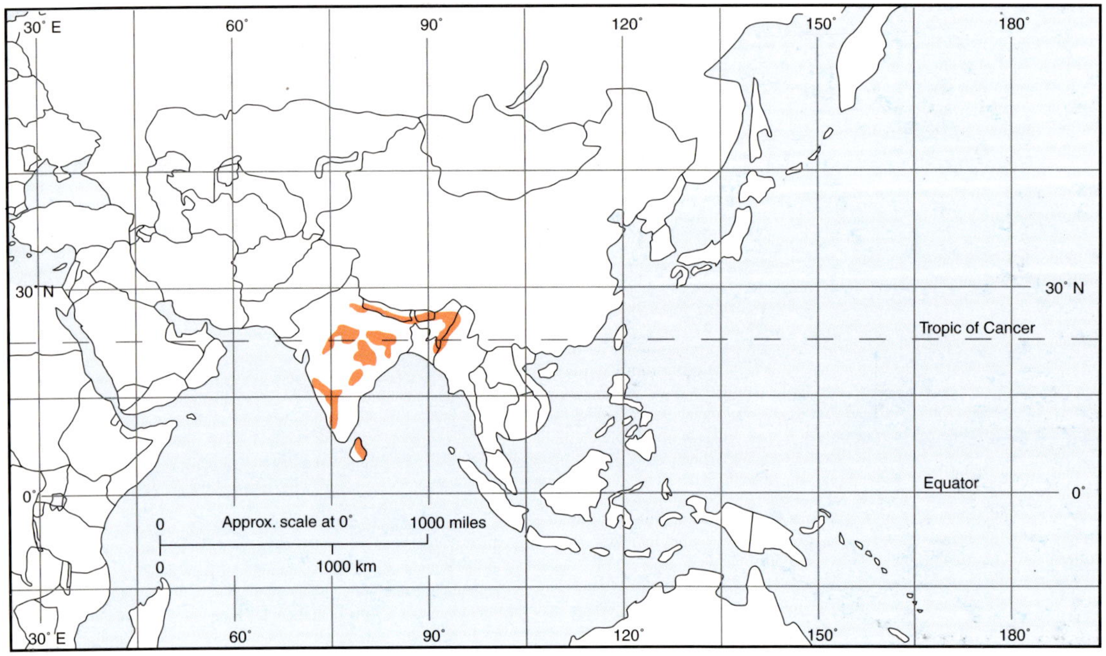

Common Name: Sloth Bear

Scientific Names: *Ursus ursinus / Melursus ursinus*

Gestation: 6 to 7 months

No of Young: 1 to 3 cubs

Size: Adult average: 150 to 190 cm (60 to 75 in)

Weight: Adult males: 80 to 140 kg (175 to 310 lb) Adult females: 55 to 95 kg (120 to 210 lb)

Diet: Termites, eggs, insects, honeycombs, carrion, vegetation.

Habitat: Forests and grasslands.

Distribution: India, Sri Lanka, Bangladesh, Nepal and Bhutan.

Spectacled Bear (*Tremarctos ornatus*)

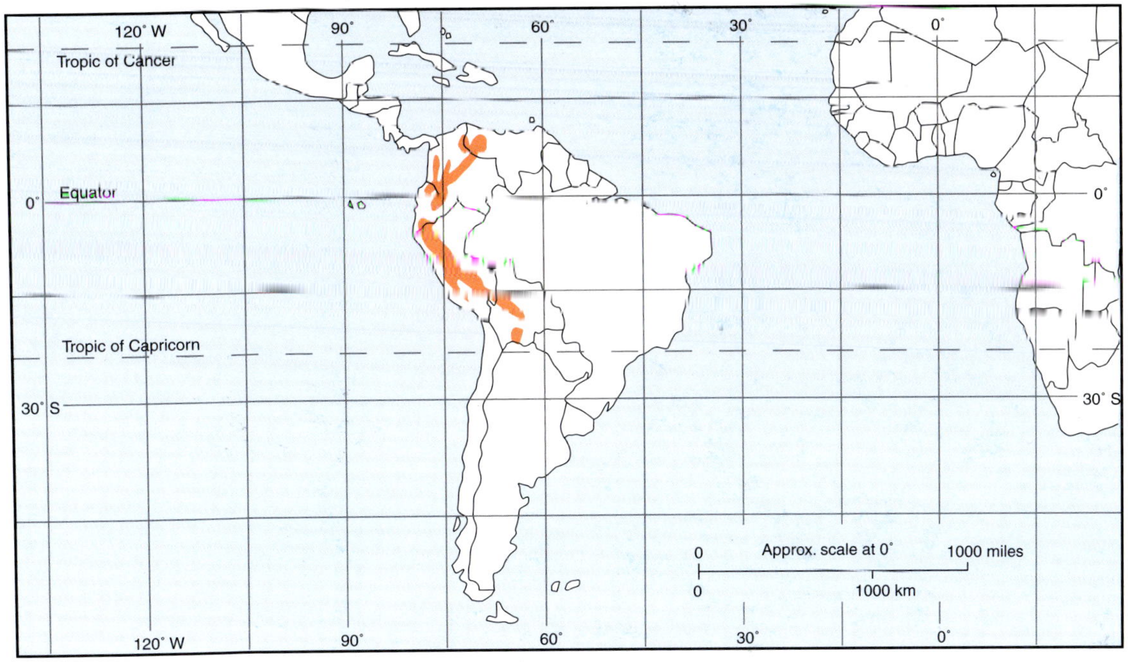

Common Name: Spectacled Bear

Scientific Name: *Tremarctos ornatus*

No of Young: 1 to 3 cubs

Size: Adult average: 150 to 180 cm (60 to 72 in)

Weight: Adult males: 100 to 155 kg (220 to 340 lb)
Adult females: 64 to 82 kg (140 to 180 lb)

Diet: Rabbits, mice, birds, berries, grasses, fruit, bromeliads.

Habitat: Rainforest, cloud forest, dry forest, steppes and coastal scrub desert.

Distribution: South America: Venezuela, Colombia, Ecuador, Peru and Bolivia.

Giant Panda (*Ailuropoda melanoleuca*)

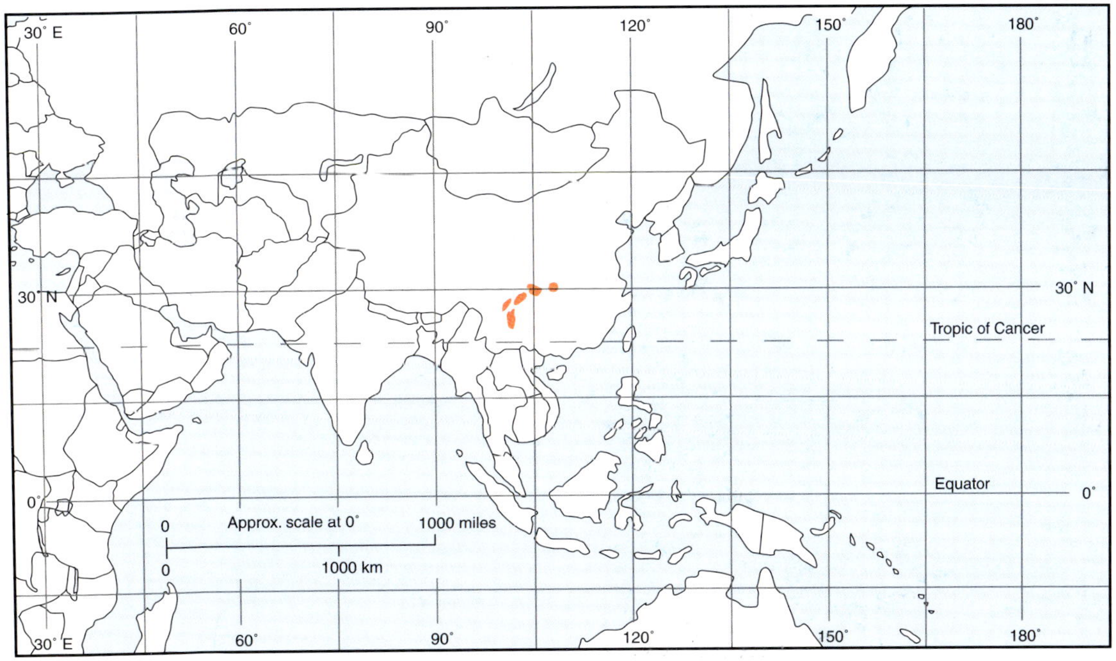

Common Name: Giant Panda

Scientific Name: *Ailuropoda melanoleuca*

No of Young: 1 or 2 cubs; rarely, 3

Age at Maturity: 5 to 6 years

Longevity: Unknown in wild, up to 30 years in captivity.

Size: Adult average: 160 to 190 cm (64 to 76 in)

Weight: Adult male: 75 to 110 kg (165 to 242 lb).

Diet: Bamboo, wild plants.

Habitat: Mountain forests.

Distribution: China.

INDEX

Entries in **bold** *indicate pictures*

Recommended Reading

Bears: status survey and conservation action plan. Christopher Servheen, Stephen Herrero and Bernard Peyton (compilers). 1999. IUCN, Gland, Switzerland and Cambridge U.K.

Bears: Majestic Creatures of the Wild. Ian Stirling. 1993. Rodale Press. Emmaus, Pennsylvania.

Polar Dance: Born of the North Wind. Thomas Mangleson and Fred Bruemmer. 1997. Images of Nature. Omaha, Nebraska.

Track of the Grizzly. Frank C Craighead, Jr. 1979. Sierra Club Books. San Francisco, California.

The Grizzly Bear. Thomas McNamee. 1984. Alfred A Knopf. New York.

The Grizzly Bears of Yellowstone. John J Craighead, John Mitchell, Jay Sumner. 1995. Island Press. Covela, California.

Spirit Bear: Encounters with the White Bear of the Western Rainforest. Charlie Russell. 1999. Key Porter Books.

Giving Voice to Bear: North American Indian Rituals, Myths, and Images of the Bear. David Rockwell. 1993. Roberts Rinehart Publishing.

Acknowledgments

I would like to acknowledge my father, Frank C Craighead, Jr, and my uncle John J Craighead who brought the scientific study of bears into the electronic age and have nurtured it ever since. I would also like to acknowledge all of the bear biologists worldwide whose work I have attempted to accurately report, all of the wildlife managers and conservationists who are dedicated to using this science to preserve and maintain bears, and all of the bear lovers and outdoor enthusiasts who feel a kinship with bears and understand the need to protect them and their habitat. The list is long and many people are deserving of recognition. I will mention just a few: Harry Reynolds, John Hechtel, Charles Jonkel, Bob Ruff, Maurice Hornocker, Charlie Russell, Andy Russell, Jay Sumner, Gordon Scaggs, Chuck Schwarz, Wayne McCrory, Brian Horesji, Barrie Gilbert, Tom Mangleson, Dave Augeri, Doug Peacock, Mardy Murie, Roland Dixon, Ian and Karen McCallister, Dennis Sizemore, Louisa Willcox, David Paetkau, all of the members of the International Bear Association, and in memorium: Michio Hosino; Olaus and Adolf Murie. Any omissions are the fault of my memory and the pressure to meet publishing deadlines.